Spatial Planning and]
Impact Analysis

The Spatial Fiscal Impact Analysis Method is an innovative approach to measure fiscal impact and project the future costs of a proposed development, recognizing that all revenues and expenditures are spatially related. The Spatial Method focuses on estimating existing fiscal impacts of detailed land use categories by their location. It takes advantage of readily available data that reflect the flows of revenues and expenditures in a city, using the tools of Geographic Information Systems (GIS). The result is a comprehensive yet transparent database for measuring existing fiscal impacts and projecting the impacts of future development or redevelopment.

This book will provide readers with guidance as to how to conduct the Spatial Method in their own cities. The book will provide an overview of the history of fiscal analysis, and demonstrate the advantages of the Spatial Method to other methods, taking the reader step by step through the process, from analyzing city financial reports, determining and developing the factors that are needed to model the flows of revenues and expenditures, and then estimating fiscal impact at the parcel level. The result is a summary of detailed land use categories and neighborhoods that will be invaluable to city planners and public administration officials everywhere.

Linda Tomaselli has a BA, MA and PhD in Geography from the University of Minnesota, USA, and has over 40 years of experience as a planner and GIS specialist. She recognized early on that cities needed a better way to measure fiscal impact. With the financial help of the National Science Foundation, she has developed a spatial methodology for estimating fiscal impact of existing development that could be used to project future impacts and develop a city's "information infrastructure."

Spatial Planning and Fiscal Impact Analysis

A Toolkit for Existing and Proposed Land Use

Linda Tomaselli

NEW YORK AND LONDON

First published 2019
by Routledge
52 Vanderbilt Avenue, New York, NY 10017

and by Routledge
2 Park Square, Milton Park, Abingdon, Oxon, OX14 4RN

Routledge is an imprint of the Taylor & Francis Group, an informa business

© 2019 Taylor & Francis

Library of Congress Cataloging-in-Publication Data
Names: Tomaselli, Linda Kay, author.
Title: Spatial planning and fiscal impact analysis: a toolkit for existing and proposed land use/Dr. Linda Tomaselli.
Description: New York, NY: Routledge, 2019.
Identifiers: LCCN 2018041591 | ISBN 9781138387942 (hardback) | ISBN 9781138387973 (pbk.)
Subjects: LCSH: Land use—Planning. | City planning—Finance. | Real estate development—Costs. | Tax revenue estimating.
Classification: LCC HD108.6 .T66 2019 | DDC 333.77/13—dc23
LC record available at https://lccn.loc.gov/2018041591

ISBN: 978-1-138-38794-2 (hbk)
ISBN: 978-1-138-38797-3 (pbk)
ISBN: 978-0-429-42591-2 (ebk)

Typeset in Sabon
by Deanta Global Publishing Services, Chennai, India
Printed by CPI Group (UK) Ltd, Croydon CR0 4YY

Contents

Figures

Colour Plate Section

Tables

About the Author

Dr. Linda Tomaselli has been a planner since the early 1970s. After graduating from the University of Minnesota, with a BA in Geography, she started out by working for the Camden County Planning Department, NJ, then at the Delaware Valley Regional Planning Commission in Philadelphia.

In 1973 she earned an MA in geography from the University of Minnesota. Later she worked as a consultant, preparing comprehensive plans in New Jersey.

Then in 1976, she moved back to Minnesota and was hired by the Metropolitan Council of the Twin Cities. At the Council, she was assigned to help cities prepare comprehensive plans under the recently passed Land Planning Act. In particular, she helped cities prepare capital improvement programs, and became aware of the need to project the fiscal impact of the proposed projects.

In 1984, she began to learn about Geographic Information Systems (GIS). With the help of the State Planning Agency, she began to pursue the idea of using GIS to measure fiscal impact. In 1988 she won a substantial research grant from the National Science Foundation (NSF) and conducted an analysis for the City of Anoka. In 1989 she wrote her PhD dissertation using the results, and in 1991 was awarded the Horwood Critique Prize from the Urban and Regional Information Systems Association (URISA) for the best paper.

Unfortunately, the idea of using GIS for fiscal impact was before its time, so she spent the next 20 years as a GIS consultant, mainly to counties, working on a wide range of projects, from aerial photography, to TIGER files, parcel mapping, soil mapping and rural addressing to name a few.

However, by 2009, many cities had developed GIS capabilities, and the quality of input data had greatly improved. Dr. Tomaselli decided to revisit the City of Anoka, and did an update of the analysis. Visit www.Anoka-Fiscal-Impact.com to see the final report. APA published two of her articles on the project in 2012 and 2013. In 2014, she contracted with the McLean County Planning Commission to prepare a Spatial Fiscal Impact study for the City of Bloomington, IL. Visit www.Bloomington-Fiscal-Impact.com to see the final report. She presented a session at the 2017 APA conference on the Bloomington project, titled "Spatial Planning and Fiscal Impact Analysis". She has written a book of the same title, relating her findings to the overall field of fiscal impact analysis.

Acknowledgments

Dr. Tomaselli has had many supporters for her efforts, culminating in this book. First, she credits the late Dr. John R. Borchert, Regents Professor of the University of Minnesota who was her advisor for her BA, MA and PhD degrees. He taught her that empirical research is generally preferable than following the theoretical work of others.

The Metropolitan Council of the Twin Cities, Minnesota was also an influential supporter. She was assigned to work with cities to implement the recently passed Land Planning Act. Helping cities to prepare capital improvement programs made her realize that there was there was a big gap between them and the city's comprehensive plan. There did not seem to be suitable methods to project the fiscal impact of their plans, and to be able to pay for their capital improvements. Mr. Jim Barton, her supervisor, supported her in her efforts at trying to develop a new method.

A very important supporter was Mr. Wayne Ersbo, who taught her to be comfortable around computers, and he helped her find ways of ferreting out useful data, especially assessor's parcel data. He also introduced her in 1984 to the State Planning Agency which was at the forefront of using Geographic Information Systems (GIS). Mr. Earl Nordstrand was instrumental in providing the resources to digitize the land parcels for a start-up effort for the City of Blaine, MN.

Mr. Robert Kirchner, Community Development Director for the City of Anoka, MN became interested in the use of GIS for fiscal impact analysis, and asked her to apply it to his city. During that time, Dr. Tomaselli applied to the National Science Foundation for a grant to pursue her research. In 1988 she was awarded a substantial grant for the Anoka project. The Environmental Systems Research Institute (ESRI) also donated a copy of PC ArcInfo. She wrote her PhD dissertation on the results, and in 1991 was awarded the Horwood Critique Prize from the Urban and Regional Information Systems Association (URISA) for her paper on the subject.

Unfortunately, the idea of using GIS for fiscal impact was before its time, so she spent the next 20 years as a GIS consultant, mainly to counties, working on a wide range of projects, from aerial photography, to TIGER files, parcel mapping, soil mapping and rural addressing, to name a few.

However, by 2009, many cities had developed GIS capabilities, and the quality of input data had greatly improved. Dr. Tomaselli decided to revisit the City of Anoka, and did an update of the analysis, again with the support of Mr. Robert Kirchner. APA published two of her articles on the project in 2012 and 2013, with the editorial support and encouragement of Mr. Jerry Weitz.

The articles caught the attention of Ms. Vasudha Pinnamaraju Gadhiraju, of the McLean County Regional Planning Commission, and in 2014, the Commission contracted with Dr. Tomaselli to prepare a Spatial Fiscal Impact study for the City of Bloomington, IL. The results of that study provided much of the material in this book.

In 2017, she presented a session at the 2017 APA conference titled Spatial Fiscal Impact Analysis, which also caught the attention of Kate Schell, who supported her proposal to write this book.

Lastly, Dr. Tomaselli would like to acknowledge the support and expertise of her assistant, Amir F. Tehrani.

1 Spatial Planning and Fiscal Impact Analysis Method

The Spatial Planning and Fiscal Impact Analysis Method is a different approach to measuring the impact of land development, particularly with regard to fiscal impact, compared to other methods. It recognizes that all revenues and expenditures are spatially related. It takes advantage of readily available data that reflect the flows of revenues and expenditures in a city, using the tools of Geographic Information Systems (GIS). The method results in a detailed planning database at the parcel level to be able to analyze existing and proposed land use. The time and effort for the method are more extensive than traditional fiscal impact, but the resulting database can be considered an investment in "information infrastructure".

I Definitions

The Spatial Planning and Fiscal Impact Analysis Method (SPFIA) is defined as:

> The determination of the direct, current, city costs and revenues associated with all types of land use in a city that can be used to project the fiscal impact of new development that is taking place or estimate the benefits of redevelopment.

This differs somewhat from the definition stated in the book *The Fiscal Impact Handbook* by Burchell and Listokin, published in 1978 (p. 1): "The projection of the direct, current, city costs and revenues associated with residential or nonresidential growth to the local jurisdiction(s) in which the growth is taking place."

The difference is that the old definition assumes that one knows the impacts of land uses and is focused on projections. The Spatial Method is based on the premise that one must first evaluate the impact of detailed land use categories in order to make accurate projections. Many methods treat residential and non-residential development as blocks of land use, assuming that they are homogeneous in their characteristics and impacts.

Here is a perfect example as to why that assumption is wrong. In the City of Bloomington, Illinois, in 2013, it was found that a single large office development had a surplus of $1,987,928, while a large discount department store had a deficit of $811,056. Both uses were classified as commercial. Making projections based on gross estimates of the average impact of commercial development would not be very meaningful, and even misleading.

II Conceptual Basis

The Spatial Method is based on the premise that nearly all revenue a city collects is based on geographically distributed factors, such as the value of land parcels that generate property taxes, or population and employment that generate sales taxes. Nearly all expenditures are delivered to places in the city based on need or demands, such as police calls, or the need for access by local public roads. It is difficult to think of anything a city does that is not based on geography. The Spatial Method uses the land parcel as the smallest unit of geography. Land parcels can be categorized as to land use, and summaries by land use can be used to indicate the fiscal impact of each type.

If one had the ideal transaction processing system for city finances that was able to indicate from where each dollar of revenue is derived or where each dollar of expenditure is spent, one could easily determine the fiscal impact of every part of the city. However, this type of system does not exist and would be prohibitively expensive to develop.

Figure 1.1 shows graphically the concepts behind the Spatial Method, adapted from Tomaselli (1991, pp. 53–54).

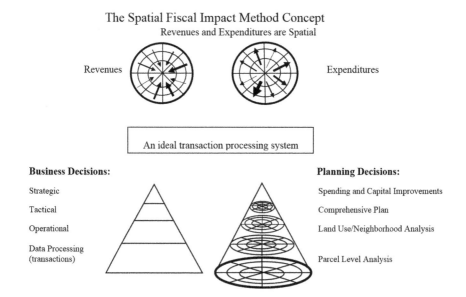

Figure 1.1 The Spatial Fiscal Impact Analysis Concept.

First, revenues and expenditures are spatially distributed. Here, parcels are conceptually represented as sections of the city, with city government in the center. Revenues come in from parcels, whether it be from the assessed values and property taxes from population or employment in the form of charges for services, or from income or sales taxes. Expenditures go out to parcels based on police and fire calls for service, local street maintenance or other general government activities.

In the lower left of the diagram, a typical management information system is shown, whether it be for businesses or cities, in the form of a triangle. At the bottom are the day-to-day transactions. These get summarized to help make operational decisions and then in turn get further summarized to make tactical decisions. At the top, there are the strategic decisions of a business or a city.

The ideal transaction processing system for a city to measure fiscal impact would convert the triangle to a cone. At the bottom are the parcel-level transactions of revenue in and expenditures out. The parcel-level impacts can be summarized by land use and/or neighborhood to help with operational decisions. Further summarizing the data yields tactical decisions, such as the impact of the comprehensive plan. At the top are strategic decisions, which the city would make to decide on spending and capital improvement decisions that support the comprehensive plan.

The Spatial Method of Fiscal Impact Analysis is based on these concepts, and the best way to evaluate the fiscal impact of land development is to try to model what such an ideal system might produce. Modeling is done by identifying those available and measurable factors that are indicators of the distribution of revenues and expenditures.

III A Parcel-Level Planning Database

The Spatial Method has its foundation built upon a parcel-level planning database. Parcels are the lowest common denominator for land use, with the exception of mixed-use parcels. Therefore, once the data is compiled by parcel, it can all be summarized by land use as well as many other cross-tabulation factors.

Parcels are the basic data unit for analysis, but not because one necessarily wants to know the impact of each and every parcel. A parcel may be a single family, but it may be different than other single-family parcels. It may be owner or renter occupied. It may have a brand-new house or a house dating back to the turn of the century. It may have only two bedrooms or five bedrooms. It may be only 800 square feet or 4,000 square feet. These parcel-building attributes provide the basis for analyzing groups of parcels by land use classification, valuation, neighborhood or year built. The reason the analysis is done at the parcel level is that one can capture all of the variations among the parcels that make up the land use categories instead of guessing.

The database includes housing units, adult and school-age population, employment, public safety calls and road frontage, which are added to all of the other attributes that the assessor has collected about the parcels.

The objective of this method is to evaluate the fiscal impact of parcels by land use and other characteristics so that the results can be summarized and used to project future revenues and expenditures, or to evaluate existing neighborhoods and identify areas in need of redevelopment so that they produce more revenue and fewer expenditures in the future.

Property taxes are the easiest to determine because they are determined by the assessed value of land and buildings for each land parcel in the city. Other revenues, such as income taxes or sales taxes, are more difficult to determine. It would be easy to estimate these taxes if one knew everyone's income in every housing unit, but that information is not available. Furthermore, one also can only estimate how many people live in each residential housing unit. However, with the value of the housing in which the estimated population lives, one can use that value to roughly estimate the incomes and therefore the distribution of income and sales taxes.

On the expenditure side, one can determine police and fire calls that are available by address. Using GIS, the amount of road frontage for each parcel can be measured. Frontage can be used to use to distribute the costs of local road maintenance, with variations of cost based on the type of road.

Furthermore, in large cities that have no incorporated suburban cities, distance also affects the cost of delivering services to the outlying areas. A distance factor can be developed to take distance into consideration.

This method is unlike other methods that rely primarily on population, or on data from other cities of a similar size. Many of the more traditional methods are used to estimate residential impacts or commercial impacts, but not both. This method analyzes all land use types in a city, including tax-exempt properties. This method is based on a city's own data, not data derived from regression analysis of other cities' data. This method is not a proprietary "black box" approach where data is fed in and then results are output from a process that is too complicated or obscure to understand. It does not rely on refinement coefficients; it is straightforward. The results can be traced back step by step to the original data and be understood. There are other methods that purport to be "GIS-based" but simply use GIS to sketch out the areas of future development so that they can be measured without using GIS in a comprehensive way to analyze existing city finances.

IV Major Limitations of the Non-Spatial Methods

Planners are often asked to determine the fiscal impact of new development, usually within a short timeframe. As a result, planners may resort to simplistic methods that produce relatively quick, but not necessarily accurate, answers. Usually, fiscal impact reports are "one-shot" studies, which are not used on a continuous or ongoing basis by the local government. And often fiscal impact studies are largely "black box" analyses that use only a few selected data inputs and rely on a variety of unstated assumptions. In such instances, the reasons and bases for the results of the fiscal impact study are not known or decipherable.

There are several simplistic methods of fiscal impact analysis currently being used in practice. Most popular is the per capita method. The per capita method uses a per person average to make expenditure projections, which assumes that local government expenditures vary simply on the basis of population and are proportional to assessed value.

A cursory list of just a few of the shortcomings of these simpler methods of fiscal impact analysis is provided below.

- They typically are used to project the fiscal impact of a single development proposal. There is usually no residual data to be used for future planning analysis.
- They use broad and simplistic assumptions as to the costs of existing development to make projections.
- Several methods attempt to measure residential impacts or commercial and industrial impacts, but not both.
- They may use total expenditures rather than separating operating from capital expenditures and evaluating them separately.
- They do not address the impact of tax-exempt property. For instance, using assessed value as a measure of revenue generation totally ignores tax-exempt property. Yet, cities with a lot of tax-exempt property need to know those fiscal impacts as well, especially if they are a government center, such as a county seat or state capital.
- Methods that measure the fiscal impacts of residential land use typically rely solely on population, but population is not the only factor by which fiscal impacts vary. For instance, the occupancy rate for housing units may be decreasing in a community, while some of the per unit costs, like road maintenance, are increasing.
- They assume that local government facility and service expenditures are proportional to assessed value. Assessed value can be used for estimating property taxes, but the use ends there. For instance, what does assessed value have to do with road expenses? And what does it have to do with generating police calls? In the latter case, there may even be an inverse relationship.
- Sometimes the fiscal impact method used may be chosen based on a desired outcome. Or, when the results are not coming out the way the practitioner wants, he or she may add an iterative feedback loop to change the method or assumptions or even adjust refinement coefficients until the desired outcome is achieved.

Detailed examples of what the non-spatial methods would produce compared to the actual results using the Spatial Method for several cities will be described in the next chapter.

This chapter will briefly show how the Spatial Method of Fiscal Impact and Planning Analysis works. Much more detail as to how it should be conducted will be shown in the remainder of the book.

V   How Does the Spatial Method Work? An Example

As stated earlier, the Spatial Method is an attempt to model what the ideal transaction processing system might produce. That ideal system would be able to tell one from where each dollar of revenue is derived or where each dollar is spent. Modeling is done by identifying those available and measurable factors that are indicators of the distribution of revenues and expenses or expenditures.

The Spatial Method begins with an analysis of the major sources of revenues that the city collects and expenditures that a city must make to provide needed services. A preliminary analysis is done by examining the latest Comprehensive Annual Financial Report (CAFR) published by the city. For some items, such as property taxes, there is a direct link between the assessed valuation of land parcels and the taxes collected. Other items, such as public safety, are less direct, but annual data on the location of each police and fire call are usually available. Local road maintenance costs can be estimated by determining the road frontage for each parcel. Other important factors include population and employment. The financial analysis also involves separating out the day-to-day, annually recurring revenues and expenses, as opposed to capital or other special project expenditures that may vary from year to year or may be attributable only to specific areas of the city.

To a large degree, the feasibility of using the Spatial Method depends on the degree to which GIS and other data are available. To show how the method works, only the operating revenues and expenses of a typical city will be used for the following example.

A   Operating Revenue

Table 1.1 shows an example of the total operating revenue for one fiscal year for "Typical City". The numbers have been rounded so that the focus is on the overall process and not the detail. The city's Finance Director and department heads have provided insight as to the factors and the weights that should be used to distribute the revenue. More detail on this process will be presented in a later chapter.

After considering the above, one can see that several distribution factors repeat. The simplest way to calculate operating revenue for each parcel would be to add up all of the per capita multipliers, all of the employment multipliers, all of the building market value multipliers, etc. As a result, the multipliers shown in Table 1.2 would be the multipliers to use to estimate operating revenue. One may wonder why so many decimal places are needed. When doing the calculations for an entire city, it is best to minimize

Table 1.1 Annual Operating Revenue, Distribution Factors and Multipliers, Typical City, USA

Operating Revenue Category	Amount	Weight	Distribution Amount	Fiscal Factor Amount	Multiplier	Description
Property Taxes	3,074,000	100%	3,074,000	1,732,000	1.77483	Per $1,000 of Assessed Value
Licenses and Permits	50,000	100%	50,000	106,000	0.47170	Per $1000 C/I Building Market Value
Intergovernmental Revenue	6,000	100%	6,000	9,600	0.62500	Per Capita
Charges for Services	106,000	70%	74,200	9,600	7.72917	Per Capita
		30%	31,800	12,000	2.65000	Per Employee
Public Safety	83,000	100%	83,000	128,000	0.64844	Per Police Call Minute
Street Aid (MSA)	78,000	100%	78,000	60,000	1.30000	Per Front Foot of Street Aid Frontage
Parks and Recreation	122,000	70%	85,400	9,600	8.89583	Per Capita
		30%	36,600	12,000	3.05000	Per Employee
Planning and Zoning	476,000	50%	238,000	9,600	24.79167	Per Capita
		50%	238,000	812,000	0.29310	Per $1000 Building Market Value
Other	237,000	45%	106,650	9,600	11.10938	Per Capita
		45%	106,650	812,000	0.13134	Per $1000 Building Market Value
		10%	23,700	12,000	1.97500	Per Employee
Total Operating Revenue	$4,232,000		$4,232,000			

Table 1.2 Summarized Operating Revenue Multipliers, Typical City, USA

Distribution Factors	Operating Revenue Multipliers
Population	$53.15104
Employment	$7.67500
Assessed Value ($1,000)	$1.77483
Building Market Value ($1,000)	$0.42445
C/I Building Market Value ($1,000)	$0.47170
Police Call Minute	$0.64844
Street Aid (MSA) Frontage	$1.30000

any rounding errors so that the results agree with the city-wide control totals for operating revenue and expenditures. That way, one can be sure not to omit or double count anything.

Tables 1.3 and 1.4 provide an example of the calculation of operating revenue for a typical single-family residential parcel, and a typical commercial parcel, which in this case happens to be offices.

B Operating Expenses

The operating expenses and the allocation factors for the city for the fiscal year are shown in Table 1.5. Again, the allocation factors and weights have been determined by working with city officials.

By summarizing by the fiscal factors, such as population, employment, building market value and police and fire calls, the multipliers shown in Table 1.6 could be calculated for operating expenses.

Using the factor amounts from the example residential parcel, the allocation of operating expenses is shown in Table 1.7 and the same calculations are shown for the commercial parcel in Table 1.8.

Table 1.3 Example of the Allocation of Operating Revenue, Residential for a Single-Family Residential Parcel

Parcel ID: 22302332XXXX

Land Use: Residential Single Family

Distribution Factor	Factor Amount	Multiplier	Operating Revenue
Population	2.68	$53.15	$142.35
Employment	0	$7.68	$0.00
Assessed Value ($1,000's)	$267.90	$1.77	$475.48
Building Market Value ($1,000's)	$157.90	$0.42	$67.02
C/I Building Market Value ($1,000's)	$0.00	$0.47	$0.00
Police Call Minutes	0	$0.65	$0.00
MSA Frontage	40	$1.30	$52.00
Total Operating Revenue			$736.84

Table 1.4 Example of the Allocation of Operating Revenue for a Commercial Office Parcel

Parcel ID: 27302342XXXX

Land Use: Commercial Office

Distribution Factor	Factor Amount	Multiplier	Operating Revenue
Population		$53.15	$0
Employment	566.00	$7.68	$4,344
Assessed Value ($1,000's)	10,198.00	$1.77	$18,100
Building Market Value ($1,000's)	5,243.00	$0.42	$2,225
C/I Building Market Value ($1,000's)	5,243.00	$0.47	$2,473
Police Call Minutes	633.00	$0.65	$411
MSA Frontage	448.00	$1.30	$582
Total Operating Revenue			$28,135

C Operating Fiscal Impact

Fiscal impact is the difference between the revenue generated by a parcel and the expenses to provide services to the parcel. Subtracting the operating expenses from the operating revenue yields the operating fiscal impact. If the difference is positive, a parcel has a positive fiscal impact. If it is negative, a parcel has a negative fiscal impact.

The example residential parcel has an allocated operating revenue of $736.84 and an operating expense allocation of $643.78. While it may appear that this parcel produces a surplus, remember that the total city operating revenue exceeded the total operating expenses by about 9.9%. Keeping this amount would tend to overstate any surpluses or understate any deficits. This excess will have to be zeroed-out or transferred to capital and special revenue. Therefore, to complete the operating fiscal-impact estimate for our example residential parcel, the revenue must be decreased by 9.9%, or $72.95. Therefore, the resulting operating revenue allocation is $663.90. Then, subtracting $643.78 in operating expenses from the operating revenue yields a surplus of $20.12. This is the residential parcel's operating fiscal impact. Table 1.9 summarizes these calculations, for both the example single-family residential parcel and the commercial office parcel.

VI Summary

This has been a general overview of what the Spatial Planning and Fiscal Impact Analysis Method is and how it works.

The Spatial Method is an attempt to model what an ideal transaction processing system might produce. The results are unique to each city since each city's fiscal and spatial patterns are different. This is not about a commercial "off-the-shelf" model; it is about a method. This book is designed to inform users about the method and provide guidance if they want to apply it on their own. If they lack the human resources to do it on their own, this

Table 1.5 Annual Operating Expenses, Distribution Factors and Multipliers, Typical City, USA

Operating Expense Category	Amount	Weight	Distribution Amount	Fiscal Factor Amount	Multiplier	Description
Admin and Finance	445,000	45%	200,250	9,600	20.85938	Per Capita
		45%	200,250	$812,000	0.24661	Per $1000 Building Market Value
		10%	44,500	12,000	3.70833	Per Employee
Planning and Zoning	200,000	10%	20,000	9,600	2.08333	Per Capita
		90%	180,000	$812,000	0.22167	Per $1000 Building Market Value
Government Buildings	211,000	45%	94,950	9,600	9.89063	Per Capita
		45%	94,950	$812,000	0.11693	Per $1000 Building Market Value
		10%	21,100	12,000	1.75833	Per Employee
Police Protection	1,000,000	50%	500,000	128,500	3.89105	Per Police Call Minute
		20%	200,000	9,600	20.83333	Per Capita
		20%	200,000	$812,000	0.24631	Per $1000 Building Market Value
		10%	100,000	12,000	8.33333	Per Employee
Fire Protection	404,000	50%	202,000	20,600	9.80583	Per Fire Call Minute
		20%	80,800	9,600	8.41667	Per Capita
		20%	80,800	$812,000	0.09951	Per $1000 Building Market Value
		10%	40,400	12,000	3.36667	Per Employee
Inspections	282,000	100%	282,000	$812,000	0.34729	Per $1000 Building Market Value
Street Maintenance	406,000	100%	406,000	291,000	1.39519	Per Front Foot of Local and MSA Frontage
Parks and Recreation	656,000	70%	459,200	9,600	47.83333	Per Capita
		30%	196,800	12,000	16.4	Per Employee
Other	208,000	45%	93,600	9,600	9.75	Per Capita
		45%	93,600	$812,000	0.11527	Per $1000 Building Market Value
		10%	20,800	12,000	1.73333	Per Employee
Total Operating Expenses	$3,812,000		$3,812,000			
Operating Surplus	$420,000		$420,000			
Percent of Operating Surplus Transferred to Capital Revenue	9.90%		9.90%			

Table 1.6 Operating Expense Multipliers Typical City, USA

Distribution Factors	Operating Expense Multipliers
Population	$119.67
Building Market Value ($1,000's)	$1.39
Employment	$35.30
Police Call Minute	$3.89
Fire Call Minute	$9.81
Local and MSA Frontage	$1.39

Table 1.7 Example of the Allocation of Operating Expense for a Single-Family Residential Parcel

Parcel ID: 22302332XXXX

Land Use: Residential Single Family

Distribution Factor	Factor Amount	Multiplier	Operating Expense
Population	2.68	$119.67	$320.49
Employment	0	$35.30	$0.00
Police Call Minutes	0	$3.89	$0.00
Fire Call Minutes	0	$9.81	$0.00
Building Market Value ($1,000's)	$157.90	$1.39	$220.05
MSA Frontage	40	$1.40	$55.81
Local Frontage	34	$1.40	$47.44
Total Operating Expense			$643.78

Table 1.8 Example of the Allocation of Operating Expense for a Commercial Parcel

Parcel ID: 27302342XXXX

Land Use: COMMERCIAL OFFICE

Distribution Factor	Factor Amount	Multiplier	Operating Revenue
Population	0	$119.67	$0.00
Employment	566	$35.30	$19,979.80
Police Call Minutes	633.16	$3.89	$2,463.65
Fire and EMS Call Minutes	85	$9.81	$833.50
Building Market Value ($1,000's)	$5,242.80	$1.39	$7,306.35
MSA Frontage	448	$1.40	$625.04
Local Frontage	0	$1.40	$0.00
Total Operating Expense			$31,208.34

will provide a guide to develop a Request for Proposals and select a consultant to do the work for them.

The example provided above deals only with operating funds but the process for capital funds is similar. Another step would be to allocate tax-exempt fiscal impact to the taxable parcels.

Table 1.9 Operating Fiscal Impact for the Example Parcels

Description	Example Parcels	
	Residential Single Family	*Commercial Office*
Gross Operating Revenue	$736.84	$28,135.36
Surplus Transferred to Capital Revenue (9.9%)	$72.95	$2,785.40
Net Operating Revenue	$663.90	$25,349.96
Operating Expenses	$643.78	$31,208.34
Fiscal Impact (Surplus or Deficit)	$20.12	–$5,858.38

The following chapters will describe how to develop the needed database, using GIS and other data processing techniques. They will also demonstrate the myriad of ways that existing and proposed land uses can be analyzed.

ArcGIS by ESRI was the major software package used to model and calculate fiscal impact, and the appendices will provide examples of tools that can be used to develop the planning database.

While it attempts to model the ideal financial system, it still involves some subjectivity as to the factors to be used as surrogates and the amount of weight that should be given to each. Therefore, the method can be considered an art as well as a science. Nevertheless, it is an attempt to be less subjective than other methods and is based on empirical rather than theoretical data.

Throughout this book, the term "city" is used, but the term also applies to communities, municipalities, towns or even townships that are the jurisdictions that collect revenue and provide services to land uses.

References

ArcGIS, Desktop (2017) Release 10.5.1, Redlands, CA: Environmental Systems Research Institute.

Burchell, R. W. and Listokin, D. (1978) *The Fiscal Impact Handbook*, New Brunswick, NJ: Center for Urban Policy Research.

Tomaselli, L. (1991) "A Geographic Systems Approach to Fiscal Analysis", *URISA Journal, Volume 2, Number 2, 50–65.*

2   A Survey of Fiscal Impact Analysis Methods

Spatial Fiscal Impact and Planning Analysis is the topic of this book, but it is useful to put it in the context of what has been used in the past and what scholars point out as to the need for further research and development.

Fiscal impact of land uses has been studied for over 75 years. It was originally used to measure the increased revenues resulting from urban renewal but has expanded to include the impact on both costs and revenues for proposed new land uses (Bise, 2010, p. 1). This chapter will describe the different methods and their strengths and weaknesses.

Fiscal impact analysis is the measurement of the costs and revenues of existing development in order to project the impact of new development. It provides planners with the information to support their recommendations or pose their critiques regarding land development proposals. The degree to which the analysis achieves this depends on how well it "helps decision-makers link planning to the local annual budget" and removes the myths that they and the citizens may have about the impact of development (Kotval and Mullin, 2006, p. 1).

There are many fiscal impact methods that have been used and described in the literature. Six were described extensively in the book *The Fiscal Impact Handbook* (Burchell and Listokin, 1978), including the average costing methods of Per Capita, Service Standard, Proportional Valuation and also the marginal costing methods of Comparable City, Employment Anticipation and (Marginal) Case Study, which examines existing infrastructure capacity (roads, sewers and water).

Since then, practitioners have developed at least four more alternative methods of analysis. The seventh method is the Hybrid approach, which combines the Per Capita Method to estimate operating revenues and expenditures and the Case Study method to deal with the existing capacity (Edwards, 2000, p. 8).

The Cost of Community Services is the eighth method. It mainly deals with operating costs and revenues and relies on interviews with local staff to estimate costs.

The ninth method is really a combination of a number of methods that incorporate some of the features of the three original average costing methods to produce "off-the-shelf" fiscal impact models.

The tenth method is the Spatial Method, which uses many factors, which are indicators of operating revenues and expenses, in addition to population, to derive the Cost of Community Services. It is more time consuming, but it creates a robust and objective database at the parcel level that allows the users to analyze the fiscal impacts of detailed land use categories at different levels of density, location and age of development. Like the Case Study method, it also identifies the existing infrastructure and remaining capacity. The method provides a strong basis on which to project operating and capital fiscal impact.

Table 2.1 summarizes the methods based on their characteristics. There may be others not listed here.

I Average Costing Methods

A *Per Capital Method*

Perhaps the easiest to use is the Per Capita Method. It is an average-costing approach to population and school-aged population (SAP) impact on costs and revenues (Burchell, Listokin and Dolphin, 1985, p. 9). It assumes that the current average patterns of revenues and expenditures will continue into the future. Revenues and expenditures are calculated based on per capita averages. The method does not consider the marginal costs for infrastructure which may have excess or deficient capacities (Bise, 2010, p. 22) and may require new capital construction.

The method assumes that the current levels of service will be the same in the future and that future residents will demand services at the same rate as the current population (Kotval and Mullin, 2006, p. 5). It also assumes that the current mix of city expenditure categories will remain constant.

Expenditures attributable to residential uses are calculated to be the proportion of the residential property valuation compared to the total valuation, multiplied times the general fund expenditures and then divided by the population. An example would be a city which has 89% of its property value in residential uses and general fund expenditures of $16 million. Multiplying the $16 million by 89% yields $14.24 million in costs, which are assumed to be attributable to residential land use. Dividing this by the population of 18,066 yields a per capita expense of $788.

The Per Capita approach is easy to use but has the disadvantage of being less accurate than other approaches if local officials want to look beyond broad levels of overall costs and expenditures (Bise, 2010, p. 26).

B *Service Standard*

The Service Standard method uses average costing to project the impact of population change (Burchell and Listokin, 1978, p. 67). It is used to project the local municipal and school district expenditures. It does examine the

Table 2.1 Summary of Selected Fiscal Impact Methods by Their Characteristics

Method or Approach	Average Costing	Marginal Costing	Factor Based	Type of Expenses		Land Use Type		Tax-Exempt	Parcel-based
				Operating	Capital	Residential	Non-residential		
1. Per Capita	X			X		X			
2. Service Standard	X			X	X	X			
3. Proportional Valuation	X			X			X		
4. Comparable City		X			X	X			
5. Employment Anticipation		X			X		X		
6. Marginal Case Study		X		X	X	X			
7. Hybrid: Allocation Rule Percentage	X	X		X	X	X	X		
8. Cost of Community Services (COCS)			X	X		X	X	X	
9. Off-the-Shelf Models	X			X	X	X	X		
10. Spatial Fiscal Impact Analysis (SFIA)		X	X	X	X	X	X	X	X

relationship of capital to operating expenses, although it does not consider the marginal costs. It does not project the impact of non-residential (commercial/industrial) change. This methodology assumes that service levels for both personnel and capital facilities are, to a large extent, a function of a jurisdiction's total population and that communities of a similar size will therefore have similar service levels (Bise, 2010, p. 26).

The process begins by estimating the population and SAP by alternative development types. Using tables for different regions of the country from the 1972 US Census of Governments, and based on the population size of the municipality, multipliers are used to estimate the number of full-time employees per 1,000 population by service category.

A problem with this approach is the accuracy of the tables, derived from data produced in 1972. Another issue is the municipal size and region categories, which tend to be very broad.

C Proportional Valuation

The Proportional Valuation method projects the impact of non-residential (primarily commercial and industrial), assuming that real property value represents municipal costs (Burchell, Listokin and Dolphin, 1985, p. 29)

The first step is to calculate the percentages of residential value and non-residential value of the total real property value. For example, if the residential value is $1.136 million and the non-residential value is $626 million, the percentages would be 64% and 36%, respectively. The 36% is then multiplied by the general government expenditures (e.g., $95.9 million) to determine the amount attributable to non-residential development, or $34.5 million. Next, this number is adjusted using refinement coefficients "derived from retrospective analyses which compared the actual expenditures generated by nonresidential facilities to those projected using a simple proportional valuation" (Burchell and Listokin, 1978, p.130). The adjustments finally result in the estimated amount of costs for the proposed development.

After the adjustments are made, percentages are used to estimate the amount of the estimated cost for governmental functions, such as general government, public safety, public works, health and welfare and recreation and culture.

While this method is reported to be quick and inexpensive, the author finds that it is not clearly understood how it works, in that the refinement coefficients are derived from retrospective analyses (Burchell and Listokin, 1978, p. 130). Explaining it to local officials and citizens could be very difficult and has the appearance of being a "black box" approach. It also groups commercial and industrial into one land use category, thus assuming that the impacts of these land use types are similar, when in fact retail development is significantly costlier than office and industrial uses (Bise, 2010, p. 6).

Another question is what constitutes real property value? Is it market value or assessed? In some states, commercial and industrial are assessed at different rates of market value compared to residential. If it is just assessed value, then what is the impact of tax-exempt uses, which are assumed to be part of "non-residential" development?

This method may make "inaccurate assumptions about residential to non-residential land use ratios. Does existing residential development account for a greater share of certain service costs than nonresidential uses?" (Kotval and Mullin, 2006, p. 20).

The Fiscal Impact Handbook was written in 1978 and the authors state that retrospective case studies are "an excellent tool to analyze fiscal impact results, yet infrequently employed" (Burchell and Listokin, 1978, p.130). To upgrade the coefficients, "these types of analyses must continue to be undertaken".

II Marginal Fiscal Impact Methods

Marginal fiscal impact methods consider the current capacities of a municipality's infrastructure, primarily sewer, water, roads and schools, and project whether these capacities are sufficient to accommodate a new development.

Although over the long term, average and marginal cost techniques will produce similar results, the real value of fiscal analysis is in the two- to ten-year time period, when a community can incur costs (Bise, 2010, p. 25).

For example, if a municipality has excess sewer and water capacity in the area where the new development is proposed, the only additional cost would be for operating expenses.

The Per Capita Method assumes that costs increase in a linear fashion. However, things like sewer and water facilities are "lumpy" in nature and capacity increases are not linear (Edwards 2000, p. 7).

A Comparable City

The Comparable City method is based on the assumption that public service expenditures vary by population size and growth rate for similar cities. The multipliers are based on Census of Governments data that are provided in *The Fiscal Impact Handbook* (Burchell and Listokin, 1978, pp. 103–108). The tables show operating multipliers for cities of differing sizes and growth rates, as well as capital multipliers for the same types of cities. A municipality with a population size of 25,001 to 50,000 that is growing at a rate of 2% per year is considered the base and the multipliers for all municipal services, including education, are equal to 1. The multipliers for other sized cities and different growth (or decline) rates will have numbers for municipal services that are greater than or less than 1.

After calculating the per capita and per student costs in the service categories (e.g., general government, public safety, etc.), costs are multiplied times the multipliers from the tables. For example, if the general government cost per capita is $15.54, then, based on the multiplier from the table of .94, the future costs per capita will be $13.99 per capita. If the general government capital cost is $1.93 per capita and the multiplier from the tables is 2.33, the future capital cost will be $4.50 per capita. After calculating the per capita and per student costs and adjusting them by the multipliers from the tables, the future impact of different development alternatives can be calculated (Burchell and Listokin, 1978, p. 111).

An issue for this method is the validity of the multipliers in the tables based on data from 1972. A literature search has found that there are no published, comparable tables reflecting more recent statistics. This methodology is used infrequently (Bise, 2010, p. 25).

B Employment Anticipation

The Employment Anticipation method is based on the assumption that commercial and industrial costs are related to per capita costs (Burchell, Listokin and Dolphin, 1985). It acknowledges that increased employment will increase expenditures. "The method relies on coefficients to express changes in per capita municipal expenditures" resulting from increased employment "for categories of cities defined by population size and direction of growth" (p. 35). The coefficients can be interpreted as "a change of one commercial or industrial employee will produce an increase in per capita local expenditures of X percent" (p. 34). A series of coefficients are available for different categories of per capita expenditures, such as general government, public safety, etc.

As with other methods, such as the Service Standard, Proportional Valuation and Comparable City, the coefficient multipliers are based on data from the 1970s, thus bringing into question whether they are still valid and whether the relationships have changed.

C Marginal Case Study

This method has traditionally been called the "Case Study" method, but there are other methods that could be considered to be case studies as well. As a result, the method has been qualified here as a Marginal Case Study.

The method is a marginal site-specific method to determine excess or slack capacity and the effect of population change (Burchell, Listokin and Dolphin, 1985, p. 15). Unlike other methods, this method views each city as unique in the way it finances governmental services and in the accepted levels of service for each.

It involves site-specific interviews with city personnel to determine whether there are excess or deficient capacities that will be affected by a new development proposal. For example, if a school has a low pupil–teacher ratio and the new development will use, but not exceed, the standard pupil–teacher ratio, the school costs will not significantly increase. However, if the school is at capacity, then the new development will be charged with the full amount of increasing the capacity.

This method seems to have more credibility with local government finance and management staff. Finance and budget staffs tend to view a per capita analysis as a planning exercise while the marginal analysis is viewed as a more serious attempt at replicating fiscal reality (Bise, 2010, p. 28). However, the method relies on individuals who may have vested interests in the outcome of the analysis (Edwards and Huddleston, 2010 p. 26).

The method requires more time to conduct compared to the previous five methods.

III More Recent Methods

A Hybrid: Allocation Rule Percentage (ARP)

The Hybrid Model using the Allocation Rule Percentage (ARP) has been described clearly and extensively by Mary Edwards in her publication "Community Guide to Development Impact Analysis" (Edwards, 2000). The method uses the Per Capita approach to project the impact of residential development and the modified Proportional Valuation Method to project the impact of non-residential development and then finally the Case Study Method to determine capital costs.

The main feature of the model is to calculate the split among expenditures between residential and non-residential uses. This measure has been labeled the Allocation Rule Percentage (Edwards and Huddleston, 2009, p. 33). For example, if the city has 89% of its property value and 62% of its parcels in residential uses, the average of the two would be 75%. This percentage is multiplied times the general fund expenditures of $16 million, the result is $12 million, which is attributable to residential. Dividing this by the population (17,990) results in a per capita cost of $667. The remaining 25% is attributable to non-residential ($4 million) and is divided by the number of employees in the city (13,830) to get the per employee multiplier of $289.

These multipliers are used to project expenditures based on population and employment.

Estimating revenue is done generally in the same manner as expenditures, with the exception of property taxes and shared revenue.

The remaining steps will not be described here, but they include estimating debt service costs and capital facility costs.

Edwards cautions the user to consider the cumulative impact of several developments rather than one case in isolation. The first development proposal may not require any new capital expenses, but the next may tip the balance and result in deficient capacities (2000 p. 9).

"No extant literature has established a conceptual or empirical basis for using the ARP to make fiscal projections, although it is used in all off-the-shelf FIA models and workbooks" (Edwards and Huddleston, 2010, p. 38).

B Cost of Community Services (COCS)

Several entities and authors have described the Cost of Community Services (COCS) approach, which attempts to determine the operating costs and revenues of existing land uses to determine if each land use "pays its way" (Kotval and Mullin, 2006, p. 4) and then uses this data to project the impact of future development. Most studies deal with a rather small number of land use categories: residential, commercial, industrial and farm or open land.

The final result of a Cost of Community Services study is a set of ratios for different categories of city operations. If a land use has a ratio of 1:1, it means that the revenue collected by the community equals the amount of expenditures needed to service the land use. Generally, results have shown that residential uses have ratios greater than 1, meaning that they cost more than the revenue they contribute. Other uses such as commercial, industrial and open or farmland have ratios that are considerably less than 1:1, for example, 1:0.27 for industrial. The main impetus behind conducting cost of community service studies has been the American Farmland Trust (AFT), in an attempt to demonstrate that residential land uses produce deficits while open and farmland land uses produce surpluses. This method has been criticized as being advocacy based, rather than objective.

Costs are averages across a land use category, such as residential, that may be comprised of old, established and compact development as well as newer development. Using the average may or may not overestimate the costs and underestimate the revenues from proposed new development. Furthermore, there can be big differences between apartments, condominiums, townhomes and single-family detached housing units. The range of land uses needs to be expanded to include more variety.

The allocation of expenses to land uses is based on "expert opinions". The validity of the results depends on the rigor with which the study is conducted. For example, some may be based on assumptions and estimates that are not necessarily backed up by empirical evidence. The estimates may be simply "guesstimates" (Bise, 2010, p. 28). Ladd also states, "we must therefore judge the reliability of the results on the basis of their plausibility and the manner in which they were derived" (1994).

Kotchen states that: "The fact that COCS studies are based on average expenditures and revenues is problematic because understanding the impacts of land-use change requires information about marginal costs and benefits." Furthermore, "future research should further investigate the effect of density with more refined measures of the actual density of development... The main concerns are the following: partitioning land uses into only three classes obscures potentially important variation within a given class" (2009, p. 377).

Kotval and Mullin characterize a COCS study as: "Resource-intensive and generates results that are not usually transferable to other communities...Calculated at a particular point in time rather than over a period of years to account for changes in public investment and variation in service demands...", they do "not account for potential economies of scale and the public good aspects of public services. That is, once the school building is built, each additional student doesn't cost nearly as much as the first students to occupy the school (at least until capacity is reached)" and that they typically report "average rather than incremental (marginal) fiscal impacts" (2006, p. 28).

C Off-the-Shelf and Spreadsheet Models

Off-the-shelf spreadsheet models have been used extensively, but space does not permit detailed descriptions. Some observations by practitioners provide a general description along with the strengths and weaknesses.

Many of the models are based on the Per Capita Method using a spreadsheet. They incorporate "a community's level of service standards for police, fire, EMS, parks, libraries, schools and roads. These services are the main drivers of government's costs" (Colie, 2003, p. 4).

According to Edwards and Huddleston, "current off-the-shelf FIA models and workbooks do not produce reliable results" (2010, p. 36). They state that planners should acknowledge the limitations of these types of models and that researchers "should develop a better theoretical and empirical underpinning for this important planning analysis tool" (p. 25). They note the "potential error associated with the determination and application of spending and revenue multipliers. Although these multipliers appear precise, they are based on assumptions that have not been verified in the literature" (p. 26). They applied a spreadsheet model to each of Wisconsin's seven largest cities using different multipliers and found a range of results.

Colie reports a concern by Dr. Fishkind, creator of the Fiscal Impact Analysis Model (FIAM), that the spreadsheet format makes it easy for "an unscrupulous user to manipulate the results to suit some particular end". Colie also notes further that obtaining marginal cost and marginal revenue measures for a specific land use decision is problematic (2003, p. 4).

D Spatial Fiscal Impact Analysis (SFIA) Method

The Spatial Fiscal Impact Analysis Method is based on the premise that all costs and revenues are spatial and that the best way to measure the costs and revenues is by allocating them to parcels. This method is the subject of this book so this description will only be a summary of its characteristics. More detail is provided in the following chapters. It was developed by the author, Dr. Linda Tomaselli, over the past 34 years (1984 to 2018).

1 Relevant Literature Review

It has been pointed out that "local government accounting practices do not systematically track expenditures by location or land use" (Heikkila and

Leckie, 1989, p. 1). The Spatial Method attempts to model what an ideal, but to date non-existent, transaction processing system would produce by using surrogate factors that reflect the flows of revenues and expenditures.

The Spatial Method is designed to eliminate the drawbacks of the other methods which purport to identify the costs of land uses but raise the question: "do we really know, or are we just guessing?". Fiscal impact analysis has been described as "an art and a science" (Bise, 2010, p. 37). The art deals with the subjectivity of the assumptions. The Spatial Method attempts to minimize subjective assumptions and come closer to reality.

Three types of fiscal impact analyses have been identified by Bise: cost-of-land-uses, area-wide analysis and project analysis (2010, p. 51). The Spatial Method initially provides the first and second of these, which set the stage for the third, project analysis, as will be described in the later chapters.

The Spatial Method is transferable to other communities, although the results may be quite different. Heikkila and Leckie point out that a method should be "quite independent of the setting chosen, and so should apply equally well to Canadian and American cities". The results, "while different should be revealing, and that the resulting database could itself be of significant value as input for general research on the links between land use and municipal finance" (1989, p. 12).

In the report by the Government Finance Officers Association (GFOA), Katz points out that "GIS data of the kind kept by many municipalities could provide information on existing conditions in a form that could be easily integrated into the fiscal impact quotient scoring process" (2013, p. 29). In particular, he refers to parcel data. Lowry and Lowry also acknowledge that large amounts of spatial data are increasingly available in the public domain (2014, p. 59).

Leiske concludes the "government's inability to mitigate the fiscal and other stresses of differing urban forms is due in part to the lack of actionable information available at the scale of land-use change, the land parcel" (2015, p. 1).

2 Key Features, Inputs and Outputs

The Spatial Method uses factors such as population, school aged population (SAP), land value, property tax collections, employment, police and fire calls and road frontage, as well as others to allocate costs and revenues to parcels. It is a method and not a "model", as in some off-the-shelf models, in that it is based on the acknowledgment that each community is unique and the financial practices are also unique. Empirical evidence is the best basis upon which cities should analyze fiscal impact.

It does require some professional judgments as to the weights that should be given to the factors to develop multipliers that can be used to determine the costs and revenues of each parcel. However, the weights generally are found to be valid, believable and understandable to local officials and citizens.

The weights could also be calibrated further if there is a concern about the preliminary results. The results must make sense to city officials. The ethical practitioner should be careful not to modify the weights to satisfy their own preconceived ideas or biases as to what the results should be.

The method also heavily reflects location, as well as the age of existing development (year built). For example, when projecting the cost of a new residential development proposal, multipliers from more recent developments should be used to project future costs and revenues, rather than using the average for the land use across the entire community. The planner or practitioner creates the detailed land use categories based on what already exists so that unique land uses can be identified and either considered or excluded from the analysis.

Parcels are usually the lowest common denominator for land use, with the exception of mixed use. By using parcel-level data, neighborhoods can be defined, tax increment financing (TIF) districts can be identified and the results can be summarized in myriads of ways. The impact of density can also be evaluated in that the results can be summarized not only by per unit but also per acre.

The availability of land-parcel data, usually from the county assessor, is what makes this method possible. The data usually includes at least the basic land use classifications, such as residential, commercial, industrial, tax-exempt and vacant. It will be up to the planner to refine the categories.

The Spatial Method provides the opportunity to estimate the impact of TIF districts or to identify areas in need of redevelopment. It also sets the stage for identifying water, sewer, road and school capacities to project the marginal impact.

As practiced for the cities of Anoka, MN (Tomaselli, 2009) and Bloomington, IL (Tomaselli, 2015), one of the final products is a detailed report that summarizes all of the assumptions and calculations that have been made, as well as describing how the information should be used.

3 Costs and Benefits

While it is certainly the most expensive method to use, it results in a robust planning and fiscal impact database that can be used for many types of projects, and for several years, before needing to be updated. The development of the database can be considered a very proactive approach to fiscal analysis and an investment for planning.

The expense in developing the database is primarily due to estimating the population and SAP by parcel. One can use general multipliers by residential land use categories or one can refine the data further by correcting for census counts by census block, which would be more realistic. Appendices D and E describe the process in detail.

The availability of employment data by parcel is a problem. In Anoka, MN, the Community Development Director had conducted a detailed employment inventory by parcel, even down to the level of home-based businesses. In Bloomington, IL, however, there was no such data. The need for employment data should be the purview of Community or Economic Development Directors and Transportation Planners and they should be brought into the study as important participants.

Another expense is allocating police and fire call time to parcels. This can be difficult if the police department only can give paper copies or print records, but the task is not insurmountable. In the case of Bloomington, IL, police and fire already had their calls located by global position system (GPS) points and, as a result, the cost was minimized.

The last major effort will be to determine the road frontage per parcel, but once it is done it can be updated rather easily. The remainder of this book, including the appendices, is designed to provide the "how to" techniques that can be used.

The Spatial Method requires a user proficient in ArcGIS (2017). The calculations can be done with linked spreadsheets in smaller communities, such as in Anoka, MN (17,990 population), but spreadsheets do have size limitations and the ability to easily select parcels based on certain parameters. For larger communities, such as Bloomington, IL (77,680 population), programming in ArcGIS Model Builder would be more effective. However, this requires more training and modeling expertise. As the education of planners evolves, the need for training in the use of GIS as well as government finance should be self-evident, as Edwards reports in her survey of planning schools (2007, p. 19).

IV   The Future of Fiscal Impact Analysis

In the past, most fiscal impact studies were demand-driven by developers seeking approvals for projects. But, Leistritz (1994, p. 8) believes that, in the future, it will be driven by decision-makers. He goes on to write that the emphasis on moving impact assessment to higher levels will likely lead to a more proactive approach. With economic development being an important part of community planning, fiscal impact analysis will become an important component.

Bise (2010, p. 9) observes that local officials and the general public have growing expectations for precise fiscal analysis. He goes on to write that studies have typically been to review direct impacts of development proposals. Problems to date with fiscal impact analysis include a lack of standards and formal procedures, the wide variation in the methods and the lack of consideration of the impact on overlapping governmental entities (Bise, 2008). Another problem, he notes, is that politicians may have their own biases as to what types of development are beneficial and "can't handle the truth" when the analysis does not support their position. He states that, in the future, communities will be interested in infrastructure replacement rather than just infrastructure expansion. Another of his observations is that fiscal impact analysis will increasingly be used to evaluate special districts and tax increment financing (TIF) district proposals. His final observation is that market analysis will be used to determine the market feasibility of development proposals or proposed land use changes, which will refine the inputs into the fiscal impact analysis and "show the pace at which infrastructure capacity will be used or filled over time" (2010, p. 2).

V Summary

Fiscal Impact Analysis has had a long history and is evolving over time. With the increased availability of spatial data, GIS software and trained users to manipulate it, it is now possible to model the flows of revenues and expenditures in a city to determine the relationship between fiscal impact and land use. It is hoped that this book will become a modest milepost along the way of that evolution.

References

Bise, L. C. (2010) *Fiscal Impact Analysis: Methodologies for Planners*, Chicago, IL: American Planning Association Planning Advisory Service.

Bise, L. C. (2008) "The Future of the Fiscal Impact Professions: Challenges and Opportunities", *Fiscal Impact Roundup: Trends in Fiscal Impact Analysis*, Orlando, FL: PowerPoint Presentation at the National Impact Fee Roundtable, slides 43–46.

Black, J. T. and Curtis, R. (1993) "The Local Fiscal Effects of Growth and Commercial Development Over Time", *Urban Land (January)*, 18–21.

Burchell, R. W. and Listokin, D. (1978) *The Fiscal Impact Handbook*, New Brunswick, NJ: Center for Urban Policy Research.

Burchell, R. W., Listokin, D. and Dolphin, W. R. (1985) *The New Practitioner's Guide to Fiscal Impact Analysis*, New Brunswick, N.J: Center for Urban Policy Research.

Burchell, R. W., Nicholas, J. C., Martin, B., Flora, P. and Bise, L. C. (2008) *Fiscal Impact Roundup: Trends in Fiscal Impact Analysis*, Orlando, FL: Powerpoint Presentation at the National Impact Fee Roundtable.

Clapp, C. M., Freeland, J. and Ihlanfeldt, K. (2017) "Fiscal Impacts of Alternative Land Uses" *Public Finance Review, Volume 46, Issue 5*, 850–878.

Colie, D. G., NAIOP of Florida, and Fishkind and Associates (2003) "Fiscal Impact Analysis Model (FIAM)", Tampa, FL: University of South Florida, *College of Business Publications, Paper 32*.

Deal, B. and Schunk, D. (2004) "Spatial dynamic modeling and urban land use transformation: a simulation approach to assessing the costs of urban sprawl", *Ecological Economics Volume 51*, 79–95.

Downs, A. (2004) "The Costs of Sprawl Revisited", Edited version of a speech presented at the ULI District Council Meeting, Washington, DC.

Edwards, M. (2000) *Community Guide to Development Impact Analysis*, Madison, WI: Wisconsin Land Use Research Program.

Edwards, M. (2007) *Public Finance and Planning: A Survey of Planning Schools*, Lincoln Institute of Land Policy Working Paper, Lincoln Institute Product Code: WP07ME1.

Edwards, M. and Huddleston, J. R. (2009) "Prospects and Perils of Fiscal Impact Analysis", Chicago, IL: *Journal of the American Planning Association, Volume 76,* Number 1.

ArcGIS, Desktop (2017) Release 10.5.1 Redlands, CA: Environmental Systems Research Institute.

Heikkila, E. J. and Kantiotou, C. (1992) "Calculating fiscal impacts where spatial effects are present", *Regional Science and Urban Economics, Volume 22, Issue 3,* 475–490.

Heikkila, E. and Leckie, P. (1989) "Expert Evaluation of Municipal Revenues and Expenditures by Land Use Category" *Journal of Planning Education and Research, Volume 8,* 35–44.

Katz, P. (2013) "The Missing Metric", *Government Finance Review,* 20–32.

Kotchen, M. J. (2009) "A Meta-Analysis of Cost of Community Services Studies", *Regional Science Review, Volume 32, Number 3,* 376–399.

Kotval, Z. and Mullin, J. R. (2006) "Fiscal Impact Analysis: Methods, Cases, and Intellectual Debate", *Lincoln Institute of Land Policy Working Paper,* Product Code: WP06ZK2.

Ladd, H. F. (1994) "Fiscal impacts of local population growth: a conceptual and empirical analysis", *Regional Science and Urban Economics, Volume 24, Issue 6,* 661–686.

Leiske, S. N. (2015) "Costs of sprawl in the metropolitan West: census block group evaluation of Public service expenditures", *Western Economics Forum, Spring 2015, pp. 1–12.*

Leistritz, F. L. (1994) "Economic and Fiscal Impact Assessment", *International Association for Impact Assessment,* https://ageconsearch.umn.edu/bitstream/1 21073/2/AAE%20No.94004.pdf.

Lowry, J. H. and Lowry, M. B. (2014) "Comparing Spatial Metrics that Quantify Urban Form" *Computers, Environment and Urban Systems, Volume 44,* 59–67.

Marlow, J. E. (2008) "Economic and Fiscal Impacts of Smart Growth Policies", *Lincoln Institute of Land Policy - Sonoran Institute Joint Venture, July, 2008, pp. 1–26.*

Meis, K. (2013) "Fiscal Impact Tools Change Local Planning", *Government Finance Review, December 2013, pp. 1–10.*

Thompson, D. (2013) "Suburban Sprawl: Exposing Hidden Costs, Identifying Innovations" *Sustainable Prosperity, October 2013, Executive Summary pp. I–VI, and 1–38.*

Tomaselli, L. (1991) "A Geographic Systems Approach to Fiscal Analysis", *URISA Journal, Volume 2, Number 2,* 50–65.

Tomaselli, L. (2009) "GIS Fiscal Impact Analysis, City of Anoka, MN 2009", *Anoka Fiscal Impact,* Retrieved from http://www.anoka-fiscal-impact.com/.

Tomaselli, L. (2015) "GIS Fiscal Impact Analysis, City of Bloomington, IL", *Bloomington Fiscal Impact,* Retrieved from http://bloomington-fiscal-impact.com/.

3 A Comparison of the Spatial Fiscal Impact Method to Other Methods

This chapter examines some of the key assumptions of other fiscal impact methods and compares the results to those of the Spatial Method. For the purpose of these comparisons, it is assumed that the Spatial Method results in measures that are closer to reality and are, therefore, more accurate. The Spatial Method results shown in this chapter are from a project for the city of Anoka, MN conducted in 2009. Anoka is presented here to keep things simple to explain since its financing methods were relatively uncomplicated. Furthermore, Anoka had a detailed breakdown of commercial/industrial uses and employment, while Bloomington did not. Anoka had a significant amount of tax-exempt properties because it was the county seat, which helps to consider their impacts as well.

I Assumption: The Costs for Tax-Exempt Properties Should Be Included in Non-residential Costs

At the outset, this assumption can easily be disputed. Tax-exempt uses are assumed to benefit all types of land use, as in schools, churches and parks, and the relationship to residential. Non-residential uses also benefit from tax-exempt uses, in that they benefit from schools which provide trained employees, recreation and affordable public housing for their employees. They also benefit from governmental offices. For this reason, under the Spatial Method, the expenses for tax-exempt uses were allocated to both residential and commercial/industrial parcels. Table 3.1 shows the expenses for tax-exempt uses found in Anoka, MN.

II Assumption: Assessed Value Reflects Real Property Value and Is Useful for Estimating Costs

By real property value, does that mean market values or assessed values? Assessed value would ignore tax-exempt property. Not all assessors provide data on the market value of tax-exempt property, although there was data for Anoka. The differences between using assessed versus market value are significant, as will be shown in the examples below. Under the Spatial

Table 3.1 Costs Attributable to Tax-Exempt Land Use Based on the Spatial Method, City of Anoka, MN, 2009

Tax Exempt Land Use	Parcels	Estimated Expenses			
		Operating	Capital	Total	Per Parcel
Schools	42	325,795	53,908	379,703	9,041
Church and Charitable	53	132,468	52,948	185,416	3,498
City Property	193	384,142	455,457	839,599	4,350
County Property	10	262,084	18,068	280,151	28,015
State Property	12	675,067	17,476	692,543	57,712
Federal Property	4	825	13	839	210
Total	314	$1,780,381	$597,870	$2,378,251	$7,574

Method, it is believed that market values, particularly building market values, provide a better way of measuring costs because they better reflect the intensity of land use. While it appears that assessed values are traditionally used to calculate per capita costs, in some states and communities, different rates by land use category and market valuation are used to calculate assessed values, so using assessed values would also affect the results. For example, the tax rate for apartments in Anoka was almost 20% greater than that for single-family units. The rates for commercial and industrial were also about 50% higher than single-family.

Assessed value is not a good measure for estimating costs.

III Assumption: Residential Costs Are Simply a Function of Population and Are Determined Based on the Proportion of Total Real Property Value

This is an important assumption in determining costs under the Per Capita Method for residential and in calculating the remaining non-residential costs under the Proportional Valuation Method. This method of calculating per capita costs may be convenient, but the results show a wide variation and a tendency to overestimate costs for dense residential development and commercial/industrial land uses.

According to the original book, *The Fiscal Impact Handbook*, the term "local taxable real property" is used (Burchell and Listokin, 1978, p. 31). A more recent publication confirms that only the taxable property values are used in a description of the Proportional Valuation Method by using the term "assessed values" (Bise, 2010, p 25).

Anoka's residential properties made up 63.19% of the "tax capacity" (proportionally equivalent to assessed value in other states). Therefore, with operating and capital costs of 16,056,014, the residential cost would be calculated to be $10,145,795. Dividing this by the population of 17,990, the per capita amount for expenses would be $564. It is not clear whether capital costs should be included as well, but they are for this example. If market values were used instead, residential land uses would make up only 60.19%, which would result in a per capita multiplier of $537, as shown in Table 3.2.

Table 3.2 Alternative per Capita Expenditure Allocations Based on Data from the City of Anoka, MN, 2009

Tax Capacity Example

Land Use	Population	Tax Capacity		Allocated Expenditures	
		Amount	Percentage	Amount	Per Capita
Residential	17,990	10,396,818	63.19%	10,146,118	$564
Non-residential		6,055,924	36.81%	5,909,897	
Totals	17,990	$16,452,743	100.00%	$16,056,014	NA

Market value Example

Land Use	Population	Market value		Allocated Expenditures	
		Amount	Percentage	Amount	Per Capita
Residential	17,990	922,639,000	60.19%	9,663,895	$537
Non-residential		610,273,400	39.81%	6,392,119	
Totals	17,990	$1,532,912,400	100.00%	$16,056,014	NA

The Spatial Method allocates costs using more than just population to determine residential costs. The factors include police and fire calls, market values and road frontage. Furthermore, it allocates costs by parcel and thus by more detailed land use categories. Table 3.3 shows a comparison of different residential types and the two methods of calculating per capita costs (assessed and market values). While the overall per capita costs may be comparable, there are substantial differences when comparing residential land use types.

If the Per Capita Method multiplier were used to project the cost of apartments, the projections would be $11 per capita too high. Using market values, the Per Capita Method multiplier would be lower ($537), yet still higher than the average under the Spatial Method by $16.

Under the Spatial Method, apartments had higher per capita operating costs due to police calls, but a lower per capita cost due to less road frontage compared to single-family detached. Nursing homes and quad homes had similar patterns. Duplexes had high police call numbers and they tended to be located more on street corners, and thus had higher costs. Single-family attached and detached, as well as twin homes, also had greater costs per capita, partially due to road frontage.

The "other" category reflects the costs borne by the city due to having a state treatment hospital that results in substantial police and fire/EMS expenses. Since the use is tax exempt, the expenses were allocated to the taxable properties (both residential and commercial/industrial).

Table 3.3 Per Capita Method Expenditures Compared to the Spatial Fiscal Impact Method Results for the City of Anoka, MN, 2009

| Taxable Residential Land Use | Spatial Method Results | | | Per Capita Method Calculations | | | |
| | | | | Assessed values | | Market Values | |
	Population	Expenses*	Per Capita	Calculated	Difference	Calculated	Difference
Apartment	3,869	1,831,007	473	564	91	537	64
Duplex	563	407,450	724	564	-160	537	-187
Nursing Home	161	31,247	194	564	370	537	343
Quad Homes	199	86,870	437	564	127	537	100
Single-Family Attached	1,586	945,413	596	564	-32	537	-59
Single-Family Detached	10,689	6,616,617	619	564	-55	537	-82
Twin Homes	54	31,387	581	564	-17	537	-44
Other Tax-Exempt Residential	869	0	0				
Totals	$17,990	$9,949,992	$553	$564	11	$537	-16

*Includes allocated tax-exempt expenses.

Another comparison that can be made is to the Hybrid Allocation Rule Percentage (ARP) approach described by Edwards and Huddleston (2010, p. 33). Anoka's residential parcels made up 84% of the parcels. Residential assessed values were 63% of the total, which yields an average of 73.5%. In that case, per capita expenditures would be estimated to be $657. Again, this would be $104 higher than the Spatial Method results.

Whatever method is used to calculate per capita costs, the methods seem to be quite arbitrary and the results vary significantly from what resulted from using the Spatial Method. If a proposal came forward to build apartment units that would add 100 persons to the population, based on the Per Capita Assessed Value Projection, the estimated cost would be $9,100 too high compared to Anoka's numbers.

Per Capita Methods may be easy to use but can lead to erroneous results, masking the differences between residential types.

IV Assumption: Assessed Value Is the Basis for Determining Non-residential Costs

Just as assessed property value is used to estimate per capita costs, it is also used to estimate non-residential costs under the Proportional Valuation Method. As stated above, assessed value is subject to some wide variations, and excludes consideration of tax-exempt uses. Using Anoka again as an example, if 63.19% represents the residential costs, then 36.81% would be the preliminary non-residential costs, for an initial amount of $5,910,219.

Following the steps described in the Fiscal Impact Handbook for the Proportional Valuation Method, the 36.81% would be adjusted by refinement coefficients, "since the relationship is non-linear" among different communities (Burchell and Listokin, 1978, p. 122). The steps are shown in Table 3.4. The author contends that following the steps was a very tedious and confusing process; what follows is an interpretation.

First, the relationship between the assessed values of properties is determined by calculating the average non-residential parcel value of $2,893 (#3) and comparing it to the average parcel value in the community ($6,456). In Anoka's case, the ratio of the average value of non-residential parcels to all parcels was 2.232. Locating this ratio on the upper line of the graph (Exhibit 6-3 of the Fiscal Impact Handbook, Burchell and Listokin, 1978, p. 124) one finds a coefficient of 1.45. This means that the allocated non-residential costs must be increased by 45%. The preliminary non-residential percentage (36.81%) would then be 53.36%. The new expenditure amount for non-residential properties would be $8,567,489.

Table 3.5 shows an example of a new industrial plant. The numbers on the left side of the table are consecutive to the numbers in Table 3.4 and the calculations are noted with reference to the numbers.

Table 3.4 Proportional Valuation Initial Calculations for Anoka, MN, 2009

1	Total assessed value for city	$16,452,743
2	Total number of parcels in city	5,688
3	Total assessed value per all parcels in city (#1 divided by #2)	$2,893
4	Total assessed value for non-residential parcels	$6,055,924
5	Total number of non-residential parcels	938
6	Assessed value per non-residential parcel (#4 divided by #5)	$6,456
7	Ratio of non-residential parcel values to all parcel values (#6 divided by #3)	2.232
8	Coefficient from upper curve	1.45
9	Initial non-residential expenditure allocation percentage	36.80%
10	Total expenditures	$16,056,014
11	Adjusted non-residential expenditure allocation percentage (#8 times #9)	53.36%
12	Adjusted non-residential expenditure allocation (#10 times #11)	$8,567,489

Table 3.5 Projected Expenditures Using the Proportional Valuation Method for a New Industrial Development

13	Total value of Anoka industrial parcels	$3,220,186
14	Number of Anoka industrial parcels	109
15	Average value of Anoka industrial parcels	$29,543
16	Assessed value of new industrial plant (from #15)	$29,543
17	Proportion of all non-residential value	0.00488
18	Proportion to average non-residential parcel value (#9 divided by #6)	4.5759
19	Coefficient from lower curve	0.6
20	Adjusted allocated expenditures times proportion of non-residential and coefficient (#10 times #17 times #19)	$25,077

The value for the new development is based on Anoka's averages for industrial parcels (see item #15 below) so the results can be directly compared to the results from the Spatial Method.

Based on the example in the *Fiscal Impact Handbook*, (Burchell and Listokin, 1978, p. 123) a proposal for a new industrial plant is presented to the city. The value of the new plant is 4.5759 (#18) times the value of all the other non-residential parcels and it is 0.00488 (.488%) of the existing non-residential property value (#17). Locating this on the lower curve of the graph, the refinement coefficient is found to be 0.6 (#19). The calculation of the amount attributable to the new development would be the $8,567,489 adjusted non-residential expenditure allocation, multiplied by .00488 and then by .6. The result would be $25,077 in expenses for the new industrial facility (#20). A comparison of this to the expenditures determined by the Spatial Method will be provided in Table 3.7.

Table 3.6 provides an example for a new shopping center, which is equal to the tax capacity (assessed value) of the average of shopping center parcels

Table 3.6 Projected Expenditures Using the Proportional Valuation Method for a New Shopping Center

21	Total value of Anoka shopping center parcels	$1,101,478
22	Number of Anoka shopping center parcels	100
23	Average value of Anoka shopping center parcels	$11,015
24	Assessed value of new shopping center (from #28	$11,015
25	Proportion of all non-residential value	0.00182
26	Proportion to average non-residential parcel value	1.70608
27	Coefficient from lower curve	0.85
28	Adjusted allocated expenditures times proportion of non-residential and coefficient (#10 times #25 times #27)	$13,245

Table 3.7 Results of Using the Spatial Fiscal Impact Method for Non-residential Parcels in the City of Anoka, MN, 2009

		Expenditures	
Taxable Non-residential Land Use	*Parcels*	*Total*	*Per Parcel*
Auto Service	27	66,036	2,446
Bank	5	5,567	1,113
General Commercial	13	26,536	2,041
Industrial	109	1,726,174	15,836
Motel	2	26,860	13,430
Office	71	407,205	5,735
Personal Service	12	60,774	5,065
Railroad	1	24,837	24,837
Restaurant	24	155,520	6,480
Shopping	100	521,551	5,216
Special Service District	3	9,600	3,200
Vacant	228	164,127	720
Other*	343	18,101	53
Total	938	$2,998,727	$3,197

*Includes tax-exempt allocated to taxable parcels.

in Anoka (see item #28). The steps are similar to the industrial parcels, but the refinement coefficients are different. The expenditures for the new shopping center under the Proportional Valuation Method would be estimated at $13,245.

What was actually found using the Spatial Method is shown in Table 3.7. The city of Anoka had 109 industrial parcels. The average value of each industrial parcel was the same as the proposed incoming industrial facility. Using the Spatial Method, the average cost per parcel was $15,836, compared to the $25,077 calculated above, meaning that the Proportional Valuation Method would have overestimated the costs by $9,241. For the average shopping center, the Spatial Method produced estimated expenditures of $5,216, compared to the $13,245 under the Proportional Valuation Method, an overestimate of $8,038.

Going through all of these calculations was found to be complicated and subject to errors. While the refinement coefficients are based on previous research, they are not easily understood, especially if one has to explain it to a citizen or decision-maker. Since the initial calculations are presumed to be based on assessed value, one would also need to be able to estimate assessed value, which is often different than projected construction costs. Furthermore, is the estimated value just the building value or does it include land? Under the Spatial Method, almost all calculations use building value alone because land does not typically demand services, except for road access, but that is also accounted for by using road frontage as an allocation factor.

A last observation regarding using the Proportional Valuation Method is that if it were used in conjunction with the Per Capita Method to estimate the future costs of a development having both residential and non-residential land uses, both costs would be overestimated. Under the Per Capita Method, the costs are estimated to be directly in proportion to land value (63%), but, in the case of the non-residential uses, the costs are increased from 35% to 53% for a total of 116%, based on the example shown previously.

V Assumption: The Proportion of Expenses among Service Categories Is Similar to Other Communities

The Proportional Valuation Method uses percentages to estimate the commercial and industrial costs for the different categories of city services, including general government, public safety, public works, health and welfare and recreation and culture. The data from the *Fiscal Impact Handbook* for non-residential uses is summarized in Table 3.8 and compared to the results for Anoka, MN (Burchell and Listokin, 1978, p. 127). Assuming that the results from the Spatial Method are more accurate, using the percentages

Table 3.8 Percentages from the *Fiscal Impact Handbook* for Government Service Categories for Commercial/Industrial Development, Compared to the Results for Anoka, MN, 2009

Service Categories	Industrial		Commercial	
	Book Average*	Anoka	Book Average*	Anoka
General government	6.00%	22.00%	6.00%	11.00%
Public Safety	45.00%	21.00%	75.00%	46.00%
Public Works	45.00%	51.00%	15.00%	36.00%
Health and Welfare	3.00%	0.00%	2.00%	0.00%
Recreation and Culture	1.00%	6.00%	2.00%	7.00%
Totals	100.00%	100.00%	100.00%	100.00%

* The Fiscal Impact Handbook, p.127.

from the book appears to be questionable. Again, they are based on retrospective analyses of old data.

VI Assumption: Per Capita Costs Can Be Used to Estimate the Increased Cost Resulting from Additional Employees

The Employment Anticipation Method is a marginal costing technique for projecting the impact of non-residential growth on municipal costs and revenues. The method is mainly focused on employment as the generator of additional costs and is based on multivariate analyses conducted between 1957 and 1975 (Burchell and Listokin, 1978, p. 135). It provides multipliers to use to project the increase in per capita municipal costs with the addition of one employee.

This is an issue that needs further study even for the Spatial Method. We know that employment affects city costs, but just how much?

Table 3.9 shows what the Employment Anticipation Method would produce for an increase of one commercial employee, using the data from the City of Anoka. Under this method, a new employee would add $302 to operating and capital expenses. Expressing employment impact using a per capita multiplier seems to be rather confusing and ambiguous. Note that the per capita amount of $895 is different than the per capita amount shown previously in Table 3.1 ($564) because all expenditures are used rather than a portion based on the proportion of assessed value. Also in this case, the per capita costs are calculated based on the category of municipal service. This shows that even among the other six methods, the multiplier can vary greatly, leading one to question the methodology and results.

Table 3.10 shows the results of the Spatial Method for the City of Anoka with regard to employment. The overall average ($328) is not that much different than the Employment Anticipation amount ($302).

However, there are significant differences among employment categories. The amounts were based on things like the numbers of police and fire calls, road frontage and market value, in addition to employment. The first three reflect the demand for city services by the presence of the different types of commercial development, not necessarily by the employees themselves. Employment was only a partial factor when it came to the need for general government, public safety, public works and parks and recreation. The author contends that basing cost projections on employees is not very effective. There are factors of the commercial and industrial and physical and operational land uses themselves that determine costs, such as police and fire calls, protection capabilities related to building market value and also road maintenance costs.

What can be concluded from the table is that employment alone is not the measure of costs for auto service, general commercial, motel,

Table 3.9 Employment Anticipation Calculations for a Commercial Development

| Government Service | Population | Expenditures | | Multiplier from Employment Anticipation Method | Increased Total per Capita Cost per One Employee |
		Amount	Per Capita		
General Government	17,990	1,917,189	106.57	0.0000018	$3.45
Public Safety	17,990	4,815,151	267.66	0.0000162	$78.01
Public Works	17,990	4,366,914	242.74	0.0000299	$130.57
Parks	17,990	1,772,377	98.52	0.0000403	$71.43
Interest on Debt	17,990	891,472	49.55	0.0000212	$18.90
Other	17,990	2,330,998	129.57	0	$0.00
Total	17,990	$16,094,101	894.61		$302.35

Table 3.10 Costs per Employee Using the Spatial Method Compared to Employment Anticipation Method, City of Anoka, MN, 2009

Land Use	Employment	Spatial Method Expenditures		Employment Anticipation Expenditures	
		Amount	Per Employee	Per One Employee	Difference
Auto Service	125	$66,036	528	302	$226
Bank	45	$5,567	124	302	−$178
General Commercial	23	$26,536	1154	302	$852
Industrial	5119	$1,726,174	337	302	$35
Motel	12	$26,860	2238	302	$1,936
Office	1805	$407,205	226	302	−$76
Personal Service	121	$60,774	502	302	$200
Restaurant	492	$155,520	316	302	$14
Shopping	1386	$521,551	376	302	$74
Total	9128	$2,996,223	$328	$302	$26

personal service and shopping. There are other factors that contribute to the greater cost. For all of the other uses, the cost per employee under the Spatial Method is less than what the employment anticipation method predicts. As noted previously, there is definitely a need for further study of the impact of employment and the factors that contribute to commercial/industrial costs. Expressing the impact of employment in per capita terms is not reliable because there are big differences among commercial/industrial types.

VII Summary

This chapter has shown several of the assumptions under several non-spatial methods and compared them to the results from the Spatial Method for Anoka, MN. Using these somewhat simpler methods would result in some big differences. In many cases, the projected costs are higher. Is that a good thing or will developments be denied based on these higher costs? It is assumed that the Spatial Method produces more accurate results because it considers several factors that realistically reflect costs. The remainder of this book is primarily based on the study for Bloomington, IL. The same patterns of results would probably be found, with the exception that results for the detailed employment and commercial/industrial land use categories did not exist for that study.

These methods were the best that were available in the past, but with spatial data and GIS, the practitioner can gain a better insight as to what really drives costs.

References

Bise, L. C. (2010) *Fiscal Impact Analysis: Methodologies for Planners*, Chicago, IL: American Planning Association Planning Advisory Service.

Burchell, R. W. and Listokin, D. (1978) *The Fiscal Impact Handbook*, New Brunswick, N. J.: Center for Urban Policy Research.

Edwards, M. and Huddleston, J. R. (2010) "Prospects and Perils of Fiscal Impact Analysis", *Journal of the American Planning Association, Vol. 76, No. 1.*

4   Preliminary Financial Analysis

This chapter will describe the process of analyzing a city's Comprehensive Annual Financial Report (CAFR) to help determine what factors are needed in the parcel database to be able to allocate revenues and expenditures. It will specifically focus on two cities in the Midwest and also provide an overview of how one would go about analyzing cities in the Northeast, South and West. To use the Spatial Method, cities need to develop a GIS database based on the complexity of the local financing system. The more complicated the city finance system is, the more types of data will probably be needed. Every city is unique in their financing but the method for analyzing their financial reports can be used for each of them.

I General Fund Analysis

The Spatial Method begins with a preliminary analysis of the city's financing methods. Typically, this starts with analyzing its Comprehensive Annual Financial Report (CAFR) and evaluating the major revenue and expenditure items. The CAFRs usually contain a table titled "Statement of Revenues, Expenditures and Changes in Fund Balances" for Governmental Funds. Table 4.1 shows the total amounts for two case study cities.

Planners may not be accustomed to working with financial data. It may be necessary to work with the Finance Director, even at this early stage of analysis, as it will almost always be required in later stages. The columns titled "Percent of Total" have been included so that one can recognize the major items. The population has also been included so that some per capita measures can also be used for a general, overall analysis.

The first observation is the similarities among the cities, such as the importance of property taxes and charges for services. However, in Bloomington, the importance of property taxes is overshadowed by sales and other taxes. There are also similarities for expenses, with public safety being the most important, followed by general government, parks and recreation and streets. Yet, note that Bloomington, with four times the population of Anoka, had almost ten times the expenses for public safety.

Table 4.1 Comparison of Revenues and Expenses, Anoka, MN and Bloomington, IL

	Anoka, MN		Bloomington, IL	
Fiscal Item	2009 Amount	Percent of Total	2013 Amount	Percent of Total
Revenues:				
Property Taxes	8,222,287	54.50%	23,572,329	24.00%
Sales and Other Taxes			54,227,817	55.30%
Special Assessments	436,729	2.90%		
Charges for Services	938,238	6.20%	11,745,246	12.00%
Intergovernmental	3,448,436	22.80%	4,168,080	4.30%
Licenses and Permits	299,718	1.99%	1,280,698	1.30%
Fines and Forfeitures	197,953	1.31%	1,192,438	1.20%
Franchise Fees	1,204,563	8.00%		
Investment Earnings	231,174	1.50%	65,667	0.10%
Other	115,220	0.80%	1,767,232	1.80%
Total Revenue	$15,094,318	100.00%	$98,019,507	100.00%
Revenue per Capita	$839		$1,262	
Expenses:				
General Government	2,015,056	12.50%	13,823,919	14.40%
Public Safety	4,572,761	28.40%	41,102,503	42.90%
Public Works	1,231,499	7.70%	9,484,042	9.90%
Park & Recreation	1,720,539	10.70%	13,821,831	14.40%
Community Development			773,068	0.80%
Interest on Debt	765,219	4.70%	2,947,855	3.10%
Debt Service Principal	235,000	1.50%	4,415,866	4.60%
Parking			439,483	0.50%
Capital Outlay	5,474,406	34.00%	9,055,786	9.40%
Other	79,619	0.50%		
Grant Pass-Thru				
Total Expenses	$16,094,099	100.00%	$95,864,353	100.00%
Expenses per Capita	$895		$1,234	
Surplus or Deficit	–$999,781		$2,155,154	
Transfer In	2,095,496		9,996,417	
Other Income			2,656,274	
Transfer Out	–1,785,500		–10,977,001	
Net Change in Fund Balance	–$689,785		$3,830,844	
Estimated Population	17,990		77,680	

Property taxes are based on the assessed value (or Tax Capacity, in the case of the Minnesota cities). Charges for services are generally accepted to be based on land use, population, employment, as well as other factors. Public safety expenses are generally based on police and fire calls, as well as the need for patrolling to protect people and buildings. General government expenditures are based on the demands of the population and employment and building market value. Parks and recreation expenses are mostly based on population and employment. Finally, street expenses are based on the amount of locally maintained road frontage.

Just from this very cursory analysis, a parcel map and basic parcel attributes are needed in the GIS database, including the following:

- Market value of land and buildings
- Assessed value (or tax capacity, in the case of the Minnesota cities)
- Land use
- Parcel address
- Housing units for multi-family
- Residential square footage and/or number of bedrooms for single-family
- Street frontage, including side streets
- Estimated population
- Estimated school-age population (if the study includes education)
- Estimated employment
- Police and fire calls for the year

Another thing that is noticeable from Table 4.1 is the differences in the amounts per capita among the two cities. That is why using a per capita approach is not reliable. It also shows that each city's finances are unique to that city and that one cannot use Anoka's results to estimate Bloomington's.

II Enterprise Fund Analysis

Cities often have "enterprise funds" to account for specific activities that operate like businesses. Typically, these include sewer, water, surface-water management and recycling. They can also include functions such as an electric utility, liquor store or a golf course. If the revenues of each fund closely balance out to the expenditures, one can assume that the funds do not need to be included in the analysis. However, if a fund is subsidized by the general fund (a transfer in) or if the fund generates more revenue than is needed to cover expenses and is transferred out, then the fund should be included in the analysis.

Table 4.2 shows the enterprise funds for the two case study cities. The values are also shown on a per capita basis for purposes of comparison since the cities vary greatly in size.

The Electric Fund for Anoka showed a significant surplus, at $209 per capita. After talking to the Finance Director, it was learned that the city buys electricity from the local large electrical company and re-sells it to city residents and businesses. Since the city buys such a large amount, it can buy it very inexpensively. It generated a large $3.6 million surplus in 2009. Therefore, the fiscal analysis included taking into consideration the electrical billing records, which were available. This surplus revenue was allocated to each parcel based on the actual billing amounts. On the other hand, the golf course generated a nearly $1 million deficit. Many of the people using the golf course come from outside the city, so it would be difficult to analyze and patronage records were not readily available. The city keeps the golf

Table 4.2 Enterprise Funds, Anoka, MN and Bloomington, IL

	Anoka, MN		Bloomington, IL	
Fiscal Item	2009 Amount	Per Capita	2013 Amount	Per Capita
Revenues:				
Electric	23,320,380	1,296		
Water	1,669,326	93	17,634,395	227
Sewer			5,353,308	69
Surface Water Management			2,730,053	35
Refuse and Recycling			4,890,868	63
US Cellular Coliseum			3,562,252	46
Liquor	3,885,844	216		
Golf	916,504	51		
Other	442,480	25	2,841,476	37
Total Revenue	$30,234,534	$1,681	$37,012,352	$476
Expenses:				
Electric	19,729,760	1,097		
Water	1,372,374	76	13,482,517	174
Sewer			5,494,245	71
Storm drainage			1,994,791	26
Refuse & Recycling			6,208,163	80
US Cellular Coliseum			4,435,803	57
Liquor	3,669,135	204		
Golf	1,372,763	76		
Other			2,908,711	37
Total Expenses	$26,144,032	$1,453	$34,524,230	$444
Surplus or Deficit:				
Electric	3,590,620	200		
Water	296,952	17	4,151,878	53
Sewer			−140,937	−2
Storm drainage			735,262	9
Refuse & Recycling			−1,317,295	−17
US Cellular Coliseum			−873,551	−11
Liquor	216,709	12		
Golf	−456,259	−25		
Other	442,480	25	−67,235	−1
Total Surplus or Deficit	$4,090,502	$227	$2,488,122	$32
Estimated Population	17,990		77,680	

course as a matter of civic pride and identity. To allocate this loss, more general factors had to be used.

Bloomington's water fund generated a significant surplus, which appears to have subsidized the other funds. However, water billing records were incomplete, making it impossible to allocate it to parcels based on the billing. The analysis could have included an analysis of refuse and recycling records and storm drainage, but they also were not readily available. The US Cellular Coliseum was like Anoka's golf course; many users come from outside the city and it is kept as a matter of civic pride and recognition. Including any of the above would have overly complicated the analysis because of the need to generate new data and records. Due to time and budgetary constraints, Bloomington's enterprise funds were not included in the analysis.

Bloomington's enterprise funds generated an overall surplus of only $32 per capita, while Anoka's was $238. If more data had been readily available for Bloomington, this could have been included in the analysis and perhaps made the final results more accurate, but the surplus was not that large and including the results may not have made a big difference.

III Separating Operating from Capital and Special Projects

It is important that a fiscal analysis take into consideration operating revenues and expenditures which maintain consistency from one year to the next, although they may increase due to inflation or changes in policy to increase or decrease the levels of service. A separate analysis must be made of the capital or special revenues and expenditures which could vary significantly from one year to the next or may be dedicated to certain special areas of the city, such as Tax Increment Financing (TIF) districts.

A Anoka, Minnesota

Figure 4.1 shows an important table from Anoka's Comprehensive Financial Report (CAFR), titled "Statement of Revenues, Expenditures and Changes in Fund Balances Governmental Funds". Table 4.3 shows the initial classification of revenues and expenditures as to whether they are operating or capital.

From this, one can see that street renewal and state aid construction had large amounts of expenditures for capital projects. Enterprise Park Tax Increment was a special fund that was also separated out from operating revenues and expenditures because it applied only to a specific area of the city. Building improvement was also separated out, although the amounts were not large. Debt service was an annual obligation of the city, even though it was probably borrowing for capital projects that happened in the past. Ideally, this should have been examined to determine exactly where the projects were done and the cost of debt service should be allocated to the land parcels that benefitted from the improvements. Unfortunately, that information was not readily available because the projects were completed many years ago. In this case, since it was considered a regular expense that recurs consistently from one year to the next, it was considered to be an operating one.

When looking at the "Other" category, one might ask, "how much detail is necessary for this analysis?". Since the fund balances out with only a minor deficit, it could probably be treated as either operating or capital.

Another thing that the table shows is the amount of intergovernmental revenue that is applicable to each fund. When allocating this revenue to

CITY OF ANOKA, MINNESOTA

STATEMENT OF REVENUES, EXPENDITURES AND CHANGES IN FUND BALANCES
GOVERNMENTAL FUNDS
FOR THE FISCAL YEAR ENDED DECEMBER 31, 2009

	General	Debt Service	Street Renewal	Building Improvement	State Aid Construction	Enterprise Park Tax Increment	Other Governmental Funds	Total Governmental Funds
Revenues:								
Taxes	$5,382,424	294,295				2,481,577	63,991	8,222,287
Special assessments	-	-	436,729	-	-	-	-	436,729
Licenses and permits	247,256	-	2,355	-	-	-	50,107	299,718
Fines and forfeitures	115,179	-	-	-	-	-	82,774	197,953
Intergovernmental	1,840,128	-	1,373,220	-	27,883	8,006	199,228	3,448,465
Charges for current services	869,298	-	-	-	-	-	68,940	938,238
Franchise fees	867,396	-	337,167	-	-	-	-	1,204,563
Investment income	41,359	7,717	62,992	346	4,173	46,185	68,402	231,174
Miscellaneous	3,781	-	-	-	10,864	5,000	95,546	115,191
Total revenues	9,366,821	302,012	2,212,463	346	42,920	2,540,768	628,988	15,094,318
Expenditures								
Current:								
General government	1,715,715	-	524	-	-	80,558	218,259	2,015,056
Public safety	4,371,785	-	-	-	-	-	200,976	4,572,761
Public works	1,190,029	-	-	-	-	-	41,470	1,231,499
Parks	1,634,783	-	-	-	-	-	85,756	1,720,539
Miscellaneous	79,619	-	-	-	-	-	-	79,619
Capital outlay	150,180	-	3,104,386	32,832	1,338,007	717,714	131,287	5,474,406
Debt service:								
Principal retirement	-	235,000	-	-	-	-	-	235,000
Interest and fiscal charges	-	515,000	-	-	-	250,219	-	765,219
Total expenditures	9,142,111	750,000	3,104,910	32,832	1,338,007	1,048,491	677,748	16,094,099
Excess (deficiency) of revenues over expenditures	224,710	(447,988)	(892,447)	(32,486)	(1,295,087)	1,492,277	(48,760)	(999,781)
Other financing sources (uses); including transfers:								
Transfer in	270,000	245,000	900,000	130,000	-	-	550,496	2,095,496
Transfer out	(1,150,000)	-	-	-	-	(390,500)	(245,000)	(1,785,500)
Total other financing sources (uses)	(880,000)	245,000	900,000	130,000	-	(390,500)	305,496	309,996
Net changes in fund balances	(655,290)	(202,988)	7,553	97,514	(1,295,087)	1,101,777	256,736	(689,785)
Fund balances (deficits) at beginning of year	5,148,834	1,099,047	2,585,481	(1,269,908)	(610,087)	(5,648,493)	3,141,649	4,446,523
Fund balances (deficits) at end of year	$4,493,544	896,059	2,593,034	(1,172,394)	(1,905,174)	(4,546,716)	3,398,385	3,756,738

See accompanying notes to financial statements.

Figure 4.1 Statement of Revenues and Expenditures and Changes in Fund Balances, Anoka, MN, 2009.

parcels, it will be necessary to understand the formulas that determine these amounts.

B Bloomington, Illinois

Figure 4.2 shows the important page from Bloomington's CAFR and Table 4.4 shows an initial categorization as to operating or capital. In this case, there were very large amounts of capital expenditures in a Non-Major Fund category. The circled items in Figure 4.2 are the major control totals that were used to check the calculations throughout the entire analysis process to make sure that nothing is omitted or double counted. The operating and capital/special revenue adds up to $98,019,507, the expenditures add up to $95,864,353 and the city had a total surplus of $2,155,154.

IV Other Cities in the US

The above examples are for a Minnesota city and another in Illinois. One may ask, "What differences might be seen in different parts of the country?".

Three additional cities have been chosen from the East, West and South: Barnstable, MA, Redlands, CA and Plano, TX. These are compared to one

Table 4.3 Governmental Funds, Categorized as Operating, or Capital and Special City of Anoka, MN

| Governmental Fund | Revenue | | Expenditures | | Surplus or Deficit | Analysis Category |
	Intergovern-mental	Other	Capital Outlay	Other		
General	1,840,128	7,526,693	150,180	8,991,931	224,710	Operating
Debt Service		302,012	0	750,000	-447,988	Operating
Street Renewal	1,373,220	839,243	3,104,386	524	-892,447	Capital
Building Improvement		346	32,832	0	-32,486	Capital
State Aid Construction	27,883	15,037	1,338,007	0	-1,295,087	Capital
Enterprise Park Tax Increment	8,006	2,532,762	717,714	330,777	1,492,277	Capital
Other	199,228	429,760	131,287	546,461	-48,760	???
Total	$3,448,465	$11,645,853	$5,474,406	$10,619,693	-$999,781	

CITY OF BLOOMINGTON, ILLINOIS
Governmental Funds

STATEMENT OF REVENUES, EXPENDITURES
AND CHANGES IN FUND BALANCES

Year Ended April 30, 2013

	General	Library	Debt Service	Nonmajor Governmental Funds	Total
REVENUES					
Taxes	$ 70,846,002	$ 4,642,935	$ 2,231,424	$ 79,785	$ 77,800,146
Intergovernmental	441,273	12,500	-	3,714,307	4,168,080
Licenses and permits	1,280,698	-	-	-	1,280,698
Charges for services	11,664,479	80,767	-	-	11,745,246
Fines and forfeitures	1,095,669	-	-	96,769	1,192,438
Investment income	55,372	4,633	499	5,163	65,667
Other	1,206,146	417,013	12,274	131,799	1,767,232
Total revenues	86,589,639	5,157,848	2,244,197	4,027,823	98,019,507
EXPENDITURES					
Current:					
General government	13,376,981	-	-	446,938	13,823,919
Public safety	40,967,988	-	-	134,515	41,102,503
Highways and streets	6,635,792	-	-	2,848,250	9,484,042
Culture and recreation	9,317,149	4,397,536	-	107,146	13,821,831
Community development	-	-	-	773,068	773,068
Parking	439,483	-	-	-	439,483
Debt service:					
Principal	1,175,866	-	3,240,000	-	4,415,866
Interest and fiscal agent fees	177,962	-	2,754,293	15,600	2,947,855
Capital outlay	1,513,191	9,328	-	7,533,267	9,055,786
Total expenditures	73,604,412	4,406,864	5,994,293	11,858,784	95,864,353
EXCESS (DEFICIENCY) OF REVENUES OVER EXPENDITURES BEFORE OTHER FINANCING SOURCES (USES)	12,985,227	750,984	(3,750,096)	(7,830,961)	2,155,154

Figure 4.2 Statement of Revenues and Expenditures and Changes in Fund Balances, Bloomington, IL, 2013.

another in Table 4.5 and to the two shown previously. Again, the percentages are based on the numbers found in the table in the Comprehensive Annual Financial Report (CAFR) titled "Statement of Revenues and Expenditures". There certainly are differences but, by approaching other cities in the same way, the method is transferable. The important thing to consider is the relative amounts of revenue and expenses, which is why the percentages are shown. When looking at the numbers, one must ask, "what is this for?" and "what does this include?". There may be other amounts within the subtotals that can be directly related to land use, rather than just within an ambiguous item.

A *Governmental Funds*

Comparing the town of Barnstable to the others, the percentages are quite different because the town is also responsible for education. As a result, the amount of property tax revenue is much higher than the others. In this case, the fiscal impact of the school-aged population (SAP) would need to be addressed. Also, the amounts for general government, public safety and

Table 4.4 Governmental Funds, Categorized as Operating, or Capital and Special City of Bloomington, IL

Governmental Fund	Revenue		Expenditures		Surplus or Deficit	Analysis Category
	Intergovern-mental	Other	Capital Outlay	Other		
General	441,273	86,148,366	1,513,191	72,091,221	12,985,227	Operating and Capital?
Library	12,500	5,145,348	9,328	4,397,536	750,984	Operating
Debt Service		2,244,197		5,994,293	−3,750,096	Operating
Non-Major Funds	3,714,307	313,516	7,533,267	4,325,517	−7,830,961	Capital
Total	$4,168,080	$93,851,427	$9,055,786	$86,808,567	$2,155,154	

Table 4.5 Comparison of Revenues and Expenditures for Five Cities in Different Parts of the US

Fiscal Item	Anoka, MN 2009 Percent of Total	Bloomington, IL 2013 Percent of Total	Barnstable, MA 2016 Percent of Total	Redlands, CA 2017 Percent of Total	Plano, TX 2017 Percent of Total
Revenues:					
Property Taxes	54.50%	24.00%	61.24%	64.47%	47.50%
Sales and Other Taxes		55.30%	4.22%	3.27%	24.60%
Special Assessments	2.89%		0.27%		
Charges for Services	6.20%	12.00%	3.33%	9.90%	5.17%
Intergovernmental	22.80%	4.30%	20.87%	11.22%	3.99%
Licenses and Permits	1.99%	1.30%	1.95%	5.64%	3.26%
Fines and Forfeitures	1.31%	1.20%			4.07%
Franchise Fees	8.00%		0.99%		6.99%
Investment Earnings	1.50%	0.10%	1.22%		0.77%
Other	0.80%	1.80%	3.49%	5.48%	3.66%
Hotel, Motel and Meal Tax			2.41%		
Total Revenue	100.00%	100.00%	100.00%	100.00%	100.00%
Population	17,202	77,680	45,193	69,211	279,100
Revenue per Capita	$877	$1,262	$3,932*	$1,092	$1,219
Expenses:					
General Government	12.50%	14.40%	4.41%	14.54%	9.69%
Public Safety	28.40%	42.90%	7.55%	50.35%	35.89%
Education			44.87%		
Public Works	7.70%	9.90%	8.81%	6.71%	1.61%
Park and Recreation	10.70%	14.40%	1.39%	3.07%	6.09%
Community Development		0.80%	3.50%		8.85%
Interest on Debt	4.70%	3.10%	1.09%	1.15%	3.70%
Debt Service Principal	1.50%	4.60%	4.93%	3.67%	6.75%
Parking		0.50%			0.00%

(Continued)

Table 4.5 (continued)

Fiscal Item	Anoka, MN	Bloomington, IL	Barnstable, MA	Redlands, CA	Plano, TX
	2009 Percent of Total	2013 Percent of Total	2016 Percent of Total	2017 Percent of Total	2017 Percent of Total
Capital Outlay	34.00%	9.40%		18.22%	22.54%
Other	0.50%		1.06%		0.25%
State and County Charges			4.49%		
Pension and Employee Benefits			15.64%		0.00%
Community Services			2.27%		1.91%
Library				2.29%	2.72%
Total Expenses	100.00%	100.00%	100.00%	100.00%	100.00%
Population	17,202	77,680	45,193	69,211	279,100
Expenses per Capita	$936	$1,234	$2,220*	$1,227	$1,440
Number of Students			5,204		
Expenses per Student			$15,695**		

* Excludes education expenses.
** Includes education expenses only.

parks and recreation seem very low. Part of the reason is that education is included in the total expenditures so the percentages are affected but, also, pension and employee benefits are shown as separate items. When performing an analysis, these items would need to be broken down by department so that the allocation of costs to land uses includes this portion of the costs. The Finance Director can provide this information.

Bloomington and Plano rely on sales and other taxes to finance their cities, and to a lesser degree, Barnstable and Redlands. This will be an issue as to how to allocate this revenue: to the population that pays the taxes or to the land uses that collect the taxes?

B Transfers and Enterprise Funds

As has already been shown for Anoka and Bloomington, one must also look at transfers in and out of the General Fund, which typically come from or go to the Enterprise Funds. Table 4.6 shows the transfers for Barnstable, Redlands and Plano. While the net result may seem relatively small, the individual amounts are also important. The relative importance, as expressed as a per capita amount is also important. For example, in Redlands, the overall surplus from the enterprise funds is $588, which is significant. Looking at the detail for the different funds, substantial surpluses are found coming from the water and waste disposal funds, and to a lesser amount from sewer funds. If one were to conduct a Spatial Fiscal Impact Study for Redlands, it would be necessary to obtain the water and waste billing records so that the surpluses could be adequately allocated to the customers.

In the case of Barnstable, there is a significant amount of loss per capita in the Enterprise Funds (–$160). The main deficit is for the airport, although there is a significant capital contribution that offsets the loss. One would need to investigate further where the contribution comes from and how it should be allocated. As for sewer and water, where the net difference is relatively small (+$23 per capita), it would be a question for the practitioner whether to use billing records to allocate this revenue.

Lastly, in the case of Plano, there is a significant contribution, mainly from developers. There also is a significant transfer out. Further investigation would need to be done as to where the transfer out is going to. Also, the city lists "Other enterprise funds" with a $7 million deficit, which is about $90 per capita. Upon digging a little deeper into the CAFR, one finds that the main source of this deficit is Convention and Tourism. More research would need to be done to determine how to allocate this cost.

In conclusion, the Spatial Fiscal Impact Method can be used in a variety of municipalities and situations. One just needs to study the Comprehensive Annual Financial Report to generate questions for the Finance Director and begin to determine what factors are needed to appropriately allocate revenues and expenditures.

Table 4.6 Enterprise Funds, Transfers and Non-operating Funds for the Three Example Communities

Fiscal Item	Barnstable, MA		Redlands, CA		Plano, TX	
	Amount	Per Capita	Amount	Per Capita	Amount	Per Capita
Enterprise Funds Surplus or Deficit	−2,746,406	−160	5,617,943	588	−3,642,014	−47
Non-Operating and Contributions	2,968,110	173	3,912,803	410	15,880,748	204
Transfers In	2,565,124	149	1,107,489	116	0	0
Transfers Out	−2,453,752	−143	−3,608,403	−378	−13,573,300	−175
Total Surplus or Deficit	$333,076	$19	$7,029,832	$736	−$1,334,566	−$17
Population	17,202		9,552		77,679	

V How Much Detail Is Needed?

How far should one go in breaking down city finances and what additional items need to be included in the GIS Database? It depends on several things:

1 How significant is the item? There is a law of diminishing returns when doing the analysis. If the item represents a significant percentage of the revenues or expenditures, then it must be examined. But if it is not significant, treat it in a general manner.

2 Does the city have intergovernmental revenue that is related specifically to certain land uses or functions?

   For example, if the city receives money for street improvements, then the allocation should be based on the spatial distribution of the streets to be improved. Furthermore, if a city receives a significant amount of outside revenue based on a formula that uses specific measures, such as population, then it should be allocated in the same manner: based on population. In Anoka, Minnesota, the city received a distribution from the Fiscal Disparities Law that showed up as property tax revenue. Under the law, the cities contribute 40% of their new commercial/industrial development to a region-wide tax base pool. The formula to redistribute the pool is based on a formula that uses the inverse of market value per capita. This means that the cities with poorer residents receive more than the ones with more well-to-do residents. Within the city, the portion of property tax revenue was distributed to residential land uses in the same manner, with apartments and mobile homes receiving more per capita than single-family homes, since their market values per capita were less than single-family.

3 Does the city have Tax Increment Financing (TIF) districts? In that case, the parcels in the districts must be identified, so that the expenditures for services can be quantified. Since the tax increment revenue goes to pay off the improvements, the district will have an operating deficit during the period in which the district is active, because the parcels must be provided with city services during that time.

4 Are specific financial items geared to only one land use? An example would be mobile home taxes.

5 Is significant development occurring? In that case, examining building permit revenue might be in order, if it is readily available and can be address-matched to the parcels. If there are significant developer contributions, how are they related to capital expenditures?

6 Are there Enterprise Funds with significant amounts of transfers either in or out? As was seen with Anoka, the electrical utility produced a lot of revenue, over and above the expenses. The billing records were readily available and were address-matched to parcels and the surplus was distributed to parcels based on the actual billing.

7 Does the city have satellite offices? In the case of Bloomington, the size of the city made it necessary to have satellite police and fire facilities so

that response time guidelines can be met. In such a case, distance would need to be considered.

8 Does the city have development that is spread far from its central core area? Or does the city have large amounts of unused infrastructure capacity? As in the case of Bloomington, information on the cost and spatial extent of the investments needed to be determined.

9 Does the city receive revenue from income or sales taxes? One will need to know how the revenue is collected. If the state collects the revenue and distributes it back to the city, one must know what the distribution formula is. For example, if sales tax revenue is distributed back based on the amounts collected in the city, then one would need to be able to identify retail commercial parcels if one decides to allocate it that way. Others contend that it should be distributed back based solely on the population which pays the taxes.

10 Is the city paying down debt that was incurred to benefit a certain part of the city in the past? If that is the case, then the costs might be allocated to the benefitted properties. (This data may be hard to come by).

The answers to these questions would shape the scope of the fiscal analysis.

VI Examples of Additional GIS Data Needed

In addition to the list of GIS shapefiles and attributes listed earlier, here are a few additional data items that were needed as fields in the parcel factor database for the two case study cities:

1. Anoka, MN

Based on special projects, metropolitan tax base sharing, and the substantial enterprise fund revenue generation, specific considerations were needed to account for them, including:

TIF district parcels
Electrical billing records
Fiscal disparities contributions and distributions
Location of capital projects

2. Bloomington

Since Bloomington had a much more complex finance system and spatial attributes, more detail was needed, including:

TIF district parcels
Site-specific parcels, such as those in special tax-sharing districts
Police and fire satellite facilities

Commercial land uses, including retail
Distance factor
Surrogate factor for low income
Sewer and water systems, capacities and the parcels they serve
Records of historical sewer and water expansion costs and amount
    recovered to date

VII Time to Analyze Fiscal Patterns

Since this is truly a fiscal analysis, a substantial amount should be devoted
to understanding the CAFR, especially focusing on the tables for Anoka and
Bloomington that have been presented as examples. The table is typically
found in any city's CAFR. Depending on the size of a city, it is recommended
that a substantial amount of time be spent reading and understanding the
report. The Finance Director should be brought into the process so that they
know about the project and can answer questions. He or she is the essential participant in this phase. As the project progresses, one probably may
need to ask them to provide the detailed spreadsheet data that went into
preparing the CAFR.

VIII Conclusions

The examples from the two cities show both similarities and wide variations in revenue and expenditure categories. As for the three cities in other
parts of the country, the Spatial Method is transferable to them because
it recognizes the uniqueness of each. By studying and analyzing the fiscal
information that is almost always available in the Comprehensive Annual
Financial Report (CAFR), the main types of revenues and expenditures can
be identified, as well as the types of data that need to be in the parcel factor
file in order to model their flows within the city. The amounts collected for
property taxes or spent on police and fire services may vary widely among
cities but the method itself would remain the same. The typical items that
are identified as needed in the parcel database are: market value of land and
buildings, assessed value, land use, parcel address, number of housing units,
square footage, number of bedrooms, street frontage, population, school-
age population, employment, and police and fire calls for the year.

References

City of Anoka, MN (2009) "Comprehensive Annual Financial Report (CAFR)",
    City of Anoka.
City of Bloomington, IL (2013) "Comprehensive Annual Financial Report (CAFR)",
    City of Bloomington, http://www.cityblm.org/Home/ShowDocument?id=5910.
City of Plano, TX (2017) "Comprehensive Annual Financial Report (CAFR)", *City
    of Plano,* http://www.plano.gov/ArchiveCenter/ViewFile/Item/6095.

City of Redlands, CA (2017) "Comprehensive Annual Financial Report (CAFR)", *City of Redlands*, http://www.cityofredlands.org/UserFiles/Servers/Server_62556 62/File/City%20Hall/Departments/Management%20Services/Finance/Com prehensive%20Annual%20Financial%20Report/2017CityofRedlandsCAFR-Final.pdf.

Town of Barnstable, MA (2016) "Comprehensive Annual Financial Report (CAFR)", *Town of Barnstable,* http://www.townofbarnstable.us/Finance/Barnst able%20FY2016%20CAFR.pdf.

5 Compiling the *Parcel_Factor* Shapefile Attributes

The *Parcel_Factor* shapefile contains the essential factors that are needed to allocate revenues and expenditures to parcels in order to model the fiscal flows using the Spatial Method. The county or local assessor's parcel file provides the basic organizing framework for the *Parcel_Factor* shapefile. This chapter will illustrate the basic contents or fields of the *Parcel_Factor* shapefile as it was used for Bloomington, IL. A smaller city with less complexity would not necessarily need all of the attribute fields. However, the most common ones include acres, land use, housing units, housing class, year built, population, employment, police and fire calls, local road frontage, market and assessed values and neighborhoods. Sums of many of the fields were used to calculate the multipliers that were used to allocate revenues and expenditures to parcels and determine fiscal impact. Developing the parcel database can be considered an investment in a city's "information infrastructure".

I *Parcel_Factor* Shapefile Fields

Bloomington's *Parcel_Factor* shapefile was somewhat detailed due to complex issues with regard to the city's finances and the size of the city, both in population and extent. Table 5.1 shows the fields in the factor database used to estimate fiscal impact and the source of the data. A description of each field is also provided in the text that follows, along with a brief summary of how the data was assembled or calculated.

II Allocation Factor Definitions

There are many allocation factors that are easy to recognize, like population, employment or market value, but there are others that must be defined.

A The Parcel Shapefile

The shapefile from the county or local surveyor provided the spatial basis for the analysis. The field *SHAPE* identifies the file as a shapefile. The attributes

Table 5.1 Factor Fields and Sources of Information for the *Parcel_Factor* Database, Bloomington, IL

FIELD NAME	Description	Data Source
SHAPE	Parcel shapefile	County surveyor
PIN	Parcel Identification Number	Assessor
AREA	Area in Square Feet	GIS software
ACRES	Area in Acres	GIS software
BLOCKID	Census Block ID (Modified)	Census, modified by consultant
TAZ	Traffic Assignment Zone (Modified)	Planner
SHP	Summary Item, All Records Equal to 1	Consultant
LUSE0	Tax Status: "TAXABLE" or "TAX EXEMPT"	Assessor
LUSE1	Generalized Land Use Categories	Assessor
LUSE1B	More Detailed Categories, Especially with Regard to Residential	Assessor, planner and consultant
LUSE2	Very Detailed Categories When Applicable	Planner and consultant
LUSE3	Concatenation of *LUSE1*, *LUSE1B* and *LUSE2*	Consultant
LUSE4	Concatenation of *LUSE0* and *LUSE3*	Consultant
ASSR_UNITS	Number of Units According to the Assessor	Assessor
YRBUILT	Year Built from Assessor, Mostly for Single-Family Residential	Assessor
NO_BDRMS	Number of Bedrooms	Assessor
CLASS10	Housing Classification for 2010	Consultant
CLASS13	Housing Classification for 2013	Consultant
BLDGSQFT	Building Square Footage	Assessor and consultant
HSG10	Estimated 2010 Housing Units	Census, modified by consultant and assessor data
POP10	Estimated 2010 Population	Census, modified by consultant
HSG13	Estimated 2013 Housing Units	Assessor and Consultant
POP13	Estimated 2013 Population	Consultant
EMPLOYMENT	Estimated 2013 Employment Based on Disaggregating TAZ Data	Planner
F_CALLS	Fire Call Equivalent	Public Safety and consultant
P_CALLS	Police Call Equivalent	Public Safety and consultant
STCALLEQ	Street Call Equivalent	Public Safety and consultant
FRTG_ART	Arterial Road Frontage	Centerline data and consultant
FRTG_COLLE	Collector Road Frontage	Centerline data and consultant

(*Continued*)

Table 5.1 (Continued)

FIELD NAME	Description	Data Source
FRTG_LOCAL	Local Road Frontage	Centerline data and consultant
FRTG_ALLEY	Alley Frontage	Centerline data and consultant
TOT_FRTG	Total Locally Maintained Road Frontage	Consultant
LAND_MV	Land Market Value from Assessor	Assessor
BLDING_MV	Building Market Value from Assessor	Assessor and consultant
ASSESSEDMV	Total Land and Building Market Value from Assessor	Assessor
NETMV	Net Market Value after Subtracting Credits from Assessed Value	Assessor
COMMERCMV	Commercial Building Market Value	Assessor based on land use
C_I_A_BMV	Commercial, Industrial and Apartment Building Market Value	Assessor based on land use
RES_BMV	Residential Building Market Value	Assessor based on land use
TOT_BMV	Estimated Building Market Value, Including Tax-Exempt Properties	Assessor and consultant
TIFMV	TIF Total Market Value	Assessor
LOW_INC_IX	Low-Income Index	Assessor data and consultant
DILAP_ST	Index Based on Pavement Condition.	Public works
FY2013DEV	Improvement Value of 2013 Building Permits	City data and consultant
BUF_MILES	Distance from the Center of the City, in Quarter Mile Increments	GIS software
POPMI	Population Times BUF_MILES	Calculated from above data
PCT_POP	Percentage of Total Population	Calculated from above data
PCT_MV	Percentage of Total Building Market Value	Calculated from above data
PCT_TOT	Total of PCT_POP and PCT_MV	Calculated from above data
PCT_MI	PCT_TOT Multiplied Times BUF_MILES	Calculated from above data
DISTF	Distance Factor: Each Parcel's Percentage of the Total PCT_MI for the City	Calculated from above data
NBHD2	Neighborhood Number	Planner and consultant
NBHD_NAME	Neighborhood Name	Planner and consultant
CI_NBHD2	Concatenation of NBHD_NAME and CI_NBHD	Consultant

(Continued)

Table 5.1 (Continued)

FIELD NAME	Description	Data Source
CI_NBHD	Commercial/Industrial Neighborhood for C/I Parcels	Consultant
NBHD_LUSE	Concatenation of NBHD_NAME and LUSE1	Consultant
METROZONE	Parcels in the Metrozone Have a Value of 1	City
DISCONTIG	Parcels Considered to Be Dis-Contiguous	Consultant

in the parcel file from the assessor provided the initial framework for the GIS database needed for Spatial Fiscal Impact Analysis. Parcels are almost always the lowest common denominator of land use and they are readily available. The only exception would be parcels classified as multi-use.

There are some limitations of the assessor's attributes. For fiscal impact analysis purposes, it was assumed that all of the attribute data was current. That was not the exact case, however. Assessors usually revisit properties on a cyclical basis, sometimes as much as every four years. For analysis purposes, it is assumed that relatively very little change has happened since the last assessment. The purpose of using assessor's data is to get the *relative* market and assessed values across the entire city.

Another limitation included the completeness of the market value data. In Bloomington, there were no market values for land and buildings on tax-exempt properties. Also, the assessor's year-built data was primarily just for single-family residential.

There are many attributes in the file that are useful in developing the database, but all of them do not necessarily have to be in the *Parcel_Factor* shapefile. They can be used to help identify the specific factor amounts used to calculate revenues and expenditures. An example would be the parcel address.

B Area and Acres

AREA is an automatic field provided in the shapefile. The GIS software allows this to be converted to the field *ACRES*. The area of a parcel, in acres, is useful for allocating features such as police calls to intersections or to blocks. Furthermore, acreage provides a common denominator when trying to map patterns. For example, comparing market values between a very large parcel and a very small one would be meaningless, unless the market value can be divided by the acreage to give a market value per acre. When the fiscal analysis is completed, the most logical way to summarize the results by mapping patterns or in tabular form will be on a per acre basis or a per unit basis as in the case of residential.

C *Land Use*

The ultimate goal of a fiscal impact study is to determine the revenues, expenditures and fiscal impact of land parcels by land use type. Land use can be as generalized or as detailed as desired. However, the most valuable results are obtained when the land use categories are as detailed as possible. The assessor provided some basic land use information that could be expanded upon by the planner and consultant. *LUSE0* was the designation by the assessor as to whether a parcel was taxable or tax exempt. *LUSE1* was also provided by the assessor and was an important distinction in developing the market and assessed values. The categories included residential, commercial, industrial, institutional, recreational and vacant. Figure 5.1 showing *LUSE1* for the city of Bloomington is shown in the color insert section. *LUSE1B* provided a more detailed breakdown of the basic land use categories, particularly for residential, which identified apartments, duplexes, multi-family, mixed-use and single-family. Information in the assessor's file provided some of this breakdown. The planner and consultant also refined the breakdown. Unfortunately, there was no basis upon which to break down the commercial category, which was a shortcoming of this particular study. *LUSE2* provided even more detail that was discovered during the study. *LUSE3* was the concatenation of *LUSE1, LUSE1B*

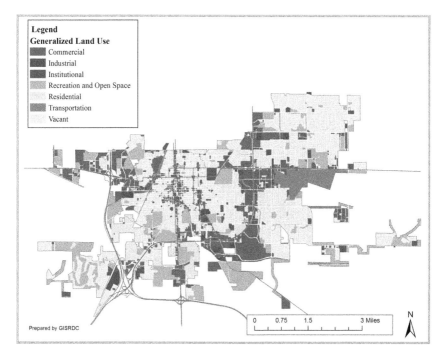

Figure 5.1 Generalized Land Use City of Bloomington, IL, 2013 (See Color Figure 5.1 in the color insert section.)

and *LUSE2*. Some examples are shown in Table 5.2. Not shown in the table is *LUSE4*, which was the concatenation of *LUSE0* and *LUSE3*. While there was not an expansion of the commercial category, *LUSE4* produced 73 separate land use categories for Bloomington. These were very useful in cross-tabulating fiscal impact and other factors.

D Census Blocks

In order to estimate population by parcel, census block data was needed and therefore each parcel must be assigned a census block ID (*BLOCKID*). The boundaries in the block file did not correspond correctly with the parcel file and had to be edited and corrected before the IDs could be assigned to the parcels. Appendix D describes this correction process for Bloomington. Depending on the accuracy of the census block file, this could take a long time. It would be a good project for a GIS technician or intern.

E Traffic Assignment Zone

Like census blocks, only much larger, each parcel was given a traffic assignment zone number (*TAZ*). Employment data by *TAZ* was used to estimate employment. In another project for the city of Anoka, MN, the Economic Development Director had an employment inventory down to the parcel level, including home-based businesses. If the city had a detailed employment inventory from the Community Development Department, the *TAZ* field and data would not be needed.

F SHP: Summarizing and Selecting Field

The field *SHP* was included as a field and given a value of 1 for all parcels. The field was useful when summarizing data or selecting matching parcels when joining files.

G Assessor's Housing and Building Data

The assessor provided the number of housing units on a parcel (*ASSR_ UNITS*) and the number of bedrooms (*NO_BDRMS*), primarily for single-family parcels. The number of bedrooms provided the basis for classifying residential parcels as to the number of bedrooms or using the "blended" category (CLASS10 and CLASS13). For example, residential single-family with 4 bedrooms would be classified as *SF_4*. In cases where the number of bedrooms was not provided, the class was *SF_BLEND*. The unit and year-built data were not always accurate. It was used and reconciled with the census data, as described in Appendix D.

Another data item provided by the assessor was building square footage (*BLDG_SQFT*). This was used to help in estimating employment, but there

Table 5.2 Example of Land Use Categories

LUSE0	LUSE1	LUSE1B	LUSE2	LUSE3
TAX EXEMPT	COMMERCIAL			TAX-EXEMPT COMMERCIAL
TAX EXEMPT	INSTITUTIONAL	EDUCATION	PUBLIC SCHOOL	INSTITUTIONAL EDUCATIONAL PUBLIC SCHOOL
TAX EXEMPT	RECREATION AND OPEN SPACE	FARM		RECREATION AND OPEN SPACE FARM
TAX EXEMPT	RESIDENTIAL	APARTMENTS	CITY PUBLIC HOUSING	RESIDENTIAL APARTMENTS CITY PUBLIC HOUSING
TAXABLE	COMMERCIAL			TAXABLE COMMERCIAL
TAXABLE	INSTITUTIONAL	EDUCATION	PRIVATE SCHOOL	INSTITUTIONAL EDUCATIONAL PRIVATE SCHOOL
TAXABLE	RECREATION AND OPEN SPACE	PUBLIC	PARK	RECREATION AND OPEN SPACE PUBLIC PARK
TAXABLE	RESIDENTIAL	APARTMENTS		RESIDENTIAL APARTMENTS
TAXABLE	RESIDENTIAL	SINGLE FAMILY		RESIDENTIAL SINGLE-FAMILY
TAXABLE	VACANT	RESIDENTIAL		VACANT RESIDENTIAL

was no data for tax-exempt parcels. This was overcome as described under market values, below.

H Year Built

The assessor also provided the year built (*YRBUILT*), mostly for single-family parcels, but this allowed the general classification of parcels in the city based on categories of year built. Figure 5.2 in the color insert section shows the categories.

I Housing Units

Housing units for the census year 2010 (*HSG_10*) and for the study year 2013 (*HSG_13*), came from an analysis of data from the assessor (*ASSR_UNITS*) and the census. Using the *YRBUILT* field, the units that existed before 2010 were identified. However, the *YRBUILT* data for apartments mostly did not exist. Appendix D describes how *HSG_10* and *HSG_13* were refined using census block totals and aerial photography.

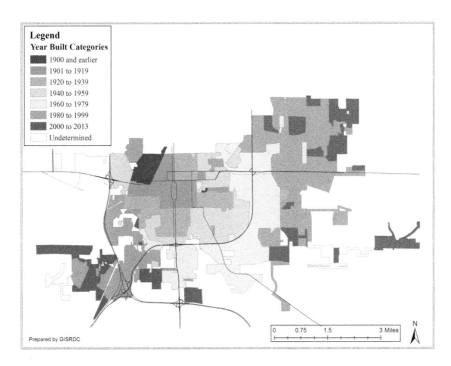

Figure 5.2 Areas Categorized by the Approximate Year Built Based on Assessor's Data City of Bloomington, IL (See Color Figure 5.2 in the color insert section.)

J Population

Since population is an important factor in allocating revenues and expenditures, it was important to develop relatively accurate estimates of population in 2010 *(POP_10)* and 2013 *(POP_13)*. Appendix E also shows how this was done using *CLASS10* and *CLASS13*. Using the information on population per housing unit type, the 2010 population was preliminarily estimated and then summed by census block. Differences in the sums and census amounts were used to identify errors and adjust so that the amounts were equal. *CLASS13* was used to estimate the additional population since the census. Figure 5.3 shows population density.

K Employment

Estimating employment was difficult because there was no breakdown of commercial land use. The only data were for Traffic Assignment Zones *(TAZ)*, which were allocated to parcels based on building market value and building square footage. As stated earlier, in the project for the city of Anoka, MN, the Economic Development Director had an employment inventory down to the parcel level, including home-based businesses.

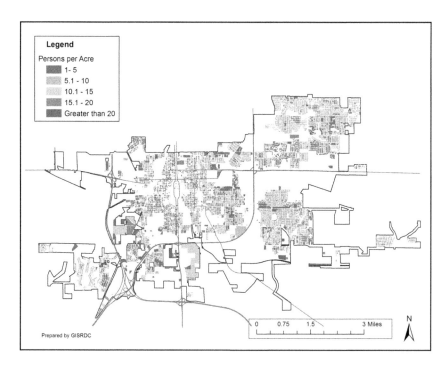

Figure 5.3 2013 Population Density City of Bloomington, IL (See Color Figure 5.3 in the color insert section.)

L Police and Fire Call Equivalents by Address

The information provided by Bloomington included not only the address and GPS point for each call but also the duration of the call, totaling 127,884 calls and 5,389,099 minutes. Of these calls, 74,548 police calls and 12,298 fire calls were matched to parcels. Another 22,411 were police or fire calls to streets or intersections, which will be described in the following section. The remainder were calls to outside the city limits or otherwise not allocable to parcels.

After the calls and minutes were allocated to parcels, it was found that both police and fire calls each averaged about 47 and 46 minutes each, respectively. Rather than dealing with minutes, it decided that it was more meaningful to express the call time as a "call equivalent". For example, if a parcel's police call took 47 minutes, it was counted as one call equivalent; if the call took 1 ½ hours, it was counted as 1.91 call equivalents (90 minutes divided by 47).

Call equivalents were then used to allocate revenues and expenditures to parcels. The allocation factors are referred to as "police call equivalents" or "fire call equivalents". The fields in the database were named *P_CALLS* and *F_CALLS*, respectively. Figures 5.4 and 5.5 show the distribution of police and Fire/EMS calls.

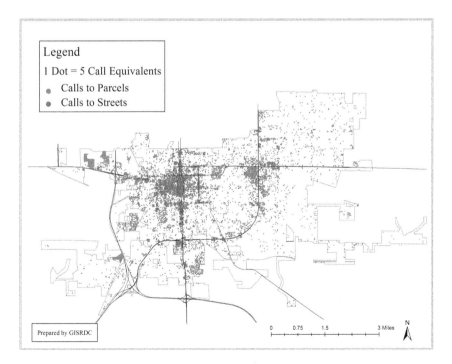

Figure 5.4 2013 Police Calls City of Bloomington, IL (See Color Figure 5.4 in the color insert section.)

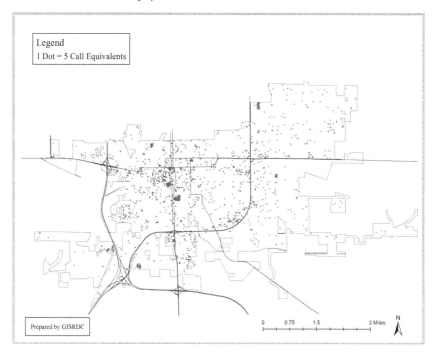

Figure 5.5 2013 Fire/EMS Calls City of Bloomington, IL (See Color Figure 5.5 in the color insert section.)

M Police and Fire Call Equivalents to Streets and Intersections

Calls to streets and intersections and the duration of each were also allocated to parcels based a distance from the street or intersection. One main intersection had as much as 365,040 minutes. Rather than allocating all of this time to the parcels immediately around the intersection, buffers were created for each intersection based on the amount of call time so that a larger number of parcels were allocated the call time. Parcels within the buffers were allocated call time based on each's proportion of acreage within the buffer. The minutes were then converted to equivalents by dividing by 47. The allocation factor is referred to as "street call equivalents" and stored in the database as *STCALLEQ*. For more detail, refer to Appendix B.

N Street Frontage and Classification

The frontage of locally maintained streets was needed to be assigned to parcels so that costs could also be allocated. Since Bloomington also had centerline designations as to arterial, collector and local streets, the frontage by category also made up fields in the database, in addition to alleys. These fields were: *FRTG_ART*, *FRTG_COLL*, *FRTG_LOCAL* and *FRTG_ALLEY*. Appendix C provides examples of how to determine frontage by parcel using GIS. Figure 5.6 shows the classes of locally maintained streets as well as roads maintained by others.

O Assessed and Market Values

Market values came directly from the assessor in the form of land market value ($LAND\_MV$) and building market value ($BLDG\_MV$), which totaled the assessed market value ($ASSESSEDMV$). Building market value was considered the most important component because it reflected the intensity of the land use. Depending on the type of revenue or expenditure, building market value by different types of land use was also needed, so fields for commercial building value ($COMMERCMV$), for commercial, industrial and apartment building value ($C\_I\_A\_BMV$) and residential building value (RES_BMV) were created to hold these subsets of building market value.

The assessor's data did not include the market values of tax-exempt property, yet these values were needed to properly allocate revenues and expenditures to all parcels. To get an accurate estimate of the impact of tax-exempt, it was necessary to use aerial photography and identify the tax-exempt parcels with buildings and then to digitize the outlines of each building. Based on the photos and the building outlines, the number of

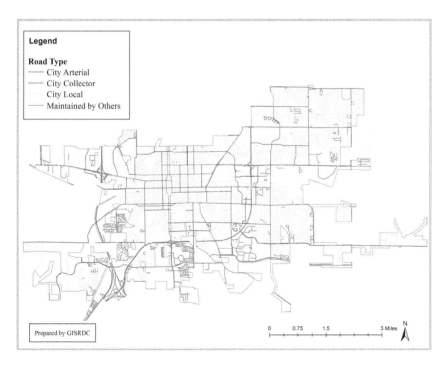

Figure 5.6 2013 Roads by Type City of Bloomington, IL (See Color Figure 5.6 in the color insert section.)

stories of the buildings had to be approximated, yielding the square footage. Then, based on the values and square footage of the neighboring taxable properties, a multiplier was developed and applied to the tax-exempt properties. As a result, the values for tax-exempt buildings was stored in the field *TOT_BMV*. The building market values just for the taxable properties were stored in the field *BLDG_MV* and *TOT_BMV*. Obviously, it would have been better if the assessor had provided this information. Figure 5.7 in the color insert section shows market values per acre.

P Low- and Moderate-Income Index

CDBG revenue and expenditures are generally attributable to areas in the city that have low and moderate income. Since specific areas or parcels are involved, a Low- and Moderate-Income Index *(LMINDX)* was developed using building market value to identify low-income areas.

Q Dilapidated Streets

The city received revenue specifically aimed at fixing streets in disrepair. Parcels with frontage on local streets that had a pavement condition of 1

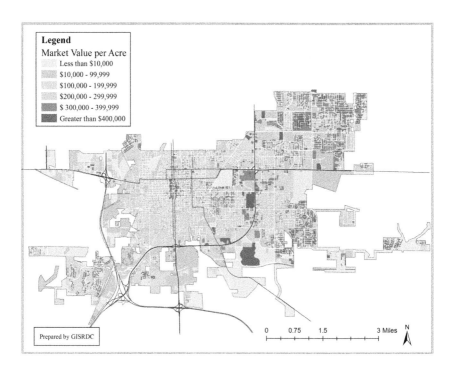

Figure 5.7 2013 Market Values per Acre City of Bloomington, IL (See Color Figure 5.7 in the color insert section.)

or 2 were given the amount of that frontage in the field *DILAP_ST* (dilapidated streets) and the revenue and cost of fixing them were allocated to them based on the multiplier for that item.

R Building Permit Revenue

The city also collected over $1 million in building permit revenue. Some of this was for new construction and some for improvements so the reported value of 2013 development was obtained by address-matching permits needed and the values were recorded in the field *FY2013DEV*.

S Population Mile

To account for the additional amount of time needed to service parcels that are outlying to the central city (as described below), an expenditure allocation factor named "population mile" (*POP_MI*) was developed for each parcel and was calculated based on the population times the distance from the central city.

T Distance Factor

The city of Bloomington extends quite far out from the central core by nearly 8 miles. Providing services to the outlying parcels costs more than for parcels that are closer in. For example, to service the population out beyond a 2.5-mile limit required the construction of satellite police and fire stations to maintain acceptable response times. The cost of these facilities was not available, so a distance factor was developed to allocate more of the costs to the outlying areas.

Population and market value have been considered to be two factors that reflect the intensity of land use and the demand for services. Each parcel's percentage of the total population was calculated (*PCT_POP*), as was the percentage of market value (*PCT_MV*). These two percentages were added together (*PCT_TOT*) and then multiplied times the distance from the central city (*PCT_MI*). Each parcel's percentage share of *PCT_MI* was calculated and stored in a field called *DISTF*, or distance factor.

The effect of distance on costs needs to be the subject of more research.

U Other Cross-Tabulation Fields

Other fields were also included in the database to identify parcels based on different criteria.

1 Neighborhoods
    Eventually, the results were summarized by neighborhoods. *NBHD2* was the neighborhood number and *NBHD_NAME* was the

Table 5.3 Appendices that Provide Guidance as to How to Develop Some of the Key Factors

Appendix A	Creating Address Matching Fields for Parcels
Appendix B	Allocating Public Safety Data to Parcels
Appendix C	Determining Local Road Frontage for Parcels
Appendix D	Reconciling Census Blocks With Parcels
Appendix E	Using Census Data to Estimate Adult and School Aged Population
Appendix F	Modeling Fiscal Impact

neighborhood name. It was also desired to be able to summarize land use by neighborhood; a field named *NBHD_LUSE* contained the neighborhood name concatenated with *LUSE1B*.

2   Metrozone

The city had an area (or zone) in the Northwest developed to share revenues with the neighboring town of Normal. The parcels in the *METROZONE* were flagged with the value of 1 to identify them.

3   TIF Districts

The city had several TIF districts that needed to have their revenue excluded from that of other parcels.

III Summary

The *Parcel_Factor* shapefile was the basis upon which fiscal impact was calculated for Bloomington, IL. Sums of many of the fields were used to calculate multipliers that were used to estimate fiscal impact. This will be shown in Chapter 6.

Table 5.1 listed the sources of the data and where consultant services were needed. If one were to conduct the analysis for one's own city, then the staff would have to assume the tasks of the consultant.

The most important set of factors to first develop in detail would be the land use classifications. It would be best to pin down the land use classifications early in the process. Classifications regarding the different types of residential need to be specifically refined because they are the basis upon which the population is estimated.

The second most important data to be developed would be the adult and school-age population. Addresses for matching transaction records, like police and fire calls, would also be a critical factor to develop, along with road frontage.

The appendices provide specific examples as to how to develop the factor data, such as public safety calls using address matching, road frontage, housing, school-age and adult population so that the amounts can be included in the *Parcel_Factor* shapefile. Table 5.3 lists them and the topic that they cover.

6 Determining Fiscal Allocation Multipliers

The most significant things needed to calculate fiscal impact under the Spatial Method are the multipliers used to calculate the impact of each parcel. This chapter will describe how they were determined for the city of Bloomington, IL.

Bloomington, Illinois had a 2013 estimated population of about 77,680 and had a complex financial system. The first step in the analysis was to separate operating items from capital and special items. Figure 6.1 shows how Bloomington's revenue was ultimately broken down with $90,577,580 (92%) categorized as operating and $7,441,927 (8%) as capital or special. There may be some gray area as far as which items are "special" versus operating. The important concept here is to identify the revenue and expenditure items that recur each year and those that might be subject to change from year to year or refer specifically to only one part of the city to make sure that the special items are fully considered rather than just arbitrarily lumped in with operating.

When separating operating from capital revenue, it is important to make sure that however things are divided, the totals must agree with the control totals and nothing is omitted or double counted.

I Operating Revenue

Table 6.1 shows the major categories of operating revenue for the city of Bloomington in 2013, along with the distribution factors, weights and multipliers. Figure 6.2 shows the proportions. Note that property taxes made up only 24% of the operating revenue, while sales and other taxes made up 32% and 27%, respectively. Beyond just using the CAFR, the city Finance Department also provided detailed spreadsheets showing the breakdowns within each category.

One may question the need to have the values for the multipliers expressed with five or more decimal places. The numbers are approximate but to do the calculations among over 25,000 parcels, the decimal places are needed so that after doing the calculations, the totals generally agree with the distribution amounts and control totals. That way, one can be assured that the calculations are being done correctly and that nothing is being omitted or double counted.

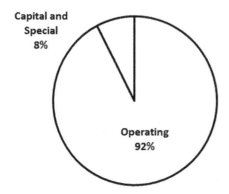

Figure 6.1 Total Revenue, by Operating and Capital Categories City of Bloomington, IL, 2013.

A Charges for Services

The total amount of $11.4 million was generated by charges for services. This was about 13% of the operating revenue. An analysis of the detail in the CAFR revealed more information on the sources of these funds. Table 6.1 shows that 31% was from the fire department and, therefore, 31% was allocated based on fire call equivalents, 6% was from the police department and allocated based on police call equivalents and 8% from streets and allocated based on proximity to the calls. The remainder of the charges for services was allocated based on population (45%) and employment (10%).

B Property Taxes and Investment Income

Property taxes generated $17.5 million in the general fund and $4.5 million in the library fund, which, combined, made up 24% of the city's operating revenue. This was the easiest revenue item to allocate because the basis for it comes directly from the assessor's data file and is based on the net assessed value of each parcel. Net assessed value is defined as the sum of the land and building market value minus credits for homestead and senior citizens. Therefore, property taxes and investment income were allocated based 100% on net assessed value.

C Sales Taxes

The largest source of revenue was sales taxes, at about $28.6 million, which made up 32% of the city's operating revenue. It was assumed that the major generators of sales taxes are population and employment. As described in a previous chapter, the city has a very large employment base. These

Table 6.1 Operating Revenue, Distribution Factors, Weights and Multipliers, City of Bloomington, Il, 2013

Revenue Category	Amount	Distribution Factor	Weight	Distribution Amount	Factor Amount	Multiplier	Description
General Government							
Charges for Services	$11,431,189	Population	45%	$5,144,035	77,680	$66.22	per capita
		Employment	10%	$1,143,119	62,300	$18.35	per employee
		Police Calls	6%	$685,871	74,548	$9.20	per police call equivalent
		Fire Calls	31%	$3,543,669	12,298	$288.15	per fire call equivalent
		Road Frontage	8%	$914,495	3,217,390	$0.28	per front foot
Property Taxes	$17,541,312	Net Assessed Value	100%	$17,541,312	1,716,746,188	$0.01	per $1,000
Sales Taxes	$28,610,085	Population	80%	$22,888,068	77,680	$294.65	per capita
		Employment	20%	$5,722,017	62,300	$91.85	per employee
Commercial Taxes	$11,411,559	Commercial MV	100%	$11,411,559	491,687,291	$0.02	per $1,000
Other Taxes	$1,511,584	Net Assessed Value	100%	$1,511,584	1,716,746,188	$0.00	per $1,000
Income Taxes	$5,418,693	Population	100%	$5,418,693	77,680	$69.76	per capita
Utility Taxes	$6,352,768	Residential Bldg. Mkt. Val.	100%	$6,352,768	1,057,480,000	$0.01	per $1,000
Intergovernmental Revenue:							
Parks	$33,375	Population	80%	$26,700	77,680	$0.34	per capita
		Employment	20%	$6,675	62,300	$0.11	per employee
Police	$161,222	Police Calls	100%	$161,222	74,548	$2.16	per police call equivalent
Fire	$9,856	Fire Calls	100%	$9,856	12,298	$0.80	per fire call equivalent
Investment Income	$55,376	Net Assessed Value	100%	$55,376	1,716,746,188	$0.00	per $1,000
Licenses	$404,343	Commercial Mkt. Val.	100%	$404,343	491,687,000	$0.00	per $1,000

(Continued)

Table 6.1 ((Continued)

Revenue Category	Amount	Distribution Factor	Weight	Distribution Amount	Factor Amount	Multiplier	Description
Fines and Forfeits	$1,192,438	Police Calls	100%	$1,192,438	74,548	$16.00	per police call equivalent
Other	$1,285,931	Population	64%	$822,996	77,680	$10.59	per capita
		Employment	20%	$257,186	62,300	$4.13	per employee
		Police Calls	10%	$128,593	74,548	$1.72	per police call equivalent
		Fire Calls	6%	$77,156	12,298	$6.27	per fire call equivalent
Library							
Charges for Services	$80,767	Population	80%	$64,614	77,680	$0.83	per capita
		Employment	20%	$16,153	62,300	$0.26	per employee
Property Taxes	$4,512,535	Net Assessed Value	100%	$4,512,535	1,716,746,188	$0.00	per $1,000
Intergovernmental	$12,500	Population	100%	$12,500	77,680	$0.16	per capita
Investment Income	$4,633	Net Assessed Value	100%	$4,633	1,716,746,188	$0.00	per $1,000
Other	$547,414	Population	100%	$547,414	77,680	$7.05	per capita
Total Operating Revenue	$90,577,580			$90,577,580			

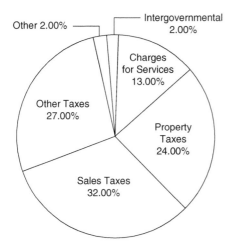

Figure 6.2 Operating Revenue Categories City of Bloomington, IL, 2013.

employees shop in city stores and buy goods and services, generating sales taxes. While it is difficult to estimate the amount that employees generate relative to the resident population, it has been assumed that 20% of the sales taxes are from employees and 80% from the resident population.

One could argue that it was the retail businesses that collected this revenue. The money was sent by the merchants to the state and then redistributed back to the city. The uses that collect most of the sales taxes typically include restaurants, automobile dealers and retail stores. Unfortunately, a detailed breakdown of the commercial land use category was not available for Bloomington, so there was no way to identify the retail businesses.

Due to these data limitations, it was decided to simply use population and employment since people and employees are the ones actually paying the taxes. Furthermore, one could argue that the commercial uses would not exist if it weren't for the customers; those uses only collect the tax but they do not actually pay it.

Katz has noted that municipalities that rely heavily on sales tax revenue let that fact "drive their decision to permit high-impact commercial and industrial uses such as big-box shopping centers. Such projects were usually sited near municipal borders, where they could attract outside customers but offload transportation-related impacts and costs to neighboring jurisdictions" (2013, p. 21). That appears to have been the case in Bloomington, where a large discount store selling both food and merchandise was located in the northwestern part of the city but the lack of more specific data on retail shopping in the rest of the city prevented measuring the impact of sales taxes by business.

D Commercial Taxes

There were various forms of taxes on commercial enterprises, totaling $11.4 million. Examples were: franchise taxes, hotel/motel taxes or food and beverage taxes. These were allocated to commercial land use parcels based on the commercial market value.

E Other Taxes

Other taxes generated $1.2 million. Examples are replacement taxes, such as those for police and fire. These were allocated to parcels based on net assessed value.

F Utility Taxes

A total of $6.4 million was generated by utility taxes, which were levied on users of the services. Examples are: natural gas, cable, electric, telecommunications and water. It was assumed that these were mostly residential customers. These taxes were allocated to residential uses based on the residential building market value. This factor may underrepresent mobile homes.

G Income Taxes

Income taxes generated $5.4 million. While the state collected income taxes based on income, this redistribution back to cities was made on the basis of population, therefore 100% of the amount was allocated based on population.

H Intergovernmental Revenue: Parks and Recreation

This was a rather small amount that the city brings in. It was assumed that the revenue reflects the users of the system, population at 80% and employment 20%. One might wonder, "why worry about such a small amount?" This was a judgment call.

I Intergovernmental Revenue: Police and Fire

As stated above, the CAFR detail provided this information and, since police and fire calls were already being used to model expenditures, it was easy to allocate the amounts.

J Licenses

Licenses generated $.4 million and this was allocated to commercial properties based on market value. Examples are: contractors, taxis, liquor or theatre. Included with licenses was permit revenue. However, this amount ($.8) million appears to be generated mostly by new development. Since this can vary from year to year based on economic conditions, it has been assigned to capital and special revenue.

K Fines and Forfeits

Fines and forfeits generated $1.2 million. They were generally the result of police action and therefore were allocated to parcels based on the number of police call equivalents.

L Notes and Summary of Operating Revenue

In most cases, the weights were 100% of the Fiscal Factor category. For example, property taxes were directly based on the Net Assessed Value, after credits and exemptions were deducted. Commercial taxes and licenses were found to be attributable to commercial land use. Utility taxes were directly related to residential uses. In some cases, some amounts directly attributable to police and fire calls and road frontage were identified in the detailed spreadsheets from the Finance Director and contributed to the weights in the charges for the services category.

Lastly, population, market value and employment were the most frequently used distribution factors. Unlike the Per Capita method, population is an important factor but it is not the sole factor.

What is the impact of employment? Intuitively, employment affects both revenues and expenditures, but the exact amount is unknown. One of the frequently used non-spatial fiscal impact methods is named "Employment Anticipation" and the method established the fact that employment does indeed affect expenditures. Employment was included in the Bloomington study and it was believed that it affects both revenues and expenditures, just as population does. For the purposes of this study, the relationship between population and employment was assumed to be about 80% to 20%, respectively. Many, if not most, of the employees are also residents of the city, or population. Including both categories gets at revenues and expenditures of people both at home and at work. This is an issue that needs more research.

To determine the multipliers, the weight was multiplied times the amount and then divided by the factor total. For example, the city received $11,431,189 in charges for services. Population was assumed to be responsible for 45% of this revenue, or $5,144,035. Dividing this amount by the population of 77,680 yielded a multiplier of $66.22 per capita.

II Operating Expenses

Operating expenses are shown in Table 6.2 and the proportions for the major categories are shown in Figure 6.3. As is typical for most cities, the

Table 6.2 Operating Expenses, Distribution Factors, Weights and Multipliers, City of Bloomington, IL, 2013

Operating Expense Category	Amount	Distribution Factor	Weight	Distribution Amount	Factor Amount	Multiplier	Description
General Government Administration	$6,936,878	Population	45%	$3,121,595	77,680	$40.19	per capita
		Total Building MV	45%	$3,121,595	$1,708,719,772	$0.00	per $1,000
Vehicle Costs	$3,271,653	Employment	10%	$693,688	62,300	$11.13	per employee
		Distance Factor	100%	$3,271,653	1	$3,271,653	% Pop. & BMV times Distance
Streets	$6,635,792	Arterial Frontage	38%	$2,521,601	442,122	$5.70	per arterial FF
		Collector Frontage	18%	$1,194,443	252,497	$4.73	per collector FF
		Local Frontage	40%	$2,654,317	2,248,800	$1.18	per local FF
		Alley Frontage	2%	$132,716	273,967	$0.48	per alley FF
		Population Distance	2%	$132,716	198,033	$0.07	population mile
Culture/Recreation	$9,317,149	Population	70%	$6,522,004	77,680	$83.96	per capita
		Population Distance	10%	$931,715	198,033	$4.70	population mile
Public Safety	$41,102,503	Employment	20%	$1,863,430	62,300	$29.91	per employee

(Continued)

Table 6.2 (Continued)

Operating Expense Category	Amount	Distribution Factor	Weight	Distribution Amount	Factor Amount	Multiplier	Description
Police and Fire		Police Call Equivalents	19%	$7,809,476	74,548	$104.76	per police call equivalent
		Street Call Equivalents	6%	$2,466,150	22,411	$110.04	per street call equivalent
		Fire Call Equivalents	22%	$9,042,551	12,298	$735.29	per fire call equivalent
Building Safety and Code Enforcement		Commercial / Industrial and Apartment MV	5%	$2,055,125	$495,953,368	$0.00	per $1,000
Patrolling and Readiness		Population	14%	$5,754,350	77,680	$74.08	per capita
		Total Building MV	15%	$6,165,375	$1,708,719,772	$0.00	per $ of value
		Distance Factor	13%	$5,343,325	1	$5,343,330	% Pop. & BMV times Distance
		Employment	6%	$2,466,150	62,300	$39.59	per employee
Parking	$439,483	Population	80%	$351,586	77,680	$4.53	per capita
		Employment	20%	$87,897	62,300	$1.41	per employee
Library	$4,397,536	Population	80%	$3,518,029	77,680	$45.29	per capita
		Employment	20%	$879,507	62,300	$14.12	per employee
Elections	$446,937	Population	100%	$446,937	77,680	$5.75	per capita
Total Operating Expenses	$72,547,931			$72,547,931			

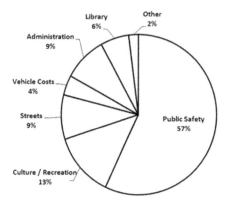

Figure 6.3 Operating Expense Categories City of Bloomington, IL, 2013.

largest item was public safety, at 57%. But, as a larger city, it also had other responsibilities, such as a library, parking, elections and major recreational attractions. Furthermore, again as a city with a large spatial extent, the cost of providing services is also affected by the distance that city staff must travel to deliver the services. For this reason, an attempt at applying a distance factor was made to adjust for development far from the city's central core. More research is needed as to how to account for distance in a large city.

A General Government

1 Administration

These were the general operational costs of city government services for which there was no specific breakdown as to the location of the services, accounting for 9% of the expenses. Therefore, population was allocated 45% of the administrative cost, building market value was allocated another 45% and employment was allocated 12%.

2 Vehicle Costs

At 4% of the operating expenses, the cost of providing services was determined to be based on the distances that staff must travel. The distance factor was used to allocate these costs.

B Streets

Streets accounted for 9% of the operating expenses. The city had classified the locally maintained streets as arterial, collector and local. City staff generally agreed that more money had been spent on the arterials and collectors compared to the local streets, even though they represented only 24% of the city's maintained frontage. For this reason, 38% of the expense was allocated based on arterial frontage and 18% for collector frontage. Local frontage was allocated 40% of the cost. The city also had many alleys, so 2% was allocated to parcels with alley frontage. Lastly, the population distance factor was used to allocate the last 2% of the cost in an attempt to compensate for the distances staff and equipment must travel to maintain streets in the outlying area.

C Culture/Recreation

The city had many cultural and recreational attractions. Culture and recreation accounted for 13% of the operating expenditures. Much of this was spent on the major cultural attractions in the central city. It has been assumed that population and employment are the beneficiaries, so they were allocated 70% and 20%, respectively. The major attractions also benefit people in the outlying area and the city also provides recreation facilities in the outlying area that require travel by city staff. To compensate for the effect of distance, 10% was allocated using the population distance factor.

D Public Safety

As with most, if not all, cities public safety is the greatest expense. In Bloomington's case, it made up 57% of the operating expenditures. There were several aspects to the public safety services that the city provided.

1 Police and Fire/EMS Call Equivalents

Of the over $41 million spent on public safety, 19% was considered to be attributable to police calls, resulting in a multiplier of $104.76 per call equivalent. Another 22% was attributed to fire/EMS calls, with a multiplier of $735.29 per call equivalent. Lastly, 6% was allocated to the parcels based on street-call equivalents. The percentages were based on more detailed information on the police and fire calls and costs based on data from the Finance Director.

2 Building Safety and Code Enforcement

These costs were primarily attributable to commercial/industrial and apartment land uses. Therefore, 5% was allocated to the building market value of these parcels.

3 Patrolling and Readiness

Police must patrol the city in order to proactively protect people and property and the fire/EMS department must always be ready for calls that may come in. Therefore, 14% was allocated based on population, 15% based on building market value and 6% based on employment. Lastly, 13% was allocated to parcels based on the distance factor.

E Parking

The need for parking was assumed to be attributable to population and employment, 80% and 20%, respectively.

F Library

It was assumed that most library patrons are either residents of the city or employees working in the city. Therefore, 80% was allocated to population and 20% to employment.

G Elections

All people involved in elections are residents of the city. As a result, 100% of the expense was allocated based on population. However, after analyzing census data as shown in Appendix E, it would have been possible to allocate it based on voting-age population.

H Summary of Operating Expenses and Surplus

Table 6.3 shows that the total of operating expenses was less than the operating revenue, resulting in a surplus of $18,029,649 million, which was 19.90520% of the operating revenue. This amount was therefore also used to pay for capital and special expenditures and was subtracted out from operating revenue and then added to the capital and special revenue. To get reliable measures of the operating fiscal impact, 19.90520% was subtracted from each parcel's operating revenue.

III Capital and Special Revenue

Capital and special revenues were for capital and special projects that were not necessarily part of city operations and may have varied from year to year or have been dedicated to specific areas of the city. Table 6.4 shows the

Table 6.3 Operating Surplus Transferred to Capital Revenue, City of Bloomington, IL, 2013

Total Operating Revenue	$90,577,580
Total Operating Expenses	$72,547,931
Operating Surplus	$18,029,649
Percent of Operating Revenue (Transfer to Capital)	19.90520%

Table 6.4 Capital and Special Revenue, Distribution Factors, Weights and Multipliers, City of Bloomington, IL, 2013

Revenue Category	Amount	Distribution Factor	Weight	Distribution Amount	Factor Amount	Multiplier	Description
Transfer in from Operating	18,029,649	Proportion of Operating Rev.	100%	18,029,649	$90,577,580	19.91%	Percent of Operating Rev.
General Metrozone	236,819	Metrozone	100%	236,819	1	$2,36,819	% Metrozone Oper. Rev.
Permits	1,109,644	FY 2013 Devel. MV Total Building Market Value	34%	377,279	$62,073,815	$0.01	per $1,000
			66%	732,365	$1,708,719,772	$0.00	per $1,000
Debt Service Property Taxes	1,642,538	Net Assessed Value	100%	1,642,538	$1,716,746,188	$0.00	per $1,000
TIF	488,886	TIF Market Value ($1,000's)	100%	488,886	$28,713,969	$0.02	per $1,000
Other	112,275	Net Assessed Value	100%	112,275	$1,716,746,188	$0.00	per $1,000
Non-Major Intergovernmental Rev. CDBG	900,806	L/M inverse BMV Index	100%	900,806	183,158,242	$0.00	per $1,000
Parks	73,553	Population	100%	73,553	77,680	$0.95	per capita
Motor Fuel Tax	2,214,382	Population	100%	2,214,382	77,680	$28.51	per capita

(*Continued*)

Table 6.4 (Continued)

Revenue Category	Amount	Distribution Factor	Weight	Distribution Amount	Factor Amount	Multiplier	Description
Elections	505,874	Population	100%	505,874	77,680	$6.51	per capita
Other	151,488	Net Assessed Value	100%	151,488	$1,716,746,188	$0.00	per $1,000
Investment Income	5,662	Net Assessed Value	100%	5,662	$1,716,746,188	$0.00	per $1,000
Subtotal Capital Revenue	$7,441,927			$7,441,927			

fiscal items, amounts, distribution factors, weights and multipliers that were used to allocate the revenue to parcels. Figure 6.4 shows the categories and the amounts as percentages. The decision as to which items are capital and special as opposed to operating can be somewhat arbitrary at the outset. The purpose is to flag those items that might be special even though they may ultimately be allocated based on a general factor, such as population or market value. The important thing is to not let them be ignored or lumped in with operating costs if they should not be.

A Transfer In from Operating

This was the operating surplus (19.90520%) that was used as revenue to finance capital and special projects. It was re-allocated in a positive manner to parcels in the same manner that it was deducted from them in the operating category: in proportion to each parcel's share of the operating revenue.

B General Revenue

These were items that were part of the city's general revenue but were attributable to specific areas or parcels in the city, amounting to 18% of the capital and special revenue.

1 Metrozone

The city had an agreement with the adjacent town of Normal to share revenue produced by the Metrozone, on the outskirts to the northwest of the city. This

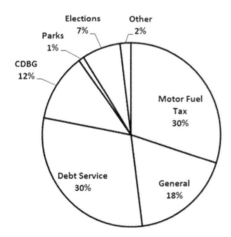

Figure 6.4 Capital and Special Revenue Categories City of Bloomington, IL, 2013.

amount was revenue that Normal collected and shared with Bloomington. It should be noted that there is a similar item in capital and special expenditures in which Bloomington paid the town of Normal over $1 million in shared revenue. It was just allocated to the parcels based on each parcel's share of the Metrozone's operating expenditures, due to a lack of more specific information.

2 Permits

Most of the permit revenue collected by Bloomington was for building per-mits. Based on information on building permits, about 34% was for new construction and 66% was for improvements to properties. It was allocated back to the parcels that paid the permit fees in proportion to the reported improvement amounts.

C Debt Service

There were several types of debt service paid by the city, amounting to 30% of the general and special revenue.

1 General

This was to pay for improvements made in the past, such as street, sewer or water bonds. It was allocated to parcels based on the assessed value because it was raised by property taxes. It could not be determined which improve-ments were financed based on information from the Finance Department. This can be a problem in doing this type of analysis. In this case, the revenue was allocated based on assessed value but, in a later part of the fiscal impact project, the costs of extending sewer and water in several outlying areas was approximately calculated based on historical data.

2 TIF

This was revenue raised from the property taxes levied against parcels in the TIF districts and was dedicated to paying off the expenditures for improve-ments in the TIF districts

3 Investment Income and Other

It was presumed that these revenues were raised by property taxes and allo-cated to parcels based on assessed value.

D Non-Major Revenue

These sources were classified by the city as non-major and fell into several categories.

1 Community Development Block Grants (CDBG)

These funds made up 12% of the capital and special revenue category and were allocated based on the low- and moderate-income index.

2 Park Dedication

A relatively small amount was allocated based on population because the source was not known.

3 Motor Fuel Tax

This was money collected by the state and allocated to local governments based on population, making up 30% of the capital and special revenue. The money must be used to fix dilapidated streets but, since it comes to the city based on population, it was allocated to parcels based on population. In retrospect, since the money must have to have been spent on dilapidated streets, some of it could have been allocated to parcels based on frontage on dilapidated streets.

4 Elections

The state provided 7% of the capital and special revenue to the city based on population.

5 Other and Investment Income

The remaining 2% of the capital and special revenue was allocated to parcels based on assessed value.

IV Capital and Special Expenditures

The amounts described below were initially identified as capital or special. They were given particular scrutiny to see if they should be allocated to specific parcels based on identifiable factors that contributed to the need for them. One will find that in some cases it was possible to do, while in others, the amounts had to be allocated based on the general factors of population, employment and building market value. If the CAFR identified them as capital, they were categorized as such. Table 6.5 shows the expenditure amount, the allocation factor, the weight on the factor and then the multiplier that was used to allocate the costs to parcels. Figure 6.5 shows the proportional amounts that each fiscal category represents.

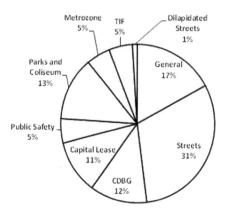

Figure 6.5 Capital and Special Expenditure Categories City of Bloomington, IL 2013.

A General Capital Expenditures

The city spent about $4 million on this category, which was 17% of the capital and special expenditures. These were allocated 60% based on population, 30% on building market value and 10% on employment.

B Parks and Coliseum

It was difficult to determine what areas of the city benefit the most from this category that made up 13% of the capital and special expenditures. More detail would have been helpful. Parks and recreation activities benefit people, whether they are residents, employees or people coming in from outside the city.

C Public Safety

Capital expenditures for public safety made up only 5% of the capital and special category. However, since there were several factors already being used to allocate public safety operating expenses, those same factors were readily available to allocate the capital expenditures.

D Streets

No information was available on the spatial distribution of street capital projects, which made up 31% of the expenditures. As a result, this amount was allocated based on the different classes of locally maintained streets and alleys. This is an area where more data would have been helpful.

Table 6.5 Capital and Special Expenditures, Distribution Factors, Weights and Multipliers, City of Bloomington, IL, 2013

Capital and Special Expenditure Category	Amount	Distribution Factor	Weight	Distribution Amount	Factor Amount	Multiplier	Description
General	$3,963,082	Population	45%	$1,783,387	77,680	$22.96	per capita
		Total Building Market Value	45%	$1,783,387	$1,708,719,772	$0.00	per $1,000
Parks and Coliseum	$3,124,648	Employment	10%	$396,308	62,300	$6.36	per employee
		Population	80%	$2,499,718	77,680	$32.18	per capita
		Employment	20%	$624,930	62,300	$10.31	per employee
Public Safety	$1,200,027	Police Calls	10%	$120,003	109,010	$1.10	per police call equivalent
		Fire Calls	40%	$480,011	14,634	$32.80	per fire call equivalent
		Population	20%	$240,005	77,680	$3.09	per capita
		Distance Factor	8%	$96,002	1	$96,002	% Pop. & BMV times Distance
		Total Building Market Value	12%	$144,003	$1,708,719,772	$0.00	per $1,000
		Employment	5%	$60,001	62,300	$0.96	per employee
		C/I and Apt MV	5%	$60,001	$495,953,368	$0.00	per $1,000
Streets	$7,222,138	Arterial Frontage	30%	$2,166,641	442,122	$4.90	per arterial ff
		Collector Frontage	20%	$1,444,428	252,497	$5.72	per collector ff
		Local Frontage	46%	$3,322,183	2,248,800	$1.48	per local ff
		Alley Frontage	2%	$144,443	273,967	$0.53	per alley ff

(Continued)

Table 6.5 (Continued)

Capital and Special Expenditure Category	Amount	Distribution Factor	Weight	Distribution Amount	Factor Amount	Multiplier	Description
		Distance Factor	2%	$144,443	1	$144,443	% Pop. & BMV times Distance
Dilapidated Streets	$100,551	Pavement Rating 1 or 2	100%	$100,551	34,976	$2.87	per front foot
CDBG	$2,737,497	L/M inverse BMV Index	100%	$2,737,497	183,158,242	$0.01	per $1,000
Metrozone	$1,204,011	Metrozone - to Normal	100%	$1,204,011	1	$1,204,011	% Metrozone Oper. Expenditures
Capital Lease	$2,560,047	Population	45%	$1,152,021	77,680	$14.83	per capita
		Total Building Market Value	45%	$1,152,021	$1,708,719,772	$0.00	per $1,000
TIF	$1,204,411	Employment	10%	$256,005	62,300	$4.11	per employee
		TIF Market Value	100%	$1,204,411	$28,713,969	$0.04	per $1,000
Subtotal Capital and Special Expenditures	$23,316,412			$23,316,412			
Capital Revenue Minus Capital Expenditures	$2,155,164			$2,155,164			

E Dilapidated Streets

A small amount (1%) was specifically spent on dilapidated streets. Using the city's pavement condition database, frontage on streets with the worst ratings (1 or 2) was the basis for allocating these expenditures. While this is such a small amount, it was decided to include this as a separate item, since spatial information was available to allocate the cost.

F Community Development Block Grants (CDBG)

The city spent $2.7 million on CDBG projects in 2013, which was 12% of the capital and special expenditures. This amount was allocated based on the low- and moderate-income index.

G Metrozone

As noted previously, the city had an agreement with the adjacent town of Normal to share revenue produced in a zone on the outskirts to the west of the city. This amount made up 5% of the capital and special expenditures and was paid to the town as part of this agreement. This expenditure was allocated to parcels in the Metrozone based on each parcel's share of the zone's operating expenses.

H Capital Lease

The city classified these expenditures as capital, making up 11% of the capital and special expenditures. While they may have been classified that way, they seem to represent regular, ongoing expenses, since they were not for purchasing things like vehicles outright, but rather to spread out the costs on a yearly basis. Nevertheless, they were included as capital and the cost was allocated based on the familiar factors of population, building market value and employment. If some was for vehicles, perhaps the distance factor should have also been used.

I TIF

Making up 5% of the capital and special expenditures, these costs were allocated directly to the TIF parcels.

V Summary of Revenues and Expenditures

The tables in this chapter show all of the revenue and expenditure items contained in the city's CAFR. Table 6.6 summarizes these amounts. By maintaining the revenue and expenditure control totals, it can be determined that nothing has been left out or double counted.

Table 6.6 Summary of Revenues and Expenditures City of Bloomington, IL, 2013

Fiscal Category	Amount
Operating	
Operating Revenue	$90,577,580
Operating Expense	$72,547,931
Operating Surplus	$18,029,649
Transfer Out of Surplus to Capital and Special Revenue	–$18,029,649
Capital and Special	
Transfer In to Capital and Special Revenue	$18,029,649
Other Capital and Special Revenue	$7,441,927
Total Capital and Special Revenue	$25,471,576
Capital Expenditures	$23,316,412
Overall Surplus	$2,155,164
Control Totals*:	
Total Revenue	$98,019,507
Total Expenditures	$95,864,343
Overall Surplus	$2,155,164

*Totals may not add exactly due to rounding.

The analysis could have continued on to allocate transfers in and out from the proprietary (enterprise) funds, including sewer, solid waste and water. The sewer fund did have a $4 million surplus that could have been allocated to parcels but there were no data to allow that to be done. Therefore, the analysis did not include the enterprise funds. This surplus would have been allocated to all occupied residential as well as commercial/industrial and tax-occupied/tax-exempt based on the billing information.

VI Revenue and Expenditure Multipliers

One will notice that several allocation factors repeat many times in the above analysis and tables, such as population, employment, building market value, police and fire calls and the distance factor. To simplify the process of calculating fiscal impact, the multipliers were summarized for each factor. The results are shown in Table 6.7. For example, all of the population revenue add up to $449.61 for operating and $35.97 for capital, resulting in a total of $485.57. On the expenditure side, the operating total was $253.79 and capital was $73.06, for a total of $326.85. It may seem surprising that the revenue is greater than the expenditure for population but there are other things that generate revenues and expenditures that must be taken into consideration, such as market values, public safety and road frontage.

At this point, the fiscal impact of each parcel can be calculated. The multipliers could also be used to estimate the fiscal impact of a proposed development, as will be described in Chapter 9.

Table 6.7 Summary of Operating and Capital Multipliers by Fiscal Allocation Factor, City of Bloomington, IL, 2013

Allocation Factor	Revenue Multiplier			Expenditure Multiplier			Description
	Operating	Capital	Total	Operating	Capital	Total	
Population	449.61000	35.97000	485.57000	253.79000	73.06000	326.85000	Per Capita
Employment	114.69000		114.69000	96.16000	21.46000	117.62000	Per Employee
Assessed Value	0.01376	0.00111	0.01488				Per $1,000
Market Values:							
Commercial/Industrial/Apartment Building Market Value				0.00414	0.00012	0.00426	Per $1,000
Residential Building Market Value	0.00601		0.00601				Per $1,000
Commercial Building Market Value	0.02403		0.02403				Per $1,000
Total Building Market Value		0.00043	0.00043	0.00544	0.00180	0.00724	Per $1,000
TIF Building Market Value		0.01703	0.01703	0.00000	0.04195	$0.041 95	Per $1,000
FY 2013 Development Building MV		6.08000	6.08000				Per $1,000
Fire Calls	295.23000		295.23000	735.29000	39.03000	774.32000	Per Call Equivalent
Police Calls	29.08400		$29.084	104.76000	1.61000	106.37000	Per Call Equivalent
Street Police and Fire Calls				110.04000	4.28000	114.32000	Per Street Call Equivalent
Road Frontage:							
Arterial Frontage	0.28000		0.28000	5.70000	4.90000	10.60000	Per Front Foot
Collector Frontage				4.73000	5.72000	10.45000	Per Front Foot

(Continued)

Table 6.7 (Continued)

Allocation Factor	Revenue Multiplier			Expenditure Multiplier			Description
	Operating	Capital	Total	Operating	Capital	Total	
Local Frontage				1.18000	1.48000	2.66000	Per Front Foot
Alley Frontage				0.48000	0.53000	1.01000	Per Front Foot
Dilapidated Streets				0.00000	2.87000	2.87000	Per Front Foot
Low- and Moderate-Income Index		4.92000	4.92000	0.00000	0.01495	0.01495	Times Index
Metrozone		236,819	236,819	0.00000	1,204,011	1,204,011	Zone Parcel % of MV
Distance Factor	0.00000	0.00000	0.00000	8,614,980	0.00000	8,614,980	Times Distance Factor Percentage*
Population Mile				5.38000	0.73000	6.11000	Per capita times miles

* % ((% population + % market value) times distance) for each parcel.

VII Summary

Determining the multipliers was perhaps the most important step in the Spatial Method, after developing the *Parcel_Factor* shapefile database.

As shown by the tables, the best way to calculate the multipliers was to create spreadsheet tables to summarize operating and capital revenues and expenditures (the *Multipliers* file). The weights were determined by working with city departments to get their agreement as to the importance of the allocation factors. Once an agreement was reached on the weights, the distribution amounts were calculated. At this point the *Parcel_Factor* shapefile had already been created, the factors were summarized for the city and divided into the distribution amounts to derive the multipliers. The next step was to use the multipliers to project fiscal impact by multiplying them times each parcel's factors, e.g., population, road frontage, police and fire calls, etc. Chapter 7 describes the process. It was important that the amounts distributed by the multipliers equaled the control totals for revenues, expenditures and the overall surplus for the project year of 2013. Since many of the allocation factors repeated, such as population, building market value or employment, the multipliers were summed by allocation factor to simplify the calculation of fiscal impact.

Reference

Katz, P. (2013) "The Missing Metric", *Government Finance Review, August*, 20–32.

7 Calculating Existing Fiscal Impact

This chapter illustrates the process by which fiscal impact was determined for the city of Bloomington, Illinois. Once the *Parcel_Factor* shapefile has been assembled containing the allocation factors and the multipliers have been identified and calculated, the task can be accomplished using programming to quickly and accurately calculate each parcel's fiscal impact. The *Fiscal_Impact* shapefile was created by copying the *Parcel_Factor* shapefile and then adding the field names that were to contain the calculations. The chapter provides some examples of naming conventions for the fields needed to do the calculations. The field *MULT_JOIN* will be introduced as the way in which the *Parcel_Factor* file was joined iteratively with the *MULTIPLIERS* File. Results of fiscal impact for taxable and tax-exempt uses will be provided. The net taxable fiscal impact by land use category, after allocating the tax-exempt and surplus amounts to the taxable parcels, will be shown. Tables and maps summarizing the fiscal impact patterns will be provided. Lastly, an example parcel will be provided, along with the calculations of net taxable fiscal impact.

I *Fiscal_Impact* Shapefile and *MULT_JOIN* Fields

The *Fiscal_Impact* shapefile was created by copying the *Parcel_Factor* shapefile and then adding the field names that were to contain the calculations. The reason that the fields were not simply added to the *Parcel_Factor* shapefile was that if the calculations needed to be redone, they would all need to be calculated back to zero to avoid errors. By adding them each time to the newly created *Fiscal_Impact* shapefile, they would automatically have values of zero.

Table 7.1 shows Bloomington's multipliers dealing with operating revenue. A column is included with the heading *MULT_JOIN*, which contains specific names of the fields to be added to the *Fiscal_Impact* file to hold the calculations of fiscal impact. For example, each of the major categories was given a prefix, such as *OR* for operating revenue, *OE* for operating expenses, *CR* for capital and special revenue and *CE* for capital and special expenditures. Allocation factors were given short nicknames, such as *POP*

Table 7.1 Operating Revenue Multipliers and the *MULT_JOIN* Field

Operating Revenue Category	Multiplier	Description	MULT_JOIN
General Government			
Charges for Services	$66.22	per capita	ORPOP
	$18.35	per employee	OREMP
	$9.20	per police equivalent	ORPCALLS
	$288.15	per fire call equivalent	ORFCALLS
	$0.28	per front foot	ORRF
Property Taxes	$0.01	per $1	ORNETAV
Sales Taxes	$294.65	per capita	ORPOP
	$91.85	per employee	OREMP
Commercial Taxes	$0.02	per $1,000	ORCMV
Other Taxes	$0.00	per $1,000	ORNETAV
Income Taxes	$69.76	per capita	ORPOP
Utility Taxes	$0.01	per $1,000	ORRESBMV
Intergovernmental Revenue:			
Parks	$0.34	per capita	ORPOP
	$0.11	per employee	OREMP
Police	$2.16	per police call equivalent	ORPCALLS
Fire	$0.80	per fire call equivalent	ORFCALLS
Investment Income	$0.00	per $1	ORNETAV
Licenses	$0.00	per $1,000	ORCMV
Fines and Forfeits	$16.00	per police call equivalent	ORPCALLS
Other	$10.59	per capita	ORPOP
	$4.13	per employee	OREMP
	$1.72	per police call equivalent	ORPCALLS
	$6.27	per fire call equivalent	ORFCALLS
Library			
Charges for Services	$0.83	per capita	ORPOP
	$0.26	per employee	OREMP
Property Taxes	$0.00	per $1	ORNETAV
Intergovernmental	$0.16	per capita	ORPOP
Investment Income	$0.00	per $1	ORNETAV
Other	$7.05	per capita	ORPOP

for population. The fields for holding the calculations were then named with the prefix and the nickname, such as *ORPOP* or *OEPOP*.

II Operating Multipliers

A *Operating Revenue*

As noted previously, population occurs many times, as well as employment and other distribution factors. In Bloomington's case, it was decided to keep things simple and summarize all of the multipliers which are based on the same distribution factor within the categories of operating revenue and expense and capital revenue and expenditures. The *MULT_ JOIN* field was the basis upon which the factors were summarized.

Table 7.2 Operating Revenue Multipliers Summarized by the *MULT_JOIN* Field

MULT_JOIN	Distribution Factor	Multiplier
ORPOP	Population	449.60118
OREMP	Employment	114.68923
ORPCALLS	Police Call Equivalents	29.08349
ORFCALLS	Fire Call Equivalents	295.22047
ORNETAV	Net Assessed Value	0.01376
ORRF	Local Road Frontage	0.28424
ORCMV	Commercial Building Market Value	0.02403
ORRESBMV	Residential Building Market Value	0.00601

For example, *ORPOP* under *MULT_JOIN* occurs 8 times in Table 7.1. All of the *ORPOP* multipliers add up to $449.6070. Table 7.2 shows the summarized multipliers.

B Operating Expense

Similarly, Table 7.3 shows the operating expenses, with the field names under the *MULT_JOIN* column beginning with the letters "OE".

Again, the operating expense distribution factors, such as population and employment, repeat several times. These were summarized to create another set of operating expense multipliers, as shown in Table 7.4.

With regard to the multipliers for *OEDISTF* (the distance factor), each parcel had been assigned a percentage for the distribution of the amounts shown under the multiplier column, described previously. The result was that parcels with high numbers of people and high building market values located far out from the central city had relatively larger percentages than parcels with the opposite characteristics. The percentages were used to calculate the share of the $12 million distance factor as an expense.

C Summarized Operating Revenue and Capital Multipliers

Finally, Table 7.5 combines both the operating revenue and expenditure multipliers summarized by the distribution factors.

The last item on the list is the Transfer Operating Surplus to Capital. The total revenue amounts categorized as "operating" far exceeded the amount of operating expense by about $18 million. This was 19.9% of the operating revenue. To make a fair comparison of operating revenue to operating expenses, 19.9% of the calculated revenue was deducted from the revenue to get net revenue. Without this deduction, all of the operating fiscal impact calculations for all of the parcels would be inflated due to the fact that operating revenue exceeds expenditures by 19.9%. Each parcel's percentage of the operating revenue was used to calculate how much should be deducted. These amounts were later added back into each parcel's revenue as part of the capital revenue.

Table 7.3 Operating Expense Multipliers and the *MULT_JOIN* Field

Operating Expense Category	Multiplier	Description	MULT_JOIN
General			
Administration	$40.19	per capita	OEPOP
	$1.83	per $1,000	OETBMV
	$11.13	per employee	OEEMP
Vehicle Costs	$3,271,653	% ((%pop + %bmv)*miles)	OEDISTF
Streets	$5.70	per arterial front foot	OEFAR
	$4.73	per collector front foot	OEFCO
	$1.18	per local front foot	OEFLOC
	$0.48	per alley front foot	OEFAL
	$132,716	% ((%pop + %bmv)*miles)	OEDISTF
Culture/Recreation	$83.96	per capita	OEPOP
	$29.91	per employee	OEEMP
	$931,715	% population * miles	OEPOPMI
Public Safety			
Police and Fire Calls			
	$89.39	per police call equivalent	OEPCALLS
	$2,466,150	% ((%pop + %bmv)*miles)	OEDISTF
	$617.91	per fire call equivalent	OEFCALLS
Building Safety and Code Enforcement	$4.14	per $1,000	OECIAMV
Patrolling and Readiness	$74.08	per capita	OEPOP
	$3.61	per $1,000	OETBMV
	$39.59	per employee	OEEMP
	$5,343,325	% ((%pop + %bmv)*miles)	OEDISTF
Parking	$4.53	per capita	OEPOP
	$1.41	per employee	OEEMP
Library	$45.29	per capita	OEPOP
	$14.12	per employee	OEEMP
Elections	$5.75	per capita	OEPOP

III Capital and Special Multipliers

A Capital and Special Revenue

Table 7.6 shows the multipliers for capital and special revenue. The categories under *MULT_JOIN* follow the naming conventions, with *CR* signifying capital and special revenue and the remainder of each category signifying the distribution factor, such as *CRPOP* or *CRNETAV*. Again, one can see

Table 7.4 Operating Expense Multipliers Summarized by the *MULT_ JOIN* Field

MULT_JOIN	Distribution Factor	Multiplier
OEPOP	Population	$253.79
OEEMP	Employment	$96.16
OEFAR	Local Arterial Road Frontage	$5.70
OEFCO	Local Collector Road Frontage	$4.73
OEFLOC	Local Road Frontage	$1.18
OEFAL	Alleys	$0.48
OEPCALLS	Police Call Equivalents	$104.76
OEFCALLS	Fire Call Equivalents	$735.29
OECIAMV	Commercial/Indust./Apartment BMV	$0.00
OETBMV	Building Market Value (BMV)	$0.01
OEDISTF	Population and BMV Distance Factor	$12,145,559

Table 7.5 Operating Revenue and Expense Multipliers Summarized by *MULT_ JOIN* and Distribution Factor

Distribution Factor	Operating Revenue		Operating Expense	
	MULT_JOIN	Multiplier	MULT_JOIN	Multiplier
Population 2013	ORPOP	$449.60700	OEPOP	$253.79450
Employment	OREMP	$114.68940	OEEMP	$96.15850
Police Call Equivalents	ORPCALLS	$29.08360	OEPCALLS	$104.75770
Fire Call Equivalents	ORFCALLS	$295.22530	OEFCALLS	$735.28630
Street Call Equivalents			OESTCALLEQ	$110.04000
Net Assessed Value	ORNETAV	$0.01376		
Local Road Frontage	ORRF	$0.28420		
Commercial Market Value	ORCMV	$0.02400		
Residential BMV	ORRESBMV	$0.00601		
Commercial/Indust./ Apartment BMV			OECIAMV	$0.00410
Building Market Value (Bmv)			OETBMV	$0.00540
Arterial Road Frontage			OEFAR	$5.70340
Collector Road Frontage			OEFCO	$4.73050
Local Road Frontage			OEFLOC	$1.18030
Alleys			OEFAL	$0.48440
Population and Distance Factor			OEPOPMI	$5.37502
Population and BMV Distance Factor			OEDISTF	$8,614,980
Transfer Operating Surplus to Capital	TRANS2CAP	−$0.19905		

Table 7.6 Capital and Special Revenue Multipliers and the *MULT_JOIN* Field

Capital and Special Revenue Category	Multiplier	Description	*MULT_JOIN*
Transfer in From Operating General	19.91%	of Operating Revenue	*TRANS2CAP*
Metrozone	$236,819	% Metrozone Parcel BMV	*CRTN*
Permits	$0.00	per $1,000	*CRFY13DEV*
	$0.00	per $1,000	*CRTBMV*
Debt Service			
Property Taxes	$0.00	per $1	*CRNETAV*
TIF	$0.02	per $1,000	*CRTIFMV*
Other	$0.00	per $1,000	*CRNETAV*
Non-Major			
Intergov. Revenue			
CDBG	$0.00	per $1,000	*CRLMINDX*
Park Dedication	$0.95	per capita	*CRPOP*
Motor Fuel Tax	$28.51	per capita	*CRPOP*
Elections	$6.51	per capita	*CRPOP*
Other	$0.00	per $1,000	*CRNETAV*
Investment Income	$0.00	per $1,000	*CRNETAV*

that these *MULT_JOIN* factors also repeat names. Note that the amount that had been deducted for the operating revenue was added back to each parcel as capital revenue (*TRANS2CAP*).

B Capital and Special Expenditures

Similarly, Table 7.7 shows the multipliers for capital and special expenditures. In this case, there were quite a number of cases of *MULT_JOIN* categories and there were also ones that repeated as well, as in the cases of population, employment and building market value. However, in the case of capital and special expenditures, there were many other factors that were unique to the expenditure patterns, such as the different categories of roads, dilapidated streets and the low- and moderate-income index.

C Summarized Capital and Special Revenue and Expenditure Multipliers

Table 7.8 shows the multipliers for capital and special revenues and expenditures, summarized on *MULT_JOIN*.

D Combined Revenue and Expenditure Multipliers

Another way to express the revenue multipliers was to combine operating and capital to provide a total revenue multiplier for each fiscal factor, as shown in Table 7.9. This can be helpful if one wants to project the revenue

Table 7.7 Capital and Special Expenditure Multipliers and the *MULT_JOIN* Field

Capital and Special Expenditures Category	Multiplier	Description	MULT_JOIN
General	22.958417	per capita	CEPOP
	0.001044	per $1,000	CETBMV
	6.361287	per employee	CEEMP
Parks and Coliseum	32.180105	per capita	CEPOP
	10.030973	per employee	CEEMP
Public Safety	1.609737	per police call equivalent	CEPCALLS
	39.031615	per fire call equivalent	CEFCALLS
	3.089708	per capita	CEPOP
	$96,002	% Distance Factor	CEDISTF
	0.000084	per $1,000	CETBMV
	0.963104	per employee	CEEMP
	0	per $1,000	CECIAMV
Streets	4.900551	per arterial front foot	CEFAR
	5.720573	per collector front foot	CEFCO
	1.477314	per local front foot	CEFLOC
	0.527227	per alley front foot	CEFAL
	$144,443	% Distance Factor	CEDISTF
Dilapidated Streets	2.874857	per front foot	CEDILAP_ST
CDBG	0.014946	per $1,000	CELMINDX
Metrozone	$1,204,011	% Metrozone Parcel BMV	CETN
Capital Lease	14.830535	per capita	CEPOP
	0.000674	per $1,000	CETBMV
	4.109225	per employee	CEEMP
TIF	0.041945	per $1,000	CETIFMV

all at once rather than by operating and capital. This would simplify the calculation process and would eliminate the need to transfer the operating surplus to capital and special, but it would mask some of the detail as to the basis for the fiscal impact results. In Bloomington's case, the operating and capital calculations were done separately.

Table 7.10 shows the combined expenditure multipliers.

V Preliminary Fiscal Impact

Using the operating and capital fiscal impact multipliers, the preliminary fiscal impact of each parcel was calculated based on the values of the factors that were developed in the *Parcel_Factor* shapefile, which were copied to the *Fiscal_Impact* shapefile. Whether the individual multipliers for operating and capital were used or the combined multipliers were used, the final results would be the same.

Table 7.11 shows the results by general land use categories. This was labeled "Preliminary" because it still included the tax-exempt properties.

Note that, as expected, the taxable commercial/industrial uses as a group produced surpluses. Taxable recreation and open-space parcels

Table 7.8 Capital and Special Revenue and Expenditure Multipliers Summarized by the *MULT_JOIN* Field

Allocation Factor	Capital Revenue		Capital Expenditures	
	MULT_JOIN	*Multiplier*	*MULT_JOIN*	*Multiplier*
Population 2013	CRPOP	$35.96620	CEPOP	73.05877
Employment			CEEMP	21.46459
Police Call Equivalents			CEPCALLS	1.60974
Fire Call Equivalents			CEFCALLS	39.03162
Street Call Equivalents			CESTCALLEQ	4.28370
Net Assessed Value	CRNETAV	$0.00111		
Residential BMV				
Commercial Market Value				
Commercial/Indust./ Apartment BMV			CECIAMV	0.00012
Building Market Value	CRTBMV	$0.00043	CETBMV	0.00180
Arterial Road Frontage			CEFAR	4.90055
Collector Road Frontage			CEFCO	5.72057
Local Road Frontage			CEFLOC	1.47731
Alleys			CEFAL	0.52723
Locally Maint. Road Frontage				
Population Miles			CEPOPMI	0.72939
% Population and BMV Distance Factor			CEDISTF	240445
% Metrozone Parcels BMV	CRTN	$236,819	CETN	1204011
TIF District	CRTIF	$0.01703	CETIFMV	0.04195
Low- and Moderate-Income Index	CRLMINDX	$0.00492	CELMINDX	0.01495
Dilapidated Streets			CEDILAPST	2.87486
FY 2013 Development	CRFY13DEV	$0.00610		
Transfer Operating Surplus to Capital	TRANS2CAP	19.9052000%		

produced deficits. Residential also produced a preliminary surplus. Transportation (the airport) and vacant produced deficits.

At this point, the impact of the tax-exempt parcels had also been determined and it was mostly all deficits when viewed by these summary categories. This information would be valuable when considering a tax-exempt development proposal. In Anoka, they used the data to establish a "Payment

Table 7.9 Operating and Capital Revenue Multipliers and the *MULT_JOIN* Field

Revenue

Operating		Capital		Total
MULT_JOIN	*Multiplier*	*MULT_JOIN*	*Multiplier*	*Multiplier*
ORPOP	449.60157	CRPOP	35.965652	$485.56722
OREMP	114.68941			$114.68941
ORFCALLS	295.22529			$295.22529
ORPCALLS	29.083619			$29.08362
ORRF	0.284235			$0.28424
ORNETAV	0.0137618	CRNETAV	0.0011137	$0.01488
ORCMV	0.0240314			$0.02403
ORRESBMV	0.0060075			$0.00601
ORTBMV	0.0004286	CRTBMV	0.0004286	$0.00086
		CRFY13DEV	0.0053641	$0.00536
		CRLMINDX	0.0049182	$0.00492
		CRTIFMV	0.0170261	$0.01703
		CRTN	236,819	$236,819

in Lieu of Taxes", or PILOT, program. Figure 7.1 shows the map of the preliminary fiscal impact, provided in the color insert section.

It is interesting to note that in the non-spatial fiscal impact methods, taxexempt property was included with the non-residential property. If this were truly the case, then residential would have substantial surpluses while the

Table 7.10 Operating and Capital Expenditure Multipliers and the *MULT_JOIN* Field

Expenditures

Operating		Capital		Total
MULT_JOIN	*Multiplier*	*MULT_JOIN*	*Multiplier*	*Multiplier*
OEPOP	253.79115	CEPOP	73.057759	$326.84891
OEEMP	96.158469	CEEMP	21.464608	$117.62308
OEFCALLS	735.28601	CEFCALLS	39.031601	$774.31761
OEPCALLS	104.758	CEPCALLS	1.60974	$106.36774
OESTCALLEQ	110.042	CESTCALLEQ	4.2837	$114.32570
OEFAR	5.7034101	CEFAR	4.9005499	$10.60396
OEFCO	4.7305198	CEFCO	5.7205701	$10.45109
OEFLOC	1.18033	CEFLOC	1.4773099	$2.65764
OEFAL	0.484423	CEFAL	0.527228	$1.01165
OETBMV	0.005435	CETBMV	0.0018022	$0.00724
OECIAMV	0.0041438	CECIAMV	0.000121	$0.00426
OEPOPMI	5.3750212	CEPOPMI	0.729389	$6.10441
OEDISTF	8614980			$8,614,980
		CEDILAP_ST	2.87486	$2.87486
		CELMINDX	0.0149461	$0.01495
		CETIFMV	0.0419451	$0.04195
		CETN	1,204,011	$1,204,011

Table 7.11 Preliminary Fiscal Impact for the Taxable and Tax-Exempt General Land Use Categories

Land Use And Tax Status	Number of Parcels	Acres	Revenue	Expenditures	Preliminary Fiscal Impact Amount	Per Acre
Taxable						
Commercial	1,544	2,723	26,577,616	20,481,749	6,095,868	2,239
Industrial	29	220	716,928	491,572	225,356	1,026
Institutional	4	1	6,451	7,643	–1,192	–927
Recreation and Open Space	92	1,583	164,947	840,110	–675,163	–426
Residential	22,012	5,662	65,857,823	62,176,255	3,681,568	650
Transportation	4	350	16,626	151,134	–134,508	–385
Vacant	1,147	545	286,405	664,015	–377,610	–692
Subtotal	24,832	11,084	$93,626,798	$84,812,479	$8,814,319	$795
Tax-Exempt						
Commercial	7	17	27,693	75,547	–47,854	–2,876
Institutional	307	643	1,470,631	4,610,825	–3,140,193	–4,884
Recreation and Open Space	155	1,592	221,505	2,104,966	–1,883,462	–1,183
Residential	181	183	2,495,635	3,140,396	–644,761	–3,521
Transportation	15	285	146,575	440,795	–294,220	–1,031
Vacant	335	477	30,885	679,607	–648,721	–1,360
Subtotal	1,000	3,197	$4,392,924	$11,052,135	–$6,659,212	–$2,083
Total	25,832	14,281	$98,019,722	$95,864,614	$2,155,107	$151

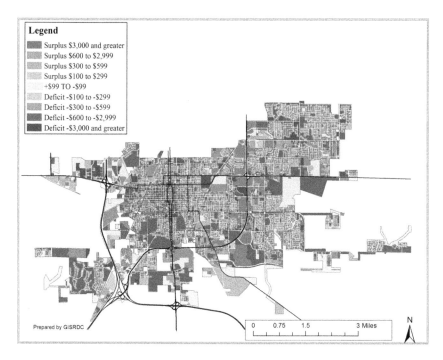

Legend

■ Surplus $3,000 and greater
▨ Surplus $600 to $2,999
▨ Surplus $300 to $599
▨ Surplus $100 to $299
  +$99 TO -$99
▨ Deficit -$100 to -$299
■ Deficit -$300 to -$599
■ Deficit -$600 to -$2,999
■ Deficit -$3,000 and greater

Prepared by GISRDC

0   0.75   1.5   3 Miles

N

Figure 7.1 Preliminary Fiscal Impact per Acre City of Bloomington, Illinois, 2013 (See Color Figure 7.1 in the color insert section).

tax-exempt deficits would be allocated to the taxable non-residential parcels (commercial, industrial, etc.) and the surpluses would be greatly reduced.

VI Allocating the Fiscal Impact of Tax-Exempt Parcels

Tax-exempt properties are believed to benefit the city as a whole and therefore are not subject to property taxes, yet they still have, on average, negative fiscal impacts. Rather than including them with the non-residential land uses, the deficits needed to be allocated to all parcels benefitting from the tax-exempt uses. Table 7.12 shows the fiscal impacts of the tax-exempt parcels by more detailed land use categories. The largest deficits came from government, recreational (golf course), educational, churches and apartments (public housing).

Figure 7.2 shows the preliminary fiscal impact for the tax-exempt properties.

The total negative impact of $6,659,212 had to be allocated to the taxable parcels. To allocate this amount, each taxable parcel's sum of operating and capital expenditures was calculated to be a percentage of the city's total operating and capital expenditures. Each parcel's percentage share was multiplied

Table 7.12 Fiscal Impact of Tax-Exempt Parcels by Detailed Land Use Category

Tax-Exempt Land Use	Number of Parcels	Acres	Revenue	Expenditures	Preliminary Fiscal Impact Amount	Per Acre
Commercial	7	17	27,693	75,547	–47,854	–2,876
Institutional:	2	1	52,574	64,304	–11,730	–10,520
Church	111	146	105,126	662,023	–556,897	–3,818
City	2	1	4,784	7,137	–2,354	–2,061
Educational	43	265	388,247	1,182,251	–794,003	–2,995
Government	44	90	566,353	1,693,560	–1,127,208	–12,533
Other	109	143	362,525	1,030,717	–668,192	–4,685
University	8	34	583,257	569,134	14,124	417
Recreation and Open Space:						
Farm	45	259	48,186	344,158	–295,972	–1,145
Public	53	381	38,673	185,272	–146,599	–385
Recreational	57	953	134,647	1,575,537	–1,440,891	–1,512
Residential:						
Apartments	60	105	1,487,637	2,051,034	–563,397	–5,367
Duplex	51	15	114,169	132,204	–18,034	–1,182
Mixed Use	2	0	9,796	13,037	–3,242	–11,403
Multi-family	33	19	264,188	302,722	–38,533	–2,019
Other	3	3	812	11,124	–10,311	–3,386
Single-Family	20	4	26,797	31,973	–5,176	–1,356
Transportation:						
Airport	1	222	142,753	367,817	–225,064	–1,013
RR	14	63	3,822	72,978	–69,156	–1,097
Vacant:						
Church	1	2	158	6,178	–6,020	–3,659
City	3	2	205	1,873	–1,668	–1,006
Commercial	3	4	292	2,001	–1,709	–383
Educational	13	3	3,363	12,414	–9,051	–3,400
Government	103	161	9,714	221,435	–211,720	–1,319
HOA	98	186	7,020	212,703	–205,683	–1,106
Residential	97	117	9,139	211,488	–202,349	–1,730
Unknown	17	3	993	11,514	–10,521	–3,390
Totals	1,000	3,197	$4,392,924	$11,052,135	–$6,659,212	–$2,083

by the total tax-exempt fiscal impact. The resulting amount was each parcel's percentage share of the tax-exempt fiscal impact. This amount was added to each parcel's preliminary fiscal impact. Actually, since the amounts were negative, they were, in effect, subtracted from the preliminary fiscal impact.

VII Zero-out the Overall Surplus for the City to Determine Net Taxable Fiscal Impact

According to the city's Comprehensive Annual Financial Report (CAFR), there was a surplus of about $2.155 million in 2013. To most

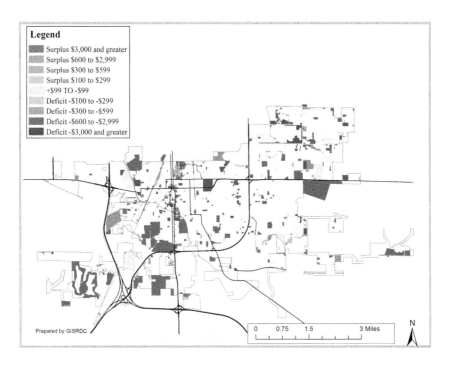

Legend
■ Surplus $3,000 and greater
▨ Surplus $600 to $2,999
▨ Surplus $300 to $599
▨ Surplus $100 to $299
+$99 TO -$99
▨ Deficit -$100 to -$299
▨ Deficit -$300 to -$599
■ Deficit -$600 to -$2,999
■ Deficit -$3,000 and greater

Prepared by GISRDC

0   0.75   1.5   3 Miles

N

Figure 7.2 Preliminary Fiscal Impact per Acre for Tax-Exempt Properties, City of Bloomington, Illinois, 2013 (See Color Figure 7.2 in the color insert section).

accurately estimate the net taxable fiscal impact, the surplus needed to be subtracted out from each parcel. This was done by adding together each parcel's operating and capital revenue and then calculating each parcel's percentage share of the city's total revenue. By multiplying each parcel's share of revenue by the overall surplus, the resulting amount was subtracted from each parcel's fiscal impact to get the net taxable fiscal impact.

Table 7.13 shows the results of allocating the tax-exempt deficit and the overall surplus by generalized land use categories.

Net taxable fiscal impact provided the best measure of fiscal for all of the taxable parcels in the city. Figure 7.3 in the color insert section shows the map of Net Taxable Fiscal Impact per Acre for the entire city.

VIII Analyzing Net Taxable Fiscal Impact Patterns

Since the spatial method is parcel-based, the results can be cross-tabulated and summarized in many different ways.

Table 7.13 Net Taxable Fiscal Impact by General Land Use Category

General Land Use and Tax Status	Number of Parcels	Acres	Preliminary Fiscal Impact	Adjustments		Net Taxable Fiscal Impact		
				Tax Exempt	Surplus	$ Amount	$ Per Acre	$ Per Unit
Taxable								
Commercial	1544	2723	6,095,865	-1,329,202	-631,660	4,135,003	1,519	
Industrial	29	220	225,357	-38,768	-17,328	169,260	770	
Institutional	4	1	-1,192	-517	-149	-1,858	-1,445	
Recreation and Open Space	92	1583	-675,163	-95,962	-3,981	-775,107	-490	
Residential	22012	5662	3,681,568	-5,055,934	-1,496,024	-2,870,390	-507	-85.00
Transportation	4	350	-134,508	-67,364	-283	-202,155	-578	
Vacant	1147	545	-377,610	-71,461	-5,652	-454,723	-834	
Subtotal*	24832	11084	8,814,317	-6,659,209	-2,155,077	0	0	-85.00
Tax-Exempt								
Commercial	7	17	-47,854	47,854	0	0	0	
Institutional	307	681	-3,140,193	3,140,193	0	0	0	
Recreation and Open Space	155	1592	-1,883,461	1,883,461	0	0	0	
Residential	181	147	-644,761	644,761	0	0	0	0.00
Transportation	15	285	-294,220	294,220	0	0	0	
Vacant	335	475	-648,722	648,722	0	0	0	
Subtotal*	1000	3197	-6,659,212	6,659,211	0	0	0	
Totals*	25832	14281	2,155,154	2,155,154	-2,155,077	0	0	-$80**

* Amounts may not add exactly due to rounding.
** Tax-exempt residential units equaled 183, thus lowering the average per unit.

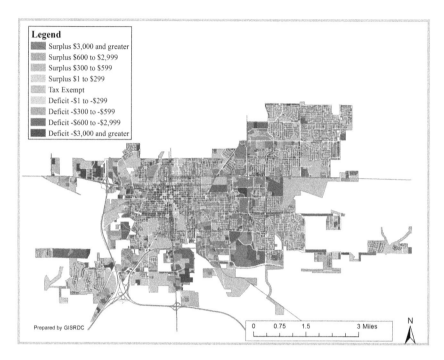

Legend
Surplus $3,000 and greater
Surplus $600 to $2,999
Surplus $300 to $599
Surplus $1 to $299
Tax Exempt
Deficit -$1 to -$299
Deficit -$300 to -$599
Deficit -$600 to -$2,999
Deficit -$3,000 and greater

Prepared by GISRDC

0   0.75   1.5   3 Miles

N

Figure 7.3 Net Taxable Fiscal Impact per Acre City of Bloomington, Illinois, 2013 (See Color Figure 7.3 in the color insert section).

A Parcel Analysis

As it has been explained previously, the purpose was not to single out any one parcel, especially residential. The purpose was to be able to summarize the impacts among similar types of parcels, both as a whole and as summarized by neighborhood or age of housing. Parcels on corners generally had deficits because they fronted on two streets but, when averaged with the other parcels in the blocks, the cost of street maintenance, including side streets, was averaged in also. A parcel may have had a police or fire call in 2013, but it just statistically represents the probability of calls within the class of land use, neighborhood or the age of housing. Table 7.14 shows the results by detailed land use category (*LUSE3*) as to the net taxable fiscal impact for the taxable parcels.

Figure 7.4 in the color insert section shows the Net Taxable Fiscal Impact per Acre for the residential parcels. One can see that residential parcels on the west (older) side produced deficits while those on the eastern side produced surpluses. Also, note the deficits in parcels on street corners.

Figure 7.5 in the color insert section shows the Net Taxable Fiscal Impact per Acre for Commercial / Industrial Properties. Note that while commercial

Table 7.14 Net Taxable Fiscal Impact by Detailed Land Use Categories

Taxable Land Use	Acres	Housing Units	Revenue	Expenditures	Allocated Tax Exempt and Surplus	Net Taxable Fiscal impact		
						Amount	per Acre	per Unit
Commercial	2,722.66		26,577,616	20,481,749	−1,960,862	4,135,006	1,519	
Industrial	219.69		716,928	491,572	−56,097	169,259	770	NA
Institutional:					0			
Church	0.24	2	825	1,467	−86	−728	−3,010	
Educational	0.92		5,194	4,566	−498	131	143	
Private School								
Other	0.13		432	1,611	−82	−1,261	−9,802	
Subtotal	1.29	2	6,451	7,643	−666	−1,858	−518	
Recreation and Open Space:					0			
Farm	1,261.01		30,953	613,255	−83,227	−665,528	−528	
Golf Course	204.93		72,496	135,811	−9,140	−72,455	−354	
Public Park	117.23		61,499	91,044	−7,577	−37,123	−317	
Subtotal	1,583.17	0	164,947	840,110	−99,944	−775,106	−63	
Residential:					0			
Apartments	518.01	10,049	10,819,282	12,255,095	−1,194,992	−2,630,804	−5,079	−262.00
Condominium	0.74	9	15,407	11,758	−1,059	2,590	3,498	288.00
Duplex	87.28	1,106	1,754,245	2,001,468	−135,443	−382,666	−4,384	−346.00
Mixed Use	2.93	9	19,019	30,442	−1,452	−12,875	−4,401	−1431.00
Mobile Home Park	322.37	1,954	2,356,277	2,514,965	−268,988	−427,677	−1,327	−219.00
Multi-family	29.18	164	270,504	282,391	−18,663	−30,549	−1,047	−186.00
Other	5.71	3	54,739	50,159	−3,620	960	168	320.00
Single-Family	4,694.08	20,546	50,442,057	44,938,624	−4,920,441	582,992	124	28.00

(Continued)

Table 7.14 (Continued)

Taxable Land Use	Acres	Housing Units	Revenue	Expenditures	Allocated Tax Exempt and Surplus	Net Taxable Fiscal impact Amount	per Acre	per Unit
University	1.74	5	126,294	91,353	-7,301	27,640	15,912	NA
Subtotal	5,662.03	33,845	65,857,823	62,176,255	-6,551,958	-2,870,390	-1,157	-85.00
Airport	349.66		16,626	151,134	-67,647	-202,154	-578	
Vacant:					0			
Commercial	116.64		107,968	157,695	-20,189	-69,916	-599	
Government City	16.04		447	2,557	-244	-2,354	-147	
Industrial	8.08		1,470	7,267	-1,244	-7,041	-871	
Residential	404.54		176,519	496,496	-55,436	-375,412	-928	
Subtotal	545.31		286,405	664,015	-77,113	-454,723	-141	
Totals	11,083.79	33,847	$93,626,798	$84,812,479	$8,814,317	$0	$795	-$85

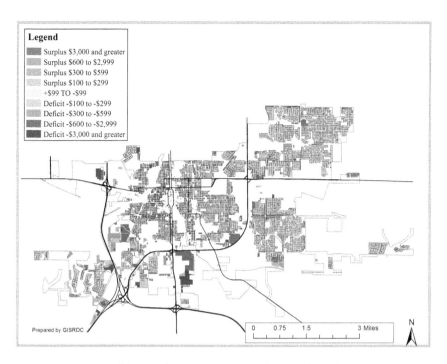

Figure 7.4 Net Taxable Fiscal Impact per Acre for Residential Properties City of Bloomington, Illinois 2013 (See Color Figure 7.4 in the color insert section.)

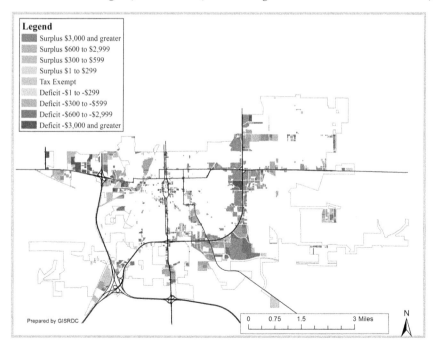

Figure 7.5 Net Taxable Fiscal Impact per Acre for Commercial and Industrial Properties, City of Bloomington, IL, 2013 (See Color Figure 7.5 in the color insert section).

and industrial parcels generally produce surpluses, there are also ones that produce deficits, particularly on the west side.

B Fiscal Impact by Year Built

It is useful to measure the fiscal impact by the year built. Figure CP.02 the color insert section shows how different areas of the city were categorized. One can see that the city developed generally from west to east. Table 7.15 summarizes the net taxable fiscal impact by year and by general land use categories. One can see that while residential produced an overall deficit, the parcels built from 1980 to 2013 produced a surplus, on average. Commercial/industrial parcels built since 1940 also produced an average surplus per acre.

Table 7.16 shows the net taxable fiscal impact by year built for residential categories. One can see that newer single-family homes have a positive impact. One can see that mobile homes seem to have a large negative impact from 2000 to 2013, but that may be due to the year-built classification, which had to be general since there were no actual year-built data for them. Furthermore, that year-built category only had 32 units. Using the average of –$219 would probably be best. The "other" category includes condominiums, mixed use, multi-family and other, which only represent 192 housing units and should also be viewed with caution.

C Surpluses and Deficits

The patterns of deficits are shown in Figure 7.6 in grayscale. One can generally see deficits in the central city within 2.5 miles of downtown. The older west side also has more deficits than the east. The mileage rings are also shown and one can see that some of the outlying areas in the southeast and

Table 7.15 Net Taxable Fiscal Impact per Acre by Estimated Year Built and General Land Use Category, City of Bloomington, IL 2013

| Estimated Year Built | Net Taxable Fiscal Impact per Acre | | | |
	Residential	Commercial / Industrial	Other	Total
1900 and Earlier	–2728.98	–144.41	–118.28	–1426.57
1901–1919	–5374.15	–4110.67	–321.74	–4046.97
1920–1939	–1347.4	–459.47	–447.76	–1102.55
1940–1959	–516.15	1304.61	–189.94	72.9
1960–1979	–883.72	4108.76	–179.51	1314.94
1980–1999	683.24	1747.12	–162.41	491.74
2000–2013	846.49	996.5	–408.59	172.21
Unknown	–4166.38	–6182.98	–331.14	–2168.77
All Parcels	–$491.07	$1,454.64	–$261.82	$0.00

Table 7.16 Net Taxable Fiscal Impact for Residential Land Use by Year Built, City of Bloomington, IL 2013

Estimated Year Built	Net Taxable Fiscal Impact per Unit					
	Single-Family	Apartments	Mobile Homes	Duplex	Other	Total
1900 and Earlier	−392	−6,659		−482	121	−578
1901–1919	−471	−630		−350	−315	−516
1920–1939	−171	−342		−432	297	−215
1940–1959	−106	−53		−330	−167	−89
1960–1979	−52	−173	−278	−189	1,822	−143
1980–1999	229	−51	−132	211	−57	141
2000–2013	317	−274	−854	461	0	172
Unknown	−748	−414	0	0	0	−431
Taxable Parcels	$28	−$262	−$219	−$346	−$64	−$85
All Residential Parcels*						−$80

* includes 181 tax exempt parcels.

southwest had significant deficits because they represent leapfrog development, which significantly increased the cost of service delivery.

In the northwest, the commercial development in the Metrozone also had significant deficits due to the fact that the city had to remit a net amount of about $1 million to the town of Normal under a revenue-sharing agreement.

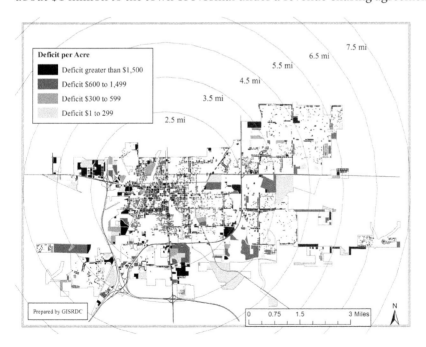

Figure 7.6 Parcels With a Net Taxable Deficit per Acre, Bloomington, IL, 2013.

It also had significant police protection costs for the over 8,000 police call equivalents that it had.

Figure 7.7 shows the parcels with surpluses in grayscale. The residential areas to the near east and northeast generally showed surpluses. As newer development, they provided higher property-tax revenues. It was also more compact and contiguous to the rest of the city, resulting in more efficient service delivery compared to the leapfrog development in the southeast and southwest. The commercial development along a major thoroughfare named Veterans Parkway around the east side of the central city had major surpluses due to commercial property taxes. Another area that had significant surpluses was the home offices of the State Farm Insurance Agency, just to the southeast of the central city and Veterans Parkway.

D Neighborhood Fiscal Impact

Another way to view the results is by neighborhood. Figure 7.8 shows some general neighborhoods that were created, representing broad areas and characteristics. Any kind of area classification could be used to summarize fiscal impact, including more detailed neighborhoods. Table 7.17 shows the summarized net taxable fiscal impact per acre.

While tabular data provides the most detail, viewing the results in map form is also very valuable to understand the spatial patterns that exist.

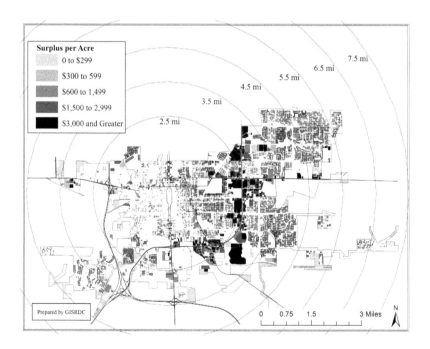

Figure 7.7 Parcels With a Net Taxable Surplus per Acre, Bloomington, IL, 2013.

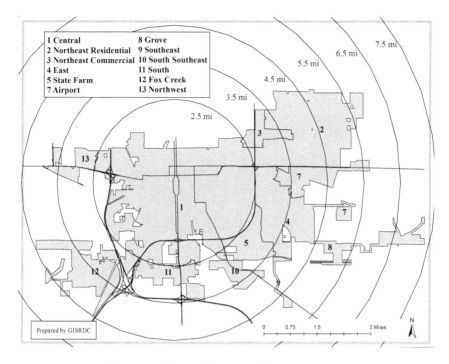

Figure 7.8 Generalized Neighborhoods, City of Bloomington, IL.

Table 7.17 Neighborhood Net Taxable Fiscal Impact per Acre

Neighborhood Number	Neighborhood Name	Net Taxable Fiscal Impact Amount ($)	$ Per Acre
1	CENTRAL	–3,451,272	–603
2	NORTHEAST RESIDENTIAL	970,821	405
3	NORTHEAST COMMERCIAL	788,493	2,227
4	EAST	1,413,523	1,059
5	STATE FARM	2,482,999	4,233
7	AIRPORT	–334,128	–450
8	GROVE	–156,025	–302
9	SOUTHEAST	–7,330	–69
10	SOUTH SOUTHEAST	2,400	7
11	SOUTH	–321,555	–489
12	FOX CREEK	–336,225	–300
13	NORTHWEST	–1,051,667	–2,759
Totals*		0	0

* Numbers may not add due to rounding.

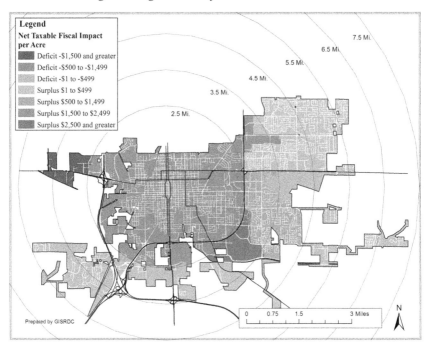

Figure 7.9 Neighborhood Net Taxable Fiscal Impact per Acre Bloomington, IL
2013 (See Color Figure 7.9 in the color insert section.)

Figure 7.9 in the color insert section shows the results for neighborhoods using color categories.

The Central neighborhood had an overall deficit of $603 per acre. Note the skipped-over areas in white within the Central neighborhood. This is an indication that services were not being efficiently delivered because the neighborhood was not wholly contiguous. The leapfrog area to the southeast, named Grove, had an overall deficit of $302 per acre. Again, the distance that the city staff have to travel contributes to inefficiency. Residential areas to the south also suffer from inefficiencies due to size and skipped-over areas. The neighborhood, known as Fox Creek, to the southwest can also be considered a leapfrog development with service inefficiencies. While the residential taxable values were higher than the rest of the city, it also had a golf course as part of the development and it was classified as tax exempt. This meant that the negative fiscal impact of the golf course was allocated to the entire neighborhood, giving it a negative fiscal impact. Lastly, the neighborhood in the northwest is commercial and within the Metrozone, which had the problems described previously.

The northeast and east neighborhoods are compact and contiguous relative to the central city and services are delivered relatively efficiently. However, the northeast neighborhood had less of a surplus than the east

Table 7.18 Net Taxable Fiscal Impact for the Northeast Residential Neighborhood

Land Use Category	Number of Parcels	Acres	Housing Units	Net Taxable Fiscal Impact		
				Amount	*Per Acre*	*Per Unit*
Taxable						
Commercial	86	135.8	0	382,416	2,817	0
Recreation	14	144.1	0	–135,605	–941	0
Residential						
Apartments	112	107.7	1,746	–266,970	–2,478	–153
Condominium	2	0.2	2	705	3,544	353
Duplex	19	2.2	24	–2,877	–1,303	–120
Single Family	5,711	1,406.7	5,711	1,506,086	1,071	264
Vacant	118	63.0	0	–41,179	–653	0
Tax Exempt						
Institutional	31	97.4	0	0	0	0
Recreation	36	247.3	0	0	0	0
Residential	30	29.6	208	0	0	0
Vacant	77	163.2	0	0	0	0
Totals	6,236	2,397.3	7,691	$1,442,577	$602	$188

neighborhood because it extends farther away from the central city and thus is more affected by the distance factor. The east neighborhood also had more commercial that contributes to the larger surplus. The neighborhood named Northeast Commercial had its surplus due to the concentration of mostly commercial land use. Lastly, the State Farm neighborhood generated the greatest amount of surplus, at an average of over $4,000 per acre. It is an office development that generally had fewer police or fire calls; the internal street system was private, so the city had no road maintenance costs, and it also generated large amounts of property taxes.

Another example of the benefit of measuring fiscal impact on a parcel basis is the fact that the data can be summarized by general or detailed land use categories and by neighborhood. Table 7.18 shows an example of the net taxable fiscal impact by land use for the Northeast Residential neighborhood. It could also have been done using the more detailed categories, especially for residential.

IX Calculating Fiscal Impact for an Example Parcel

The multipliers and the fiscal factors in the *Fiscal_Impact* shapefile are what are needed to estimate the fiscal impact of each parcel. They can also be used to project the fiscal impact of a new development, as will be shown in a later chapter. A residential parcel has been selected at random to provide an example of how its fiscal impact was calculated. Table 7.19 shows the relevant values for the parcel from the *Parcel_Factor* shapefile that were copied to the *Fiscal_Impact* shapefile.

Table 7.19 Values in the *Fiscal_Impact* Database for an Example Residential Parcel

Factor Description	Parcel_Factor Database Field	Factor Value
PIN	*PIN*	1425103XXX*
ACRES	*ACRES*	0.246
Land Use Tax Status	*LUSE0*	TAXABLE
General Land Use	*LUSE1*	RESIDENTIAL
Additional Land use	*LUSE1B*	SINGLE-FAMILY
More Detail Land Use	*LUSE2*	
LUSE1, 1B AND 2	*LUSE3*	RESIDENTIAL SINGLE-FAMILY
All Land Use Categories	*LUSE4*	TAXABLE RESIDENTIAL SINGLE-FAMILY
Population 2013	*POP13*	3.235
Housing 2013	*HSG13*	1
Employment	*EMPLOYMENT*	0
Fire Call Equivalents	*F_CALLS*	1.713
Police Call Equivalents	*P_CALLS*	0
Street Call Equivalents	*STCALLEQ*	0
Arterial Frontage	*FRTG_ART*	0
Collector Frontage	*FRTG_COLLE*	0
Local Frontage	*FRTG_LOCAL*	93
Alleys	*FRTG_ALLEY*	0
Total Frontage	*TOT_FRTG*	93
Net Assessed Value	*NETAV*	70672
Commercial Building Market Value	*COMMERCMV*	0
Commercial/Industrial and Apartment Building Market Value	*C_I_A_BMV*	0
Residential Building Market Value	*RES_BMV*	60584
Total Building Market Value	*TOT_BMV*	60584
Fiscal Year 2013 Development	*FY2013DEV*	0
TIF Market Value	*TIFMV*	0
Low Income Index	*LOW_INC_IX*	0
Dilapidated Streets	*DILAP_ST*	0
Metrozone	*METROZONE*	0
Population Miles	*POPMI*	11.96
Distance Factor	*DISTF*	0.0000535

Tables 7.20 and 7.21 show how the operating revenue and expenditure amounts for this parcel were calculated and Table 7.22 shows the calculation of the operating fiscal impact.

Tables 7.23, 7.24 and 7.25 show the capital and special revenues and expenditures and fiscal impact calculations for the example residential parcel.

The preliminary fiscal Impact for the example parcel is shown in Table 7.26. The operating fiscal impact and the capital fiscal impact were added together to get the preliminary fiscal impact of –$66.10.

Table 7.20 Operating Revenue Calculations for an Example Residential Parcel

Parcel_Factor		*Operating Revenue*		
Database Field Name	Factor Amount	MULT_JOIN	Multiplier	Calculated Amount
POP13	3.19	ORPOP	449.607	$1,434
EMPLOYMENT	0	OREMP	114.6894	$0
P_CALLS	0	ORPCALLS	29.0836	$0
F_CALLS	1.713	ORFCALLS	295.2253	$506
NETAV	70672	ORNETAV	0.01376	$973
COMMERCMV	0	ORCMV	0.02403	$0
RES_BMV	60584	ORRESBMV	0.00601	$364
C_I_A_BMV	0			$0
TOT_BMV	60584			$0
FRTG_ART	0			$0
FRTG_COLLE	0			$0
FRTG_LOCAL	93			$0
TOT_FRTG	93	ORRF	0.2842	$26
FRTG_ALLEY	0			$0
POPMI	11.96			$0
DISTF	0			$0
		OPER_REV		$3,303
		TRANS2CAP	−0.19905	$657
		NET_O_REV		$2,646

Table 7.21 Operating Expense Calculations for an Example Residential Parcel

Parcel_Factor	Example Factor	Operating Expense		
Database Field Name	Amount	MULT_JOIN	Multiplier	Calculated Amount
POP13	3.18961	OEPOP	253.79	$809
EMPLOYMENT	0	OEEMP	96.16	$0
P_CALLS	0	OEPCALLS	104.76	$0
F_CALLS	1.713	OEFCALLS	735.29	$0
STCALLEQ		OESTCALLEQ	110.04	$0
FRTG_ART	0	OEFAR	5.7034	$0
FRTG_COLLE	0	OEFCO	4.7305	$0
FRTG_LOCAL	0	OEFLOC	1.1803	$0
FRTG_ALLEY	0	OEFAL	$0.48	$0
TOT_FRTG	93			
NETAV	70,672			
COMMERCMV	0			
RES_BMV	60,584			
C_I_A_BMV	0	OECIAMV	0.00414	$0
TOT_BMV	60,584	OETBMV	0.00544	$809
POPMI	11.961	OEPOPMI	$5.38	$64
DISTF	0.000053473	OEDISTF	$8,614,980	$329
Total Operating Expense		OPER_EXP		$2,013

Table 7.22 Operating Fiscal Impact for an Example Residential Parcel

Total Operating Revenue	$3,302.73
Transfer to Capital Revenue	–$657.41
Total Operating Expense	–$3,033.04
Operating Fiscal Impact	–$387.72

Table 7.23 Capital and Special Revenue Calculations for an Example Residential Parcel

Parcel_Factor	Factor	Capital and Special Revenue	
Database Field Name	Amount	MULT_JOIN Multiplier	Calculated Amount
POP13	3.18961	CRPOP 35.97	$115
NETAV	70,672	CRNETAV 0.00111	$78
TOT_BMV	60,584	CRTBMV 0.000429	$26
TRANS2CAP			$657
Total Capital and Special Revenue			$876

Table 7.24 Capital and Special Expenditure Calculations for an Example Residential Parcel

Parcel_Factor	Factor	Capital and Special Expenditures		
Database Field Name	Amount	MULT_JOIN	Multiplier	Calculated Amount
POP13	3.18961	CEPOP	73.05877	$233.03
EMPLOYMENT	0	CEEMP	21.46459	$0.00
P_CALLS	0	CEPCALLS	1.60974	$0.00
F_CALLS	1.713	CEFCALLS	39.03162	$66.86
STCALLEQ		CESTCALLEQ	4.2837	$0.00
NETAV	70672		0	$0.00
RESBMV				$0.00
CMV				$0.00
C_I_A_BMV	0	CECIAMV	0.00012	$0.00
TOT_BMV	60584	CETBMV	0.0018	$109.18
FRTG_ART	0	CEFAR	4.90055	$0.00
FRTG_COLLE	0	CEFCO	5.72057	$0.00
FRTG_LOCAL	93	CEFLOC	1.47731	$137.39
FRTG_ALLEY	0	CEFAL	0.52723	$0.00
TOT_FRTG	93		0	$0.00
POPMI	11.96	CEPOPMI	0.72939	$8.72
DISTF	0.000053473	CEDISTF	240,445	$0.00
METROZONE	0	CETN	1,204,011	$0.00
TIF_MV	0	CETIFMV	0.04195	$0.00
LOW_INC_IX	0	CELMINDX	0.01495	$0.00
DILAP_ST	0	CEDILAP_ST	2.87486	$0.00
FY13DEV	0	CEFY13DEV	0	$0.00
Total Capital and Special Expenditures				$555.18

Table 7.25 Capital and Special Fiscal Impact for an
Example Residential Parcel

Total Capital Revenue	$876
Total Capital Expenditures	–$555
Capital Fiscal Impact	$321

Table 7.26 Net Taxable Fiscal Impact for an Example
Residential Parcel

Operating Fiscal Impact	–387.72
Capital Fiscal Impact	320.82
Preliminary Fiscal Impact	–66.1
Share of Tax-Exempt	–400.91
Taxable Fiscal Impact	–467.01
Zero-out City-Wide Surplus	–82.33
Net Taxable Fiscal Impact	–549.34

Finally, the Net Taxable Fiscal Impact for the example residential parcel is also shown. The amount of allocated tax-exempt cost was $401. The surplus allocation was $82.33. These amounts were deducted from the parcel's preliminary fiscal impact to get the net taxable fiscal impact of –$549.34.

These same calculations were made in the *Fiscal_Impact* shapefile for each parcel. As noted before, the purpose was not necessarily to single out any one parcel for examination but rather to be able to summarize the fiscal impact for similar types of parcels.

For example, this home was built in 1997, it had 2,658 square feet of building and 10,731 square feet of lot area and was located in the Northeast neighborhood. A summary of all the single-family housing units built in 1997 with 2,500 to 3,000 square feet of building area would provide the average fiscal impact for that group of land uses in that neighborhood. The example parcel had a fire/EMS call equal to 1.713 fire call equivalents in 2013, which cost $1,260. But probably in 2014 it had none, it would have resulted in a positive fiscal impact in 2014. Yet, there may have been a similar parcel located a few blocks over with a fire/EMS call in 2014. As a result, the average for the land use category in the neighborhood would still be nearly the same.

X Summary

Calculating fiscal impact would be unbelievably tedious if one had to do it parcel by parcel. However, once the *Parcel_Factor* shapefile has been assembled containing the allocation factors and the multipliers have been identified and calculated, the task can be accomplished using programming to quickly and accurately calculate each parcel's fiscal impact. Appendix F will provide some programming examples. The Bloomington example has numerous factors that needed to be considered. In smaller cities, the number may be far less. This chapter has provided suggestions as to revenue- and expenditure-naming conventions that help to understand the processing steps amidst all the factor names and fiscal calculations. Ways to summarize and analyze the results have also been shown. The actual processing was done with ArcGIS and Model Builder, as shown in Appendix F.

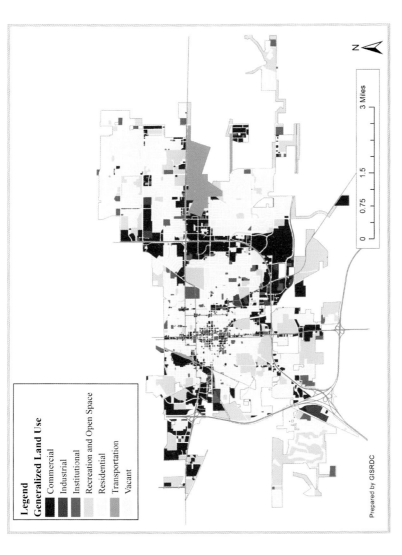

Legend

Generalized Land Use

- Commercial
- Industrial
- Institutional
- Recreation and Open Space
- Residential
- Transportation
- Vacant

Prepared by GISRDC

0   0.75   1.5   3 Miles

N

Color Figure 5.1 Generalized Land Use City of Bloomington, IL, 2013.

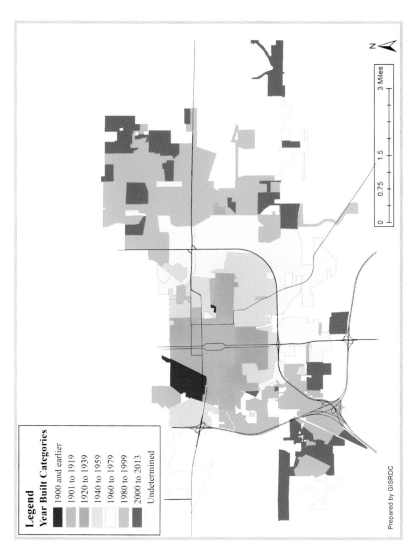

Legend
Year Built Categories

- 1900 and earlier
- 1901 to 1919
- 1920 to 1939
- 1940 to 1959
- 1960 to 1979
- 1980 to 1999
- 2000 to 2013
- Undetermined

N

0   0.75   1.5   3 Miles

Prepared by GISRDC

Color Figure 5.2 Areas Categorized by the Approximate Year Built Based on Assessor's Data City of Bloomington, IL.

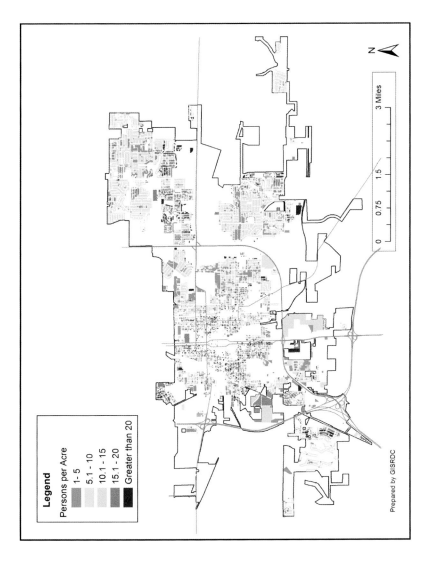

Legend

Persons per Acre

- 1 - 5
- 5.1 - 10
- 10.1 - 15
- 15.1 - 20
- Greater than 20

0   0.75   1.5   3 Miles

N

Prepared by GISRDC

Color Figure 5.3 2013 Population Density City of Bloomington, IL.

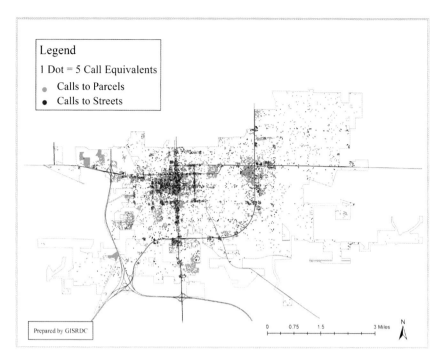

Color Figure 5.4 2013 Police Calls City of Bloomington, IL.

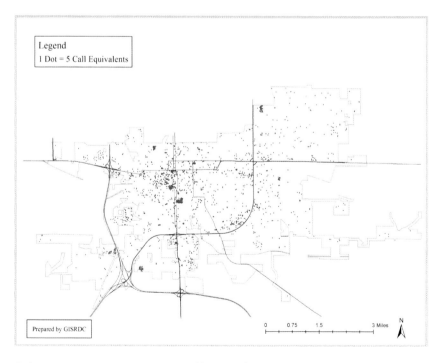

Color Figure 5.5 2013 Fire/EMS Calls City of Bloomington, IL.

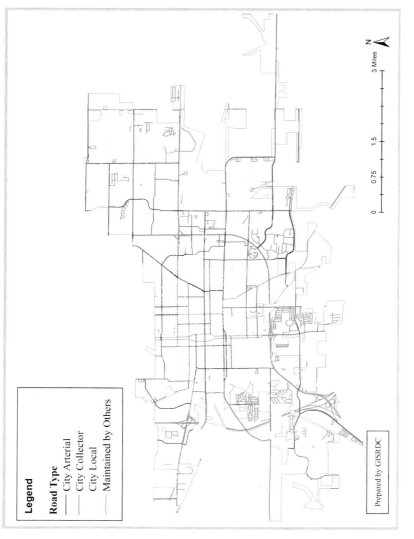

Legend

Road Type

—— City Arterial
—— City Collector
—— City Local
—— Maintained by Others

Prepared by GISRDC

0   0.75   1.5   3 Miles

N

Color Figure 5.6 2013 Roads by Type City of Bloomington, IL.

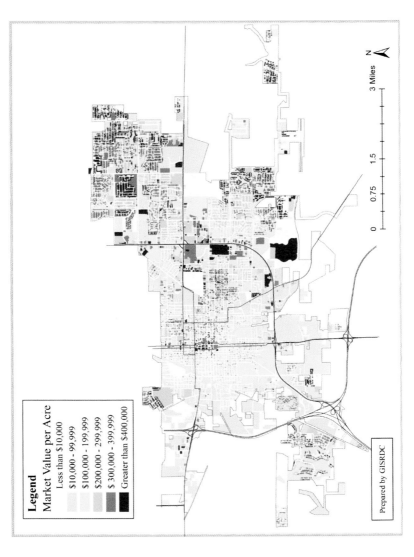

Legend
Market Value per Acre
Less than $10,000
$10,000 - 99,999
$100,000 - 199,999
$200,000 - 299,999
$ 300,000 - 399,999
Greater than $400,000

0   0.75   1.5   3 Miles

N

Prepared by GISRDC

Color Figure 5.7 2013 Market Values per Acre City of Bloomington, IL.

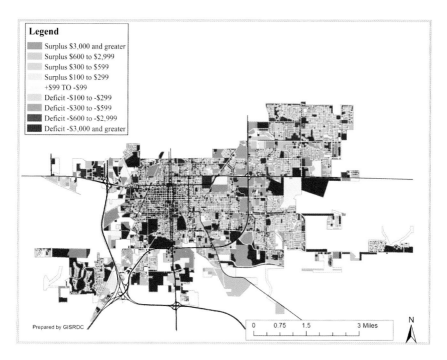

Color Figure 7.1 Preliminary Fiscal Impact per Acre City of Bloomington, Illinois, 2013.

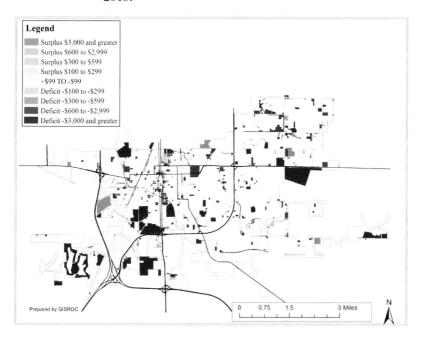

Color Figure 7.2 Preliminary Fiscal Impact per Acre for Tax-Exempt Properties, City of Bloomington, Illinois, 2013.

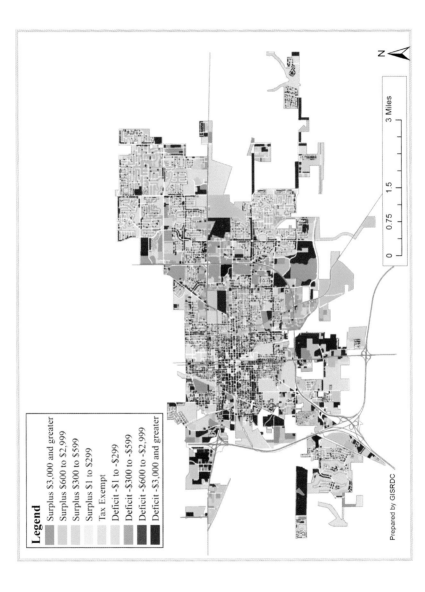

Legend

Surplus $3,000 and greater
Surplus $600 to $2,999
Surplus $300 to $599
Surplus $1 to $299
Tax Exempt
Deficit -$1 to -$299
Deficit -$300 to -$599
Deficit -$600 to -$2,999
Deficit -$3,000 and greater

N

0   0.75   1.5   3 Miles

Color Figure 7.3 Net Taxable Fiscal Impact per Acre City of Bloomington, Illinois, 2013.

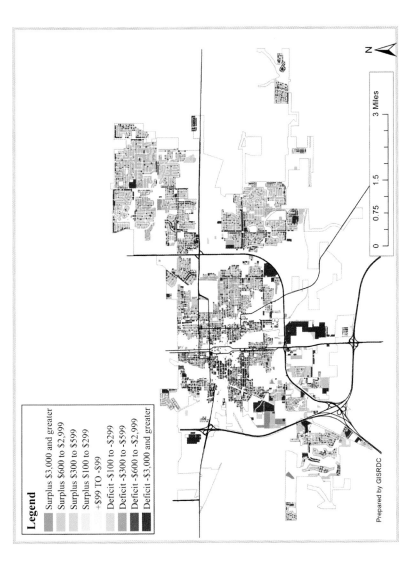

Color Figure 7.4 Net Taxable Fiscal Impact per Acre for Residential Properties City of Bloomington, Illinois 2013.

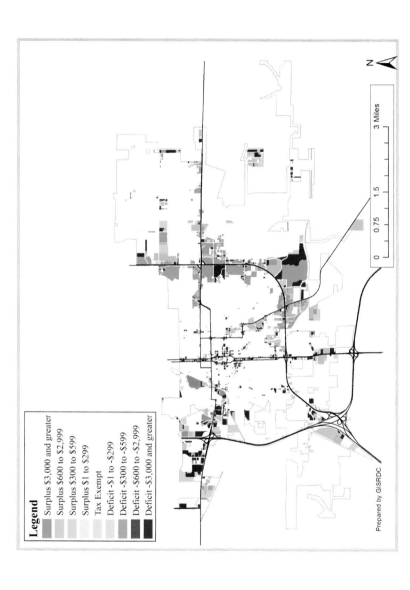

Legend

Surplus $3,000 and greater
Surplus $600 to $2,999
Surplus $300 to $599
Surplus $1 to $299
Tax Exempt
Deficit -$1 to -$299
Deficit -$300 to -$599
Deficit -$600 to -$2,999
Deficit -$3,000 and greater

N

0   0.75   1.5   3 Miles

Prepared by GISRDC

Color Figure 7.5 Net Taxable Fiscal Impact per Acre for Commercial and Industrial Properties, City of Bloomington, IL, 2013.

Color Figure 7.9 Neighborhood Net Taxable Fiscal Impact per Acre Bloomington, IL 2013.

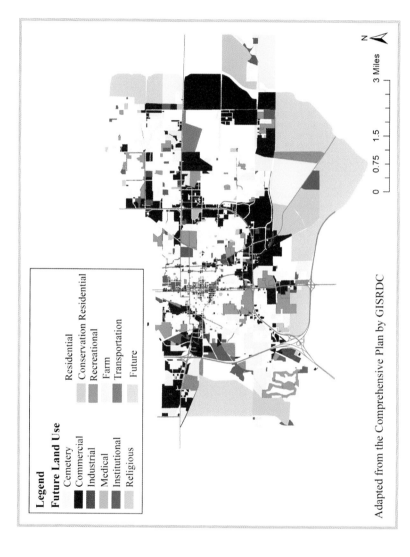

Legend

Future Land Use

Cemetery
Commercial
Industrial
Medical
Institutional
Religious

Residential
Conservation Residential
Recreational
Farm
Transportation
Future

N

0   0.75   1.5   3 Miles

Adapted from the Comprehensive Plan by GISRDC

Color Figure 9.1 Generalized Land Use Plan City of Bloomington.

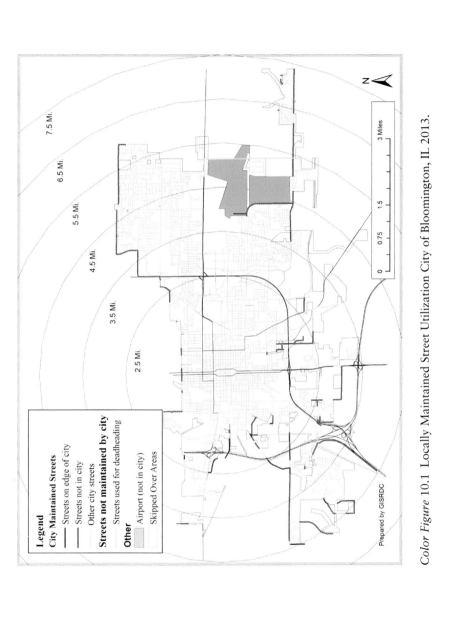

Color Figure 10.1 Locally Maintained Street Utilization City of Bloomington, IL 2013.

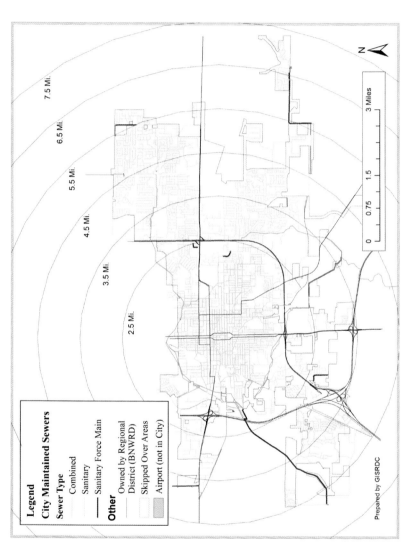

Color Figure 10.2 2013 Sanitary Sewers City of Bloomington, IL.

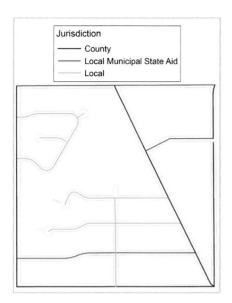

Color Figure C.3 Right-of-Way Polygon and Centerlines.

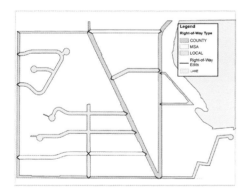

Color Figure C.4 Edited Right of Way Polygons.

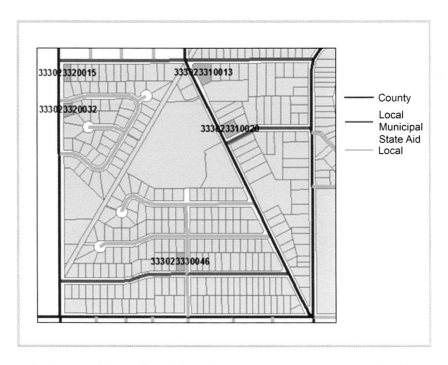

Color Figure C.6 Example of Selected Parcels Located on Corners With Different Street Jurisdictions.

8 Analyzing School Fiscal Impact

This chapter will show the many ways that the parcel-level data can be summarized to help with analyzing school fiscal impact. The project for Bloomington did not consider school fiscal impact. School finances were borne by two independent districts covering the city. However, in the process of estimating population by parcel using census block population, a city could also estimate the school-aged population (SAP), as presented in Appendix E. Furthermore, the assessor's file included the amounts of property-tax revenue raised for each district. Since the *Parcel_Factor* shapefile included detailed residential land use categories and the assessor's file had the number of bedrooms, the amount of school revenue could be summarized by residential type as well as the estimated students per parcel. The revenue per student could also be summarized. Each district's financial report provided the operating expenses and the amounts per pupil (OEPP); therefore, the number of students could be calculated. The *Parcel_Factor* shapefile also included the approximate year built and, as a result, the students per unit could also be summarized by the age of housing. In this case, the newer housing had greater numbers of students. This information would be very useful in projecting the number of students coming from a proposed development.

The spatial data on schools was provided by the McLean County GIS Department. All tables refer to the city of Bloomington in 2013, unless noted otherwise.

I The Districts

The original city district was much smaller than the larger city boundary in 2013. At some time in the past, the school administration for newer areas was probably taken over by an outlying district. Figure 8.1 shows the map of the original district and the outlying district, which extends out beyond the city border. The big differences in boundaries have made it difficult to do any type of complete analysis.

However, the city could have considered some of the school district impact by including an analysis of school students by parcel in addition

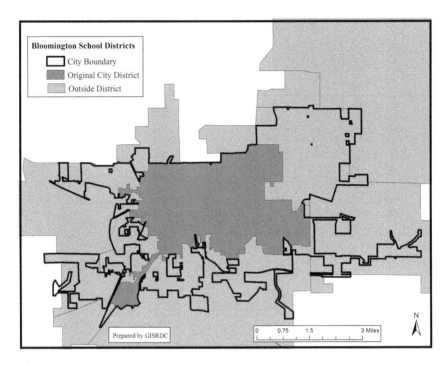

Figure 8.1 School Districts Covering the City of Bloomington, IL.

to the estimation of population. Appendix E shows how this could have been done by considering not only census block population but also the voting-age population. Subtracting the voting-age population from the total population yields the 0–17 population in the census year. Some adjustments had to be made to subtract out the 0–4 population and adding in the estimated age-18 population. Census data also has more detailed information on population by age and sex, which could have been used as well, and perhaps would have been more accurate, but the process would have been more complicated.

II Revenue Considerations

The assessor's parcel data included the revenue raised by parcel for each school district, which made it possible to identify the district in which each parcel was located and to calculate the number of students per housing unit and also the revenue per unit. The averages for the different residential classes are shown in Table 8.1. This data is from Appendix E, after the population and school-aged population was estimated. The classes and their definitions are also included. The term "blended" means that there was no assessor's data under the field *NO_BDRMS* so that an average category

Table 8.1 2013 Revenue and Estimated Students per Unit, By Residential Housing Classification

Residential Class	Description	Revenue			Students	
		Housing Units	Amount	Per unit	Number	Per unit
APTBLEND	Apartment Blend	11,776	5,805,421	493	2,748	0.23
CONDO1	Condo 1 Bedroom	3	3,722	1,241	1	0.17
CONDO2	Condo 2 Bedroom	2	3,632	1,816	1	0.34
CONDO3	Condo 3 Bedroom	4	8,857	2,214	2	0.41
DUP1	Duplex 1 Bedroom	2	1,342	671	1	0.46
DUP2	Duplex 2 Bedroom	2	2,811	1,406	1	0.59
DUP3	Duplex 3 Bedroom	9	4,751	528	5	0.52
DUPBLEND	Duplex Blend	1,208	782,350	648	422	0.35
GQ	Group Quarters	4	44,448	11,112	53	13.29
MFBLEND	Multi-family Blend	321	108,979	339	145	0.45
MHBLEND	Mobile Homes Blend	1,954	293,400	150	763	0.39
MIXBLEND	Mixed-Use Blend	18	17,804	989	4	0.25
SF1	Single-Family One-Bedroom	113	185,692	1,643	25	0.22
SF2	Single-Family Two-Bedroom	2,215	4,038,221	1,823	683	0.31
SF3	Single-Family Three-Bedroom	6,132	13,706,029	2,235	3,197	0.52
SF4	Single-Family Four-Bedroom	6,297	23,165,490	3,679	4,815	0.76
SF5	Single-Family Five-Bedroom	242	1,325,666	5,478	188	0.78
SF6	Single-Family Six-Bedroom	36	221,032	6,140	28	0.77
SF7	Single-Family Seven-Bedroom	5	24,431	4,886	2	0.37
SFBLEND	Single-Family Blend	5,525	8,429,283	1,526	2,396	0.43
Total	All Housing Units	35,868	$58,173,360	$1,622	15,479	0.43

was used when allocating population and school students, as explained in Appendix E. These numbers would be useful in projecting the number of school students per unit for a proposed development.

Table 8.2 shows a summary of the revenue collected by each school district, the number of students that were allocated to each parcel and the average revenue per student by the district and residential classification. District 87 and Unit 5 data were obtained from each of their websites and were for 2013 and 2014, respectively.

School district revenue included more than just property taxes. Other local sources included payments in lieu of taxes, food service and other levies. Federal and state aids were also included. Table 8.3 shows that federal aid was between 19% and 20%. State aid varies by district, with the original district receiving 8% and the outlying Unit 5 receiving only 4.7%. Perhaps this is due to the greater need for aid in a more central district and the effect of keeping the property-tax burden comparable to the outlying area. For projecting state aid for new development in the outlying area, the 4.7% rate would be the most appropriate. One would need to investigate the distribution formula for state aid to be more precise. The data sources were the Illinois Department of Education Financial Reports for District 87 (2013) and Unit 5 (2014).

III   Expenditure Considerations

On the expenditure side, Table 8.4 compares the Operating Expenditures per Pupil (OEPP) from the financial reports for both districts. While neither financial report specifically lists the number of pupils, it can be estimated by dividing the operating expenses by the OEPP.

Not all school-aged students attend public schools. By comparing the estimated SAP to the estimated number of pupils for District 87 for 2013, one can calculate an approximate percentage that attend public school, as shown in Table 8.5. This percentage could be used to estimate the public-school attendance for new development, but it may be different in different parts of the city.

IV   School Students by Age of Housing

The analysis so far has included all estimated school students by type across the entire city. However, this does not give an idea of the SAP over time. Figure CP.02 in the color insert section shows the categories of year built, which start with 1900 and earlier and end with the past 13 years by 20-year increments. Summarizing the SAP by residential class over the time periods gives an idea of the numbers in different ages of housing.

Table 8.6 shows the year-built classes and the estimated number of students per housing unit over time. The most recent years, from 2000 to 2013, provide a basis for estimating the SAP for proposed new development. Also,

Table 8.2 Revenue per Student by School District and Residential Housing Classification

| | Bloomington School District – 87 | | | Outlying School District – 5 | | | Combined Average per Student |
| | Property Taxes | | | | Property Taxes | | |
Residential Class	School-Aged Population	Amount	Per Student	School-Aged Population	Amount	Per Student	
APTBLEND	1,553.31	3,462,296	2,229	1,194.65	2,343,125	1,961	$2,113
CONDO1	0.52	3,722	7,122	0.00	0	0	$7,122
CONDO2	0.00	0	0	0.67	3,632	5,384	$5,384
CONDO3	0.69	4,226	6,119	0.95	4,631	4,874	$5,398
DUP1	0.92	1,342	1,455	0.00	0	0	$1,455
DUP2	1.18	2,811	2,382	0.00	0	0	$2,382
DUP3	4.71	4,751	1,009	0.00	0	0	$1,009
DUPBLEND	392.97	703,458	1,790	29.28	78,893	2,694	$1,853
GQ	2.15	20,702	9,638	51.00	23,746	466	$836
MFBLEND	93.70	82,195	877	51.00	26,783	525	$753
MHBLEND	35.67	15,989	448	727.82	277,411	381	$384
MIXBLEND	4.44	17,804	4,011	0.00	0	0	$4,011
SF1	18.27	97,251	5,322	6.80	88,441	13,011	$7,407
SF2	367.44	1,552,004	4,224	315.51	2,484,503	7,874	$5,910
SF3	1,463.79	6,085,241	4,157	1,732.85	7,620,787	4,398	$4,288
SF4	1,172.30	5,898,216	5,031	3,642.53	17,267,274	4,740	$4,811
SF5	58.25	472,108	8,105	129.55	853,558	6,589	$7,059
SF6	14.39	115,783	8,046	13.47	105,250	7,811	$7,932
SF7	1.06	10,803	10,235	0.78	13,628	17,398	$13,286
SFBLEND	2,248.51	7,757,171	3,450	147.39	672,112	4,560	$3,518
All Classes	7,434.26	$26,307,874	$3,539	8,044.26	$31,863,773	$3,961	$3,758

Table 8.3 Revenue Sources by School District

	Original City District 87		Outlying Area Unit 5	
Revenue Sources	*Amount*	*Percent*	*Amount*	*Percent*
Local Sources	47,005,772	73.44%	109,440,337	75.31%
Federal	12,180,428	19.03%	29,023,323	19.97%
State	4,815,379	7.52%	6,856,014	4.72%
Totals	$64,001,579	100.00%	$145,319,674	100.00%

Table 8.4 Operating Expenditures per Pupil and Estimated Number of Students

Category	*Dist. 87*	*Unit 5*
Operating Expenses	$59,488,686	$130,560,312
Operating Expenses per Pupil (OEPP)	$11,704	$10,341
Estimated Number of Pupils	5,083	12,626

Table 8.5 Estimated Percentage of School-Age Population in District 87 Attending Public Schools

Category	*District 87*
Estimated School-Age Population	7,434
Estimated Pupils	5,083
Percentage of School-Age Population	68.38%

the categories of 1980 to 1999 and 2000 to 2013 cover a span of 33 years which would be useful in projecting the life-cycle changes in housing units as students graduate and move away from their parents.

The city-wide average of 0.43 students per housing unit would not necessarily be useful when estimating the SAP for new development since the rate varies greatly based on the year and type of development. Over all of the residential categories, shown at the bottom, the rate increases with more recent development.

For apartments or one- and two-bedroom condominiums, using the city-wide average rate of 0.43 would inflate the number of students. When estimating the students for a proposed single-family development, the rates increase with the number of bedrooms, except for the rare seven-bedroom houses. The rates within each category generally increase for more recent development.

Some of the categories have very few numbers of units so the rates should be used with caution.

Table 8.6 School-Age Population per Housing Unit by Residential Class and Age of Housing

Residential Class	1900 and earlier	1900–1919	1920–1939	1940–1959	1960–1979	1980–1999	2000–2013	Number of Units	Average Per Unit
APTBLEND	0.92	0.159	0.205	0.13	0.24	0.33	0.25	11,776	0.23
CONDO1		0.174						3	0.17
CONDO2						0.34		2	0.34
CONDO3						0.41		4	0.41
DUP1				0.46				2	0.46
DUP2				0.59				2	0.59
DUP3		0.666	0.345					9	0.52
DUPBLEND	0.26	0.366	0.322	0.28	0.36	0.41	0.34	1,208	0.35
MFBLEND	0.51	0.423	0.625	0.17	0.23	0.42	0.58	321	0.45
MHBLEND					0.33	0.44	0.71	1,954	0.39
MIXBLEND		0.278	0.090					18	0.25
SF1	0.22	0.292	0.213	0.23	0.22	0.16	0.43	113	0.22
SF2	0.26	0.353	0.310	0.22	0.30	0.36	0.28	2,215	0.31
SF3	0.41	0.494	0.433	0.29	0.47	0.61	0.61	6,132	0.52
SF4	0.61	0.529	0.530	0.39	0.48	0.77	0.89	6,297	0.76
SF5	1.03	0.772	0.485	0.49	0.51	0.74	1.04	242	0.78
SF6	0.35	0.892	0.956	0.54	0.47	0.78	0.93	36	0.77
SF7		0.326			0.40	0.51	0.28	5	0.37
SFBLEND	0.40	0.511		0.30	0.45	0.62	0.65	5,525	0.43
All Classes	0.43	0.323	0.364	0.24	0.33	0.58	0.60	35,864	0.43
Classified Housing Units	685	4,517	5,265	4,028	6,396	9,590	4,771	35,251	
Other								617	
Total Housing Units								35,868	

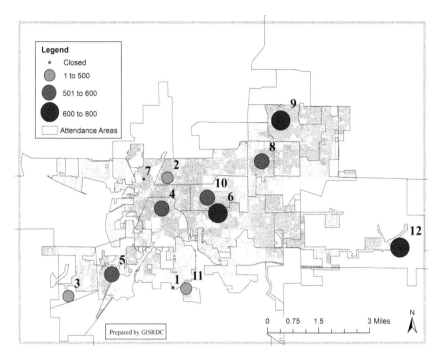

Figure 8.2 Elementary Schools within the City, Their Districts and Estimated School-Aged Students that Come from the City.

Table 8.7 Elementary Schools and the Estimated Elementary School-Aged Students

		Estimated School-Aged Population	
School Number	Elementary School Name	Total	Elementary
1	Brigham	0	0
2	Bent	1,005	503
3	Fox Creek	911	456
4	Irving	1,204	602
5	Pepper Ridge	1,119	560
6	Oakland	1,490	745
7	Sheridan	0	0
8	Stevenson	1,283	642
9	Northpoint	1,596	798
10	Washington	1,231	616
11	Cedar Ridge	873	436
12	Benjamin	1,620	810
Total Attending Schools in the City		12,333	6,167

V Elementary School Attendance Zones

The main concern with evaluating school fiscal impact would be the locations and utilization of elementary schools, which are more sensitive to residential changes, compared to middle and high schools. Figure 8.2 shows the locations of the different elementary schools, their districts and the estimated number of elementary school students coming from within the city. There has been no deduction for students attending private schools. When actually doing an evaluation of school attendance, more detail would need to be collected but this shows, in general, how, using the parcel data, attendance could be estimated.

The important thing to see on this map is that the relationships between different schools and their location. Schools 6, 9 and 12 have the largest attendance and are mostly located on the growing edge of the city. Numbers 4, 5, 8 and 10 have an average attendance. School 2 has light attendance, being located in the older part of the city. Numbers 1 and 7 appear to be closed, with number 7 in the oldest part of the city. Other schools, such as 3 and 11, are located in the outer extremes of the city and may have students coming in from out beyond the city boundary. That information is not available. There is also a part of the city where students attend an elementary school in the town of Normal. That information is not available.

VI Summary

This chapter has described the various ways that the parcel level data can be used in combination with other GIS shapefiles and readily available data regarding schools. In particular, the number of students coming from more recent development could be used to project the number of students coming from a proposed new development. For an example of how an impact analysis might be approached, see Chapter 9 on the impact that a new subdivision would have on the Benjamin School in the southeastern part of the city, located in the Grove neighborhood.

References

Illinois Department of Education (2013) "Bloomington School District Number 87 2013 Annual Financial Report", *Illinois Department of Education*, https://www.district87.org/cms/lib/IL02212106/Centricity/Domain/405/AFY%202013.pdf.

Illinois Department of Education, "McLean County Unit School District No. 5 2014 Annual Financial Report", *Illinois Department of Education*, https://www.unit5.org/cms/lib/IL01905100/Centricity/Domain/54/Annual%20Financial%20Reports/Unit%205%20AFR%20FY2014.pdf.

9 Projecting Fiscal Impact

This chapter demonstrates how to project the impact of a new development shown in the city's comprehensive plan based on the fiscal impact of existing development. Two methods of projecting fiscal impact will be shown and are named Comparable Development and Factor Based. The data in the *Parcel_Factor* and *Fiscal_Impact* shapefiles could be used to evaluate significant patterns in the city, allowing one not only to project fiscal impact but also to understand the interactions between land use and things like population, housing, property values, school-aged population (SAP), road frontage, public safety, the age of housing, neighborhoods and distance. The data for more recent development, as opposed to those for city-wide, are useful because older areas may have much different issues.

The city officials in Bloomington used the overall city-wide analysis maps to see the fiscal impact of existing development. A big benefit of using GIS to analyze fiscal impact is the ability to visualize the results and summarize them by a wide variety of cross-tabulations. These were shown in Chapter 7. Just by looking at several maps, the city officials and citizens could see some important patterns without having to dig down into tables and statistics. But if there were questions as to the fiscal patterns, there were always the data in the tables that quantified the patterns.

I The Comprehensive Plan

The city of Bloomington has a Comprehensive Land Use Plan, prepared by the McLean County Regional Planning Commission and adopted in 2015 (pp. 229–230). The plan included the existing city and the outlying areas and it has been combined into a single map by the author. It is shown in as Figure 9.1, contained in the color insert section. The development priorities are expressed as tiers. Tier 1 prioritized development in areas within the city that already have infrastructure, as well as infilling some of the "skipped-over" areas that are currently surrounded by the city boundary. Tier 2 was areas adjacent to the city that had access to existing infrastructure and Tier 3 included areas out beyond Tier 1 and 2 that would need additional infrastructure, shown in gray.

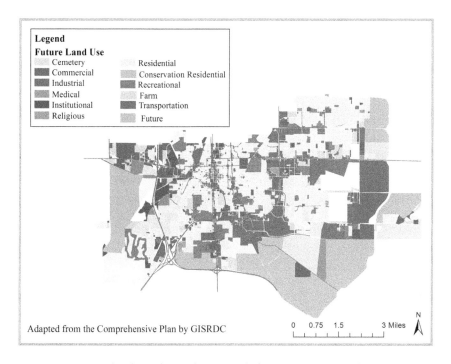

Figure 9.1 Generalized Land Use Plan City of Bloomington (See Color Figure 9.1 in the color insert section.)

Some practitioners suggest that the entire future land use plan should be projected as to fiscal impact, taking into account the factor of time when the plan would be fully implemented. Bise refers to this as an "areawide" analysis (2010, p. 5). Due to some ambiguities in the city's plan, more detail and specifications would be needed to undertake such a task.

II Project Analysis Fiscal Impact Methods

The data that has been developed thus far would be considered a "cost-of-land-uses-FIA" (Bise, 2010, p. 5). This section will illustrate how to do what Bise describes as a "project analysis", in which the data derived thus far would be used to project the impact of a proposed new development.

There are two ways to approach this task. If the new development was residential and it was similar to an existing neighborhood in the city, the neighborhood results could be used to project fiscal impact. The method is named Comparable Development.

However, one could also estimate all of the fiscal factors that the new development would have and then use the multipliers. This method would work for commercial, recreation and tax-exempt uses, as well as residential. That method is named Factor Based.

A Comparable Development Method of Projecting Fiscal Impact

The Grove I single-family residential subdivision provided a significant negative fiscal impact in 2013. According to the land use plan, the subdivision may be expanded to the north as "Grove II" and there was some current interest in developing it. Figure 9.2 shows the existing and proposed subdivision.

Table 9.1 shows information about the existing development in Grove I that will be used to illustrate how the fiscal impact of the completed and proposed Grove II subdivision can be estimated using the Comparable Development Method.

As of 2013, there were 288 developed and 90 undeveloped lots. The net taxable fiscal impact of the developed lots was $20,950 or $72.74 per unit. The impact of the undeveloped lots was –$68 per lot, mostly due to road maintenance costs. The impact of the farm and recreational use was very high, with a combined total of –$109,086. This is because most of the land fronts on the main access road to the subdivision and the property taxes derived from the amount of land were very small or not even taxed at all.

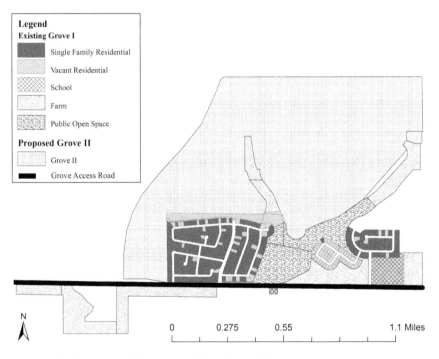

Figure 9.2 Existing and Future Land Use Grove Subdivision Area.

Furthermore, more than half of the access road frontage had taxable parcels on only one side of the road, thus doubling the cost burden on those parcels. This example deals with the Grove area alone but, if there was annexation and residential development to the south side of the road, then the road cost would be less. This example can be viewed as an "all other things being equal" situation, with no other development taken into consideration. It also assumes that the land has already been annexed to the city and that construction of the new connecting lines for sewer and water and the local roads would take place while the remaining 90 lots are developed.

Table 9.1 shows information about the existing development in Grove I that will be used to illustrate how the fiscal impact of the completed and proposed Grove II subdivision can be estimated.

Since there is no specific plan for the area to the north, it has been assumed that the new area will have a land use mix similar to the existing subdivision, excluding farms and other institutional acreage: 35% in recreation and open space, 51% in single-family lots and 14% in streets. The total acreage is 526, meaning that about half of it will be in single-family residential use. Table 9.2 summarizes this.

Table 9.3 shows the Net Fiscal Impact for the 288 developed lots in the Grove development (Grove I) that existed in 2013.

Table 9.4 shows some parameters that would be used to project fiscal impact, derived from the existing Grove development. The average number of lots per acre was 3.4 and the number of new lots and housing units would be 911. It is assumed that the access road cost will continue into the future, but as more lots are developed, the total fiscal impact of the entire subdivision will improve. The original Grove lots were available for development in 2007, so as of 2013, the rate of development averaged 41 units per year over 7 years.

Table 9.1 Existing Grove Subdivision Statistics as of 2013

Grove Existing Land Use	Acres		Percent of Total	Net Taxable Fiscal Impact	Number of Lots	Net Taxable Fiscal Impact per Lot
	Amount					
Single-Family Residential	77.61		32%	16,574	288	$57.55
Single-Family Residential Lots	32.49		13%	–6,096	90	–67.73
Recreation and Open Space*	53.55		22%			
Government and School*	16.36		7%			
Farm	61.06		25%	–1,09,086		
Totals	241.08		100%	–98,608.00	378	–260.87

* tax-exempt.

Table 9.2 Assumed Land Use Acreage for Grove Subdivision II

Land Use	Percent of Acreage	Acres
Recreation and Open Space	35%	185
Single-Family Residential	51%	268
Streets	14%	73
Total	100%	526

Table 9.3 Net Taxable Fiscal Impact for Grove I in 2013

	Fiscal Impact		
Fiscal Allocation Factor	Operating	Capital	Total
Population	143,676	−27,216	116,460
Fire Call Equivalents	−12,510	−1,110	−13,620
Police Call Equivalents	−3,235	−69	−3,304
Street Call Equivalents	−614	−24	−637
Arterial Frontage	−7,637	−6,562	−14,199
Local Frontage	−33,649	−42,115	−75,764
Total Frontage	8,484	0	8,484
Residential Building MV	117,346	0	117,346
Total Building MV*	−106,165	−26,830	−132,995
Net Assessed Market Value	338,526	27,396	365,922
Building Permit Value	0	18,436	18,436
Population Mile	−24,974	−3,389	−28,363
Distance Factor	−193,626	0	−193,626
Allocate Exempt to Operating Exp.	−88,949	0	−88,949
Allocate Exempt to Capital Exp.	0	−34,201	−34,201
Allocate Surplus	0	−20,039	−20,039
Subtotal	136,673	−115,723	20,950
Access Road	0	0	−115,237
Undeveloped Lots	0	0	−6,096
Total			−$100,383

* Includes tax exempt market value.

It is assumed that the net taxable fiscal impact will be the same for the new development as it was for the existing development, at the rate of about $73 per unit. There still were 90 undeveloped lots as of 2013 which had a negative fiscal impact. Combining these with the lots in Grove II results in the total number of projected new housing units to be 1,001. Recreation and Open Space would be tax-exempt and therefore included in the average per unit.

Based on these parameters, the net taxable fiscal impact can be projected for the entire Grove subdivision, as provided in Table 9.5. If the area is developed at the same rate as in the past, it will take 24 years to be fully developed. However, if the rate of development is faster or slower, the length of time would change. Over time, the total surplus would grow but the net overall fiscal impact would still be negative (−$21,472) due to the

Table 9.4 Projection Parameters Based on Existing Grove Development

Grove Single-Family Residential Characteristics	Projection Parameters
Existing Residential Lots/Units	
Acres	78
Number of Units	288
Average Lots/Units per Acre	3
Total Net Taxable Fiscal Impact	$20,950
Net Taxable Fiscal Impact per Developed Lot	$73
Existing Platted Undeveloped Lots	
Number of Lots	90
Total Net Taxable Fiscal Impact per Lot	–$6,096
New Development	
Acres	268
New Lots to Be Developed	911
Total Number of Future Housing Units	1,001
Other Parameters	
Years to Develop	7
Units Developed per Year	41
Continuing Farm and Access Road Cost	–$1,15,237

ongoing access road costs, assuming that no additional development occurs to the south.

Table 9.6 provides an example of projecting the development in five-year increments based on the rate of 41 units per year.

B Factor Based Method of Projecting Fiscal Impact

Another way of projecting fiscal impact would be to estimate each of the applicable factors that are indicators of fiscal impact and then use the multipliers to calculate revenues and expenditures.

This method is also preferable in areas where there is no adjacent development from which to extrapolate the future impact but the key features of the proposed development are already known.

Table 9.5 Projected Fiscal Impact, Grove I and Grove II, Comparable Development Method

Projected Item	Existing Units	New Units	All Units
Undeveloped Lots	–6,096	6,547	6,547
Projected Fiscal Impact	20,950	66,269	87,219
Continuing Farm and Access Road Cost	–$115,237	–$115,237	–$115,237
Total Net Taxable Fiscal Impact	–$100,383	–$42,422	–$21,472
Lots and Duration			
Number of Lots	288	1,001	1,289
Years to Develop	7	24	31

Table 9.6 Projected Grove Fiscal Impact by Five Year Increments, Comparable Development Method

Land Use	2018 Units	Net Taxable Fiscal Impact	2023 Units	Net Taxable Fiscal Impact	2028 Units	Net Taxable Fiscal Impact	2033 Units	Net Taxable Fiscal Impact	2038 Units	Net Taxable Fiscal Impact	Fiscal Impact Change
Existing											
Single-Family Residential	288	$20,950	288	$20,950	288	$20,950	288	$20,950	288	$20,950	0
Farm and Access Road		–$115,237		–$115,237		–$115,237		–$115,237		–$115,237	0
Undeveloped											
Single-Family Residential Lots	90	$6,547	90	$6,547	90	$6,547	90	$6,547	90	$6,547	
New Subdivision											
Recreation and Open Space											
Single-Family Residential Lots	115	$8,365	320	$23,278	525	$38,190	730	$53,102	911	$66,269	
Totals	493	–$79,375	698	–$64,463	903	–$49,550	1,108	–$34,638	1,289	–$21,472	
Five-Year Change	205	$21,008	205	$14,912	205	$14,912	205	$14,912	181	$13,166	$78,912
Cumulative Change	205	$21,008	410	$35,921	615	$50,833	820	$65,745	1,001	$78,912	$78,912

For this example, some of the factors are easy to estimate, such as population, road frontage and market values. Other factors such as police and fire calls, the distance factors, and the transfers of tax-exempt costs to the parcels, among others, would be more difficult but using the information from similar surrounding areas would help.

For the Grove II expansion, some of the factors can be estimated based on the original Grove I subdivision, as shown in Table 9.7. In Grove I, there were land uses that would not be in Grove II, which included an elementary school, governmental facilities and additional farmland fronting on the main access road to the subdivision. For this reason, only the factors related to the residential use were considered. Dividing the residential factors by the number of housing units provided a measure to estimate the factor per unit. Multiplying the factor per unit by the proposed 1,001 housing units (911 new lots plus the existing 90 that were undeveloped as of 2013) provided the projected factors for the Grove II subdivision.

The projected factors shown in Table 9.7 could then be used to project the revenue for the Grove II subdivision, as shown in Table 9.8, by multiplying the factors by the revenue multipliers.

Table 9.9 shows the calculations for expenditures. Note that the multipliers for road capital expenditures are quite significant. They are based on the city-wide capital costs divided by the total frontage, rather than allocated to specific areas and projects. It has been assumed that the capital costs that have been allocated will accumulate over the years until the time that the funds are needed to make improvements. The same could be said for the need for police and fire capital improvements.

Table 9.10 summarizes the fiscal impact of the new residential development in Grove II.

Table 9.11 summarizes the combined fiscal impact for Grove I and Grove II. It has been assumed that the operating and capital fiscal impact for Grove I will remain the same. Adding together the Grove I and Grove II fiscal impacts yields the total fiscal impacts for the entire subdivision. The original Grove I produced a negative fiscal impact due to the costs of the access road. With the development of Grove II, an overall surplus is projected to be generated and will absorb most of the negative fiscal impact brought about by Grove I.

C Comparison of the Methods

Both methods are designed to produce approximate estimates of fiscal impact. The differences between the two sets of numbers are probably due to rounding errors.

Of course, this all assumes that the new lots will be platted and then built upon in a short period of time. In reality, this does not happen. That would also have to be considered as well.

Table 9.7 Estimating and Projecting the Fiscal Factors for Grove I and Grove II

Fiscal Allocation Factor	Grove I				Grove II	
	Amount	Residential Area Only	Existing Housing Units	Factor per Unit	Projected Housing Units	Projected Factors
Population	734	734	288	2.55	1,001	2,550
Fire Call Equivalents	28	28	288	0.1	1,001	99
Police Call Equivalents	63	43	288	0.15	1,001	149
Street Call Equivalents	43	6	288	0.02	1,001	19
Arterial Frontage	19,728	1,339	288	4.65	1,001	4,654
Local Frontage	37,939	28,508	288	98.99	1,001	99,085
Total Frontage	57,667	29,847	288	103.64	1,001	103,739
Residential Building MV	$19,533,357	$19,533,357	288	$67,824.16	1,001	$67,891,980
Total Building MV	$20,833,816	$19,533,357	288	$67,824.16	1,001	$67,891,980
Net Assessed Market Value	$24,749,117	$24,598,947	288	$85,413.01	1,001	$85,498,423
Building Permit Value	$5,498,972	$3,033,241	288	$10,532.09	1,001	$10,542,619
Population Mile	4,646	4,646	288	16.13	1,001	16,149
Distance Factor	193,626	193,626	288	672.31	1,001	672,986
Allocate Exempt to Operating Exp.	0	88,949	288	308.85	1,001	309,160
Allocate Exempt to Capital Exp.	0	34,201	288	118.75	1,001	118,871
Allocate Surplus	0	20,039	288	69.58	1,001	69,650

Table 9.8 Projected Grove II Operating and Capital Revenue, Factor Based Method

Fiscal Allocation Factor	Revenue Multipliers			Projected Factor Amounts	Revenue		
	Operating	Capital	Total		Operating	Capital	Total
Population	449.60157	35.965665	485.56724	2,550	11,46,615	91,723	1,238,337
Fire Call Equivalents	295.22529	0	295.22529	99	29,170	0	29,170
Police Call Equivalents	29.08362	0	29.08362	149	4,321	0	4,321
Street Call Equivalents	0	0	0	19	0	0	0
Local Frontage	0	0	0	99,085	0	0	0
Total Frontage	0.28424	0	0.28424	103,739	29,487	0	29,487
Residential Bldg MV	0.006008	0	0.00601	67,891,980	407,861	0	407,861
Total Building MV	0	0.00043	0.00043	67,891,980	0	29,099	29,099
Net Assessed MV	0.013762	0.001114	0.014876	85,498,423	1,176,611	95,221	1,271,832
Building Permits	0	0.006078	0.006078	10,542,619	0	64,077	64,077
Allocated Surplus	0	0	0	0	0	−69,650	−69,650
Totals					$2,794,065	$210,469	$3,004,534

Table 9.9 Projected Grove II Operating and Capital Expenditures, Factor Based Method

Fiscal Allocation Factor	Expenditure Multipliers			Projected Factor Amounts	Projected Expenditures		
	Operating	Capital	Total		Operating	Capital	Total
Population	253.79115	73.05776	326.84891	2,550	647,240	186,318	833,558
Fire Call Equivalents	735.28601	39.0316	774.31761	99	72,651	3,857	76,508
Police Call Equivalents	104.758	1.60974	106.36774	149	15,564	239	15,803
Street Call Equivalents	110.04198	4.2837	114.32568	19	2,132	83	2,215
Arterial Frontage	5.7	4.9	10.6	4,654	26,528	22,804	49,332
Local Frontage	1.18033	1.47731	2.65764	99,085	116,953	146,379	263,333
Total Frontage	0	0	0	103,739	0	0	0
Residential Bldg. MV	0	0	0		0	0	0
Total Building MV	0.00544	0.0018	0.00724	$67,891,980	368,996	122,353	491,349
Net Assessed MV	0	0	0	$89,988,253	0	0	0
Building Permits	0	0	0	$19,112,746	0	0	0
Population Miles	5.3750021	0.729389	6.10441	16,149	86,802	11,779	98,581
Distance Factor	672.31407	0	672.31407	1,001	672,986	0	672,986
Allocated Exempt	NA	NA	NA	0	309,160	118,871	428,031
Allocated Surplus	NA	NA	NA	0	0	69,650	69,650
Total					$2,319,012	$682,334	$3,001,346

Table 9.10 Projected Fiscal Impact for Grove II, Factor Based Method

Fiscal Allocation Factor	Projected Grove II		
	Revenue	Expenditures	Fiscal Impact
Population	1,238,337	8,33,558	404,779
Fire Call Equivalents	29,170	76,508	–47,338
Police Call Equivalents	4,321	15,803	–11,483
Street Call Equivalents	0	2,215	–2,215
Arterial Frontage	0	49,332	–49,332
Local Frontage	0	263,333	–263,332
Total Frontage	29,487	0	29,486
Residential Building MV	407,861	0	407,858
Total Building MV	29,099	491,349	–462,250
Net Assessed Market Value	1,271,832	0	1,271,832
Building Permit Value	64,077	0	64,077
Population Mile	0	98,581	–98,581
Distance Factor	0	672,986	–672,986
Allocated Exempt	0	428,031	–428,031
Allocated Surplus		69,650	–69,650
Totals	$3,074,184	$3,001,346	$72,834

Table 9.11 Summary of Grove I and Grove II Fiscal Impact, Factor Based Method

Fiscal Allocation Factor	Fiscal Impact		
	Existing	Projected	Total
Population	116,460	404,779	521,239
Fire Call Equivalents	–13,620	–47,338	–60,957
Police Call Equivalents	–3,304	–11,483	–14,786
Street Call Equivalents	–637	–2,215	–2,853
Arterial Frontage	–14,199	–49,332	–63,531
Local Frontage	–75,764	–263,332	–339,096
Total Frontage	8,484	29,486	37,970
Residential Building MV	117,346	407,858	525,203
Total Building MV	–132,995	–462,250	–595,245
Net Assessed Market Value	365,922	1,271,832	1,637,754
Building Permit Value	18,436	64,077	82,513
Population Mile	–28,363	–98,581	–126,943
Distance Factor	–193,626	–672,986	–866,613
Allocate Exempt	–123,150	–428,031	–551,180
Allocate Surplus	–20,039	–69,650	–89,689
Subtotal	20,950	72,834	93,784
Undeveloped Lots*	–6,096	6,096	0
Access Road	–115,237	0	–115,237
Total	–100,384	78,931	–21,453

* Included with developed lots.

D School Fiscal Impact

When the original Grove I subdivision was built, it also required the building of the new Benjamin Elementary School. Chapter 8 showed the location. Table 9.12 shows an example of what a fiscal impact study for schools might include.

As of 2013, there were only approximately 170 school-aged students coming from Grove I. Assuming that half were high-school and middle-school aged, it would leave about 85 elementary-school-aged students. The remainder of the students attending the school were bussed in from other areas.

The rate of school-aged students was about .59 per occupied housing unit. In 2013, the residential parcels were taxed $1,201,440 for school costs, averaging $4,172 per unit and $7,067 per student. The city-wide average was $3,758 per student. Therefore, the subdivision had a $3,309 surplus compared to the average, which resulted in a combined total of $638,910.

The projected Grove II subdivision would have 1,001 new housing units and therefore an estimated 610 school-aged students. All other things being equal, the new subdivision would bring in a surplus of $2,220,656 for the schools.

However, that would not be the only consideration. The new school that was needed for Grove I only had about 85 students actually attending it as of 2013. When the subdivision was initially proposed in 2007, a fiscal impact analysis for schools should have provided not only a projected impact on operating costs but also the cost of building the new school.

E Marginal Costs

Marginal costs of the new Grove II development also need to be considered. The fact that the above analysis deals with the total net taxable fiscal impact including both the capital revenues and expenditures means that the marginal costs have been factored in to some degree. If one wanted to consider

Table 9.12 School Impact for Grove I and Grove II

Comparison Factors	Grove I	Grove II	Total Subdivision
Number of Students	170	591	761
Elementary	85	295	390
Middle and High School	85	295	390
Number of Residential Units	288	1,001	1289
Students per Unit	0.59	0.59	0.59
Property tax Revenue	$1,201,440	$4,175,838	$5,377,278
Per Housing Unit	$4,172	$4,172	$4,172
Per Student	$7,067	$7,067	$7,067
City Average	$3,309	$3,309	$3,309
Difference	$3,758	$3,758	$3,758
Total Difference for Subdivision	$638,910	$2,220,656	$2,859,566

marginal costs separately, then only the operating revenues and expenditures should be used in the analysis.

1. Road Improvement Costs

The addition of 1,001 units would mean that the population would increase by more than 2,500, bringing the total to about 3,300. This increase may require some major road improvements, but since the road costs include average capital as well as operating, there was a built-in assumption that the costs are not necessarily incurred each year. The revenue and costs would accumulate over time and have already been factored in.

2. Police and Fire

The addition of 2,500 people may require the establishment of a police and fire substation since the development is located about five miles from an existing one. Including a distance factor was one way to factor in those costs, but it was determined using a straight-line distance from the central city. This new development actually increases the travel distance because it is located to the north of the existing development. The distance factors may not cover all of the costs of a substation. Nevertheless, the capital multiplier for police and fire also builds up revenue that will accumulate over time for such improvements.

3. Schools

While the above analysis does not include schools, some general observations can be made. Because of the development of Grove I, a new elementary school needed to be built. Many of the students have been bussed in quite far from other areas to supplement those from Grove I. With the development of Grove II, more students will attend the school so no additional school costs are anticipated and those that have been bused in can be handled by schools that are more nearby, thus reducing the busing costs.

4. Sewer and Water

The above analysis does not include the costs of the major sewer and water trunk lines that were incurred in 2007. It is assumed, however, that the developer will pay for local sewer and water connections as well as local road construction.

The city borrowed $6.3 million to build the sewer force main and lift station that was required to service the Grove I subdivision. The debt was to be repaid over 23 years, with the interest will adding on another $4.1 million for a total cost of $10.4 million. Part of this has been paid for with "tap on fees" of $1,300 and "property owner contribution" fees of $43 per unit. As of 2013, the city had collected about $386,784 in connection fees ($1,343 times 288), which was less than 4% of the total cost. With the development of an additional 1,001 units, $1,344,343 more in revenue will have been collected, bringing the percentage to 16%. The city also spent $974,453 to bring a water main to the development, paid for with water-billing revenue, which was paid by the city-wide water users.

F Comparison to the Land Use Plan

The above analysis is based on the results in 2013 and the land use plan adopted in 2015. The area named as Grove II was not part of the city and would have had to be annexed to the city. As of this writing (2018), the city must have annexed other land to the east of Grove I because there is new development showing on aerial photography that was not part of the city in 2013. The annexed area was not part of the plan. Nevertheless, the same type of analysis would also be applicable to this new development.

IV Other Data Useful for Factor Based Analysis

When using the Comparable Development Method, the measurements of fiscal impact have the allocation factors built into the results, like the cost of road frontage, and have the probability of having the same relative costs for police and fire, the distance factor, etc. However, if there are no nearby developments that can be used, one would need to use the Factor Based Method. Estimating the factors for a new type of development can be based upon the many ways that the data can be summarized, as shown in Chapter 7. With a development proposal, the amount of road frontage, projected adult and school-aged population or employment, and the distance factor might already have been specified. Assessed and building market value could also be estimated. When it comes to police and fire costs, estimates can also be based on statistics from the parcel base file. Another consideration would be the allocation of tax-exempt deficits. The examples provided below show how parcel statistics can be used.

A Police and Fire Call Patterns

Police and fire costs are the major factors driving expenses so the parcel data allows the summarization of calls by land use. Table 9.13 shows the numbers of calls by general land use and by the year built. One can see that the numbers of calls in all categories decrease with newer development. This helps to explain why the older areas in the central city have fiscal impact deficits.

   Table 9.14 shows the police calls per unit by residential category and year built. The calls include both the calls to individual parcels as well as the street calls allocated to surrounding parcels. Note again that the older

Table 9.13 Police and Fire Calls per Acre for Generalized Land Use, City of Bloomington, IL, 2013

Estimated Year Built	Commercial			Residential			Other			All Land Uses		
		Calls per Acre			Calls per Acre			Calls per Acre			Calls per Acre	
	Acres	Fire	Police	Acres	Fire	Police	Acres	Fire	Police	Acres	Fire	Police
1900 and Earlier	78.11	0.02	1.54	135	3.04	10.66	57.84	0.24	6.09	271	1.57	7.06
1901–1919	196.65	1.83	32.61	402.8	5.71	34.91	146.87	2.9	85.22	746	4.14	44.2
1920–1939	95.32	1.06	19.11	757.97	2.72	12.76	189.82	0.81	5.68	1,043	2.22	12.05
1940–1959	458.28	0.79	7.2	663.51	1.52	3.9	660.59	0.32	3.52	1,782	0.89	4.61
1960–1979	1,152.38	0.66	6.43	956.58	1.5	8.22	746.99	0.09	1.23	2,856	0.79	5.67
1980–1999	712.39	0.65	3.02	1,929.98	0.53	2.64	1,932.14	0.05	0.51	4,575	0.35	1.8
2000–2013	32.61	0.85	3.21	940.91	0.78	2.76	1,138.64	0.01	0.28	2,112	0.37	1.43
Unknown	545.58	0.28	23.86	53.23	1.95	12.05	545.58	0	0.36	1,144	0.23	12.11
Total	2,958.99	0.75	11.6	5,839.98	1.56	7.52	5,418.46	0.18	3.45	14,217	0.87	6.82

Table 9.14 Police Calls per Unit by Residential Category and Year Built, City of Bloomington, IL, 2013

Estimated Year Built	Single-Family Police calls	per unit	Apartments Police calls	per unit	Duplex Police calls	per unit	Mobile Homes Police calls	per unit	Other Police calls	per unit
1900 and Earlier	1208.7	2.04	168.83	3.07	59.77	2.72	0	0	2.29	0.57
1901–1919	5490	3.06	6436.5	3.2	1684.4	2.92	0	0	451.69	3.18
1920–1939	5388.9	1.55	2986.5	2.18	911.77	2.64	0	0	381.7	5.38
1940–1959	1754.3	0.79	731.36	0.43	92.46	1.4	0	0	8.11	0.81
1960–1979	1911.9	0.84	4203.1	1.41	92	1.18	1626.6	1.62	25.66	0.39
1980–1999	2709.1	0.41	791.33	0.42	21.62	0.22	1508.9	1.64	54.72	1.09
2000–2013	1124	0.32	1457.4	1.2	0.79	0.04	12.72	0.4	2.26	1.13
Unknown	14.18	0.41	620.61	1.11	0	0	0	0	6.47	0.19
Total	19601	0.95	17396	1.48	2862.8	2.37	3148.2	1.61	932.91	2.47

units have a higher rate of calls compared to the newer units. Of particular note are the duplexes, which have high rates in the older categories, when they were mostly built.

A better way of understanding residential fire calls is to evaluate them on a per unit basis by land use category, as shown in Table 9.15. Note again that the older units generally have higher rates of calls and the newer units have smaller rates. Fire calls also include EMS calls, so some of this pattern relates to the fact that newer units will have a younger population which is less in need of emergency medical services.

B Commercial/Industrial Examples from Anoka, MN

If there was more detail as to the commercial categories in Bloomington, the same type of analysis by commercial category could be done. Unfortunately, there was none. It has been found in previous studies that there is a big difference as to the impact of different types of commercial development. Table 9.16 shows the fiscal impact for commercial and industrial for the city of Anoka in 2009. This is just an example of how commercial and industrial could be summarized if there was more detail about the land use.

Table 9.17 shows the distribution of police calls for the city of Anoka in 2009 by commercial and industrial land use categories, as another example of analyzing the factors that contribute to fiscal impact. It should be noted that in Anoka's case, only the number of calls was available but not the duration. In Bloomington's case, the calls were expressed as call equivalents, thus factoring in the amount of time per call. This would certainly be preferable.

The last example of the differences among classes of commercial and industrial for Anoka, MN is the amount of property taxes paid by each, as shown in Table 9.18

C Tax-Exempt Allocation

The non-spatial methods assume that negative tax-exempt fiscal impact should be included in non-residential land use. However, in reality, the impact should be allocated to all taxable parcels in the city, including residential. For the Bloomington project, the Central tax-exempt impact was allocated to all parts of the city, while the more localized impact was allocated by neighborhood. Table 9.19 summarizes the results.

Note that the Central allocation was about 5% of each taxable parcel's expenses and should be added to the expenses (or subtracted from the fiscal impact). Among the neighborhoods, there is a wide variation, with the Airport neighborhood having the expenses of the tax-exempt airport allocated to all the surrounding taxable parcels, amounting to a 50% increase in costs. Other neighborhoods have no tax-exempt and thus no neighborhood allocation. The Fox Creek and Grove neighborhoods have substantial

Table 9.15 Fire Calls per Unit by Residential Category and Year Built, City of Bloomington, IL, 2013

Estimated Year Built	Single-Family		Apartments		Duplex		Mobile Homes		Other	
	Fire calls	per unit	Fire calls	per unit	Fire calls	per unit	Fire calls	per unit	Fire calls	per unit
1900 and Earlier	147.8	0.25	250.2	4.55	12.2	0.55	0	0	0	0
1901–1919	716.3	0.4	1,342.30	0.67	178.6	0.31	0	0	63.4	0.45
1920–1939	859.4	0.25	899.3	0.66	205.2	0.59	0	0	99.4	1.4
1940–1959	590.4	0.26	399.7	0.23	19	0.29	0	0	0	0
1960–1979	544.9	0.24	521.5	0.18	19.2	0.25	340.7	0.34	6.1	0.09
1980–1999	606.2	0.09	125.6	0.07	6.1	0.06	286	0.31	3.1	0.06
2000–2013	369.8	0.11	347.4	0.29	0	0	16.9	0.53	3.5	1.73
Unknown	1.6	0.15	100.5	0.18	0	0	0	0	1.4	0.04
Total	3,836.40	0.19	3,986.50	0.34	440.2	0.36	643.6	0.33	176.9	0.47

Table 9.16 Fiscal Impact for Commercial / Industrial Land Uses, City of Anoka, MN, 2009

Commercial/Industrial Land Use	Number of Parcels	Acres	Revenue	Expenditures	Fiscal Impact		
					Amount	Per Parcel	Per Acre
Auto Service	27	12.31	72,361	60,780	11,581	429	940
Bank	5	0.39	8,873	5,123	3,751	750	9,706
General Commercial	13	8.78	26,025	24,423	1,602	123	182
Industrial	54	300.02	1,746,696	1,136,597	610,098	11,298	2,034
Light Industrial	55	127.7	819,482	492,792	326,690	5,940	2,558
Motel	2	4.34	44,460	24,722	19,738	9,869	4,547
Office	71	32.58	482,463	391,672	90,792	1,279	2,787
Personal Service	12	6.69	102,830	55,936	46,893	3,908	7,012
Restaurant	24	12.44	201,196	143,138	58,058	2,419	4,666
School–Commercial	3	3.05	19,585	13,813	5,772	1,924	1,896
Shopping	100	65.22	787,674	480,029	307,646	3,076	4,717
Total	366	574	$4,311,646	$2,829,025	$1,482,621	$4,051	$2,585

Table 9.17 Police Calls for Commercial / Industrial Land Uses, City of Anoka, MN, 2009

Commercial/Industrial Land Use	Number of Parcels	Acres	Police Calls		
			Number	Per Parcel	Per Acre
Auto Service	27	12.31	139	5.17	11.33
Bank	5	0.39	2	0.39	5.03
General Commercial	13	8.78	51	3.92	5.8
Industrial	54	300.02	229	4.24	0.76
Light Industrial	55	127.7	179	3.25	1.4
Motel	2	4.34	54	27.24	12.55
Office	71	32.58	514	7.24	15.79
Personal Service	12	6.69	139	11.59	20.8
Restaurant	24	12.44	488	20.32	39.21
School–Commercial	3	3.05	27	8.89	8.75
Shopping	100	65.22	1,214	12.14	18.61
Totals	366	573.51	3,036	8.3	5.29

Table 9.18 Property Taxes for Commercial / Industrial Land Uses, City of Anoka, MN, 2009

Commercial/Industrial Land Use	Number of Parcels	Property Taxes	
		Amount	Per Parcel
Auto Service	27	59,435	2,201
Bank	5	2,819	564
General Commercial	13	20,519	1,578
Industrial	54	766,524	14,195
Light Industrial	55	461,770	8,396
Motel	2	16,677	8,338
Office	71	289,618	4,079
Personal Service	12	55,571	4,631
Restaurant	24	85,265	3,553
School–Commercial	3	22,462	7,487
Shopping	100	421,857	4,219
Total	368	$2,203,868	$5,989

amounts of tax-exempt land use, resulting in neighborhood allocations of about 20%. These mostly include recreation and open space, with a tax-exempt golf course in Fox Creek and institutional land uses in both. Of course, these patterns reflect how the neighborhood boundaries were drawn, but Fox Creek and Grove are pretty well defined.

When using the Factor Based Method, one will need to make these adjustments. In Bloomington's case, if a development is in the central city, only 5% should be added to a parcel's expenses. However, for development in the other neighborhoods, the neighborhood allocations should also be used.

Table 9.19 Allocation of Tax-Exempt Deficits by Neighborhood, City of Bloomington, IL, 2013

Neighborhood	*Tax Exempt Allocation*		
	Central	*Neighborhood*	*Total*
Airport	−5.03%	−50.80%	−55.83%
Central	−5.03%	0.00%	−5.03%
East	−5.03%	−3.77%	−8.80%
Fox Creek	−5.03%	−14.80%	−19.83%
Grove	−5.03%	−15.21%	−20.24%
Northeast Commercial	−5.03%	−4.02%	−9.05%
Northeast Residential	−5.03%	−7.03%	−12.06%
Northwest	−5.03%	−0.31%	−5.34%
South	−5.03%	−20.91%	−25.94%
South Southeast	−5.03%	0.00%	−5.03%
Southeast	−5.03%	0.00%	−5.03%
State Farm	−5.03%	−3.12%	−8.15%
Weighted Average	−5.03%	−7.43%	−12.46%

When considering the city as a whole, the weighted average total allocation was about 12%.

V Redevelopment Analysis

Beyond projecting the impact of new development, the results of the study also provide a basis upon which to identify problem areas in the city that could benefit from redevelopment. The following provides just one example of how this was done.

In 2018, the city adopted the "TIF Redevelopment Plan and Project, Downtown East Washington Street Redevelopment Project Area" study. In that plan, the results of the fiscal impact study were cited as one of many reasons for establishing it. According to the fiscal impact study, the district had a net taxable fiscal impact deficit of −$28,042 in 2013, as shown in Table 9.20.

Table 9.20 Net Taxable Fiscal Impact in 2013, for the TIF Redevelopment Plan and Project, Downtown East Washington Street Project

Tax Status	Land Use	Acres	*Net Taxable Fiscal Impact*	
			Amount	*Per Acre*
Taxable	Commercial	5.38	−23,137	−4,298
Taxable	Residential Single-Family	2	−616	−308
Taxable	Residential Apartments	5.49	−4,289	−782
Tax Exempt	Vacant Government City	0	0	0
Tax Exempt	Institutional Other	0	0	0
Total		12.87	−$28,042	−$2,179

As stated in the report, the district had numerous deficiencies brought about by deteriorating infrastructure, vacant buildings and overall blighted conditions. The former high school was planned to be converted to a 58-unit affordable, age-restricted apartment building after retrofitting, repairing and renovation. The ground floor would also provide space to be leased by commercial or other tenants. Other parcels would be acquired, demolished and prepared for redevelopment. The streets would be upgraded and would help to address the police-street-call costs. Of course, the upgrades would help to improve their overall attractiveness and functionality.

The total cost of the project was estimated to be $7,625,000. The increase in the assessed value was projected to be $3.6 million. Other revenue would come from the sales of the property once the sites were prepared for development. In addition, other sources of revenue would be sought to pay for the improvements, such as state or federal grants. Lastly, more revenue would come in the form of population and employment growth and sales taxes.

VI Summary

This chapter provided examples of how to project fiscal impact for one portion of the city's comprehensive plan. Two ways of projecting fiscal impact were demonstrated: Comparable Development and Factor Based. When using the Comparable Development Method, the fiscal impact of all of the factors is built in. When having to use the Factor Based Method, data from the *Parcel_Factor* and *Fiscal_Impact* shapefiles can provide help in determining specific factors such as police calls and the allocation of tax-exempt deficits. The chapter also showed how to use the data to evaluate areas for redevelopment and TIF districts.

The shapefiles can be used to evaluate significant patterns in the city, allowing one to understand the interactions between land use and things like population, housing, property values, SAP, road frontage, public safety, the age of housing, neighborhoods and distance as well as fiscal impact. Many more tables showing other relationships could also have been shown but they were too numerous, and seemingly limitless, to include.

Should other cities use the statistics in these tables and apply it to their own situation? The answer is *no*. The statistics reflect what was happening in the above cities at a certain point in time and they are examples of how the results can be used. The statistics would probably remain fairly constant for each city for a few years but would need to be updated, probably at least every five years. Other cities may have totally different issues that affect public safety, housing types and property values. Each city should develop the factors and fiscal impact based on their own unique patterns of land use, spending, and level of service issues.

References

Bise, L. C. (2010) *Fiscal Impact Analysis: Methodologies for Planners*, Chicago, IL: American Planning Association Planning Advisory Service.

City of Bloomington, Illinois (2018) "Downtown East Washington Street TIF District", *City of Bloomington, Illinois*, http://www.cityblm.org/doing-busine ss/economic-development/tax-increment-financing-tif/downtown-east-washingto n-street-tif.

McLean County Regional Planning Commission (2015) "Comprehensive Plan 2015–2035", *City of Bloomington, Illinois*, http://www.cityblm.org/governm ent/departments/planning-zoning/comprehensive-plan.

10 Marginal Impacts and Sprawl

Ideally, marginal fiscal impact should be considered, particularly when new development is proposed at the outer edges of the city, especially when sprawl or leapfrog development is being proposed.

To some degree, marginal costs have already been built into the Spatial Method when using both operating and capital expenditure multipliers. In Bloomington's case, there was no information on the location of capital expenditures and so the capital amounts were allocated to all parcels. For example, the total amount of street expenditures was allocated to all parcels based on the type of locally maintained road frontage. The same was true for police and fire capital costs, which were allocated using the factors of population, employment, building market value and service calls. This meant that capital costs were allocated to development but the costs would not necessarily be incurred until actually needed. If one wanted to deal with specific marginal costs, then one would project only the operating fiscal impact and then estimate the marginal costs separately.

Unfortunately, the marginal costs for the examples shown in this chapter were evident only after the fact. Just by looking at the parcel maps of Net Taxable Fiscal Impact and Neighborhood Fiscal Impact, city officials in Bloomington saw that the compact and contiguous areas in the northeast and eastern sides of the city were the best type of development and that the areas of sprawl were not.

The most important marginal costs for sewer, water and schools apparently were not considered when the developments were proposed.

This chapter will illustrate ways to consider marginal impacts using examples from Bloomington, IL.

I Road Capacity and Utilization

Please refer to Figure 10.1 in the color insert section. It shows several aspects regarding the utilization of Bloomington's road system. The roads in red are ones that only have taxable parcels on one side, even though the city maintains the entire road. On the northern side of the city is the town of

Normal and, therefore, the city cannot expand in that direction to include more taxable parcels.

However, on the south side, there is the possibility for expansion so that development can take advantage of the excess road capacity. There are several "skipped-over" areas, shown in light yellow, with taxable parcels only on one side of the road. This skipped-over land is taking advantage of city street services but not being taxed to pay for them. If these areas were annexed into the city, the parcels would contribute property tax revenue. In the city's comprehensive plan, the development of these areas was considered a priority.

There are roads shown in magenta that are maintained by the city but pass through areas that are not even part of the city and therefore not taxable on either side. The map also shows in cyan roads that are not maintained by the city but city vehicles must travel over them ("deadheading") to service parts of the city.

The area to the southeast, known as the Grove neighborhood, is an obvious example of sprawl or leapfrog development. This has already been described extensively in Chapter 9 as an example of how additional development could take advantage of the excess road capacity, shown in red.

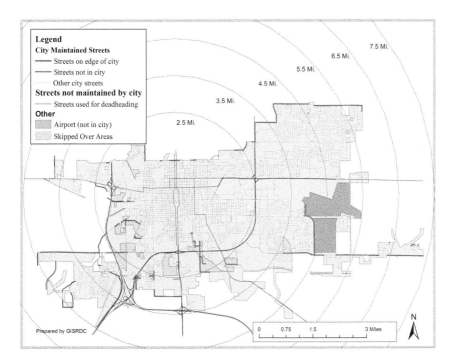

Figure 10.1 Locally Maintained Street Utilization City of Bloomington, IL, 2013 (See Color Figure 10.1 in the color insert section.)

The area to the southwest, known as Fox Creek, is another example of sprawl, with its many one-sided roads shown in red, plus roads maintained by the city passing through the unincorporated area to provide access to the parcels.

When these developments were proposed, fiscal impact analyses should have shown the costs to develop and maintain these streets.

II Sewer Capacity and Utilization

Refer to Figure 10.2 in the color insert section. It shows the sewer system with major force main extensions, shown in red, to serve both the Grove and Fox Creek areas. Force mains themselves are not expensive to build but they also require lift stations to pump the sewage uphill to the treatment plant and thus affect operating and maintenance costs. Again, when these developments were proposed, there should have been analyses projecting the costs to build the sewer lines along with the water system extensions that would be needed. To some degree, there were reports to provide this analysis but the historical records were very sketchy.

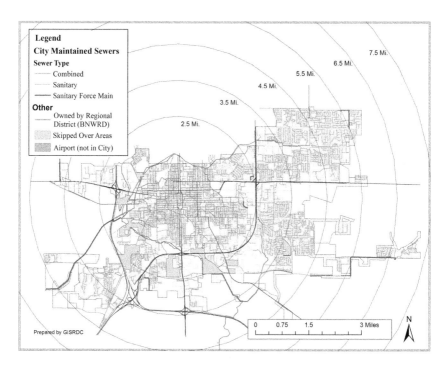

Figure 10.2 2013 Sanitary Sewers City of Bloomington, IL (See Color Figure 10.2 in the color insert section.)

A Grove

In 2007, the city borrowed $6.3 million to build the sewer force main and lift station that was required to service the Grove I subdivision. The debt was to be repaid over 23 years, with the interest will adding on another $4.1 million, for a total cost of $10.4 million. Part of this has been paid for with "tap on fees" of $1,300 and "property owner contribution" fees of $43 per unit. As of 2013, the city had collected about $386,784 in these connection fees ($1,343 times 288), which was less than 4% of the total cost. The city also spent $974,453 to bring a water main to the development, paid for with water billing revenue, which was paid by the city-wide water users. In effect, this was a kind of hidden cost of the development. In effect, the marginal costs were significant but, as of 2013, there only had been a small amount of utilization of the capacity and repayment by connection fees.

B Fox Creek

The information on the Fox Creek sewer extensions was very limited. Starting in 1995, the city built a force main from the northwestern tip of the main residential neighborhood to the treatment plant. In 2001, another force main and gravity trunk lines were built. The total cost was estimated to have been about $10 million. There was no record as to how these lines were financed. The "tap-on" fees for the area were $1,049 and it was assumed that there also was another $43 "property owner contribution" fee. With 1,360 platted lots in 2013, the city had recouped about $1.5 million, or only 15% of the cost.

There also was no record as to the cost of water line extensions. Using the numbers from Grove, about 15% may have been the cost for the water line extensions, or $1.5 million.

These retrospective numbers, however sketchy, for both Grove and Fox Creek provide some insight as to what a marginal cost analysis might have been provided regarding sewer and water extensions.

III Schools

It does not appear that the city considered the impact on schools when it approved the Grove subdivision. But if it did, it should have considered the number of elementary school students that would need a school to attend. Figure 10.3 shows the very large attendance area for the Benjamin Elementary school that was built near, and as a result of, the Grove subdivision.

As of 2013, the Grove subdivision had approximately 170 students. Assuming that half were high-school and middle-school-aged would leave about 85 elementary-school-aged students. Also, in 2013, it was estimated that there were 810 elementary students in the entire Benjamin District, although some of these may have attended private schools. That means that

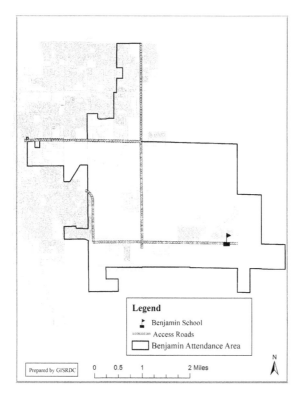

Figure 10.3 Benjamin Elementary School Attendance Area.

725 students may have had to be bused in from other areas, thus increasing the school transportation costs. The main access roads are shown in Figure 9.02. The large gap between the north and south is the airport.

The other district just to the northwest also had at least 750 elementary school students, so it would appear that the school was near to capacity. It appears that the new school would have been needed anyway if more development had occurred in the north. Nevertheless, the new school was built near the Grove subdivision.

A fiscal impact analysis that included consideration of schools would have identified not only the school construction costs but also the transportation costs. Another consideration would have been the impact of young students having to cope with relatively long bus rides.

IV Summary

The availability of an estimate of marginal costs before a new subdivision was approved would be the best way to avoid the overextension of city services and prevent sprawl.

Just by looking at the parcel map of Net Taxable Fiscal Impact, labeled CP.10 in the color insert section, and also CP.13 showing neighborhood fiscal impact, one can see that the compact and contiguous areas in the northeast and eastern sides of the city were the best types of development. The maps also showed that the areas of sprawl were not the best.

Without going over a lot of facts and figures, local officials understood these major points just by looking at the maps. The response to the Comprehensive Plan, adopted in 2015, was very favorable considering the key development policy priorities (p. 231), which have been paraphrased below:

Tier 1: Develop existing vacant areas in the city, land that is not within the city boundaries that has been "skipped over" by historical development, plus lots that have been platted, but not yet built upon (Grove I's 90 lots are an example).

Tier 2: Land immediately adjacent to the city that has access to all city services, including sewer and water.

Tier 3: Land adjacent to the city but lacking city services. In particular, sewer and water extensions would be needed.

In an ideal world, a marginal impact study would enable city officials to see problem areas in advance and use the study results to inform their decisions.

References

McLean County Regional Planning Commission (2015) "Comprehensive Plan 2015–2035", *City of Bloomington, Illinois*, http://www.cityblm.org/government/departments/planning-zoning/comprehensive-plan.

Thompson, D. (2013), "Suburban Sprawl: Exposing Hidden Costs, Identifying Innovations", *Sustainable Prosperity Research Network*, Ottawa, ON: University of Ottawa.

Transportation Research Board (2000) "The Costs of Sprawl", *Transit Cooperative Research Program, Report 74*, Washington, DC: National Academy Press.

11 Working Toward an Enterprise Spatial Planning and Fiscal Impact Analysis System

The Enterprise Spatial Planning Fiscal Impact Analysis System is a forward-looking way toward achieving the ideal transaction processing system, in which every dollar of revenue and expenditure could be traced to location. The Spatial Fiscal Impact Analysis system was initially described as an attempt to model the ideal system, but it is unlikely that such a system could be developed since municipal finance systems are not designed that way. However, municipal operations could be structured and streamlined in such a way that everyday operations could be tracked by location, thus creating an Enterprise Spatial Planning and Fiscal Impact Analysis System. Each department in a city has in common their expenditures. They also need to budget for their operations and present their requests based on the factors that contribute to the cost. In other words, finance is the one common element that ties it all together.

In Chapter 1, the conceptual basis for the Spatial Method was presented, comparing city land-development decisions to business decisions, and there were some strong similarities. Cities can take a business approach to planning, in addition to other considerations, like providing affordable housing and attracting businesses that will create jobs.

The Spatial Method described so far deals with one point in time but, if there was a way to update the data on an annual basis or as development occurs, it would remain useful from one year to the next. For cities not experiencing major changes, the data might only need to be updated every five years or so.

The key organizing mechanism to the enterprise system would again be the parcel base map, using the tools of geographic information systems (GIS). As described previously, the purpose is to measure fiscal impact by land use. Therefore, the place to store the information would be one built upon the assessor's parcel file. The staff responsible for maintaining and reporting the results would be in the GIS department, with the support of top-level management who would oversee coordination with the operating departments. Within the departments, staff would collect the information using standard geographic identifiers, such as address, parcel number, GPS point, street names and blocks, address range or intersection. With this standardized data, it would be updated in the parcel base file by the GIS staff. There may be some reluctance to changing the way things are done, however.

1 Stages of GIS Development

Tomaselli describes the development of Geographic Information Systems (GIS) in an organization as an evolutionary one, with Enterprise GIS as the last and highest stage (2004, p.5). The adoption of the Spatial Method will typically occur in cities that have made it to later stages of GIS development, which she has identified:

Stage 1 – GIS Interest and Awareness
Stage 2 – GIS Development Begins
Stage 3 – GIS Acknowledgment
Stage 4 – GIS Support Expands
Stage 5 – Organizational Integration (Enterprise GIS)

In Stage 3, GIS has the acknowledgment of the top levels of the organization. While it would be very useful if the Finance Director was among the supporters, the impetus may come from the decision-makers who want to know the fiscal impact of new development. The Economic Development Director would also play an important role in creating an inventory of employment by business or parcel. As recognized by several authors, in the past, most fiscal impact studies were demand-driven by developers seeking approvals for projects. But Leistritz believes that it in the future it will be driven by decision-makers (1994, p. 8). He goes on to write that the emphasis on moving impact assessment to higher levels will likely lead to a more proactive approach. With economic development being an important part of community planning, fiscal impact analysis will be an important component.

Stage 4 would be when city staff in the departments begin to organize their work using geographic identifiers and the GIS staff would develop tools to easily update the parcel factors with the results.

Stage 5 would be when city decision-makers expect to be briefed regularly on the fiscal impact of neighborhoods, land uses and new development. They will expect the Economic Development Director to pursue new development that makes fiscal sense, rather than development just for development's sake. They will try to promote low- and moderate-income housing that has the best net impact on the city, even though it may produce deficits. Furthermore, they will require new development proposals to prepare detailed operating and marginal-impact cost estimates and expect staff to be able to evaluate their accuracy.

Some of the data needs for the Spatial Method to work within a Fiscal Impact Enterprise System are described below.

II Revenues

The assessor's file provides an indicator of property-tax collections based on assessed value. What is missing from the file in many, if not most, cases is the actual tax collections. If these explicit data were contained in the enterprise file, the municipality would have a more precise measure since using the tax rate and assessed value to calculate property taxes may not agree with the actual tax collections due to appeals, lack of payment and other equalization practices.

A deficiency in the assessor's data for Bloomington was the lack of building market value data for tax-exempt properties. Ideally, the assessor should provide this, perhaps updated every 3–5 years.

In Bloomington, IL, sales and other taxes proved to be much greater than property taxes. To the extent that taxes are directly collected by the city, these collections could be summarized by address and input into the enterprise system. A problem was presented with the issue of sales taxes. The sales taxes are collected by the state and then a portion is distributed back to the city based on what was collected, but not from where it was collected. The state will most likely not reveal the amounts attributable to each establishment. In Bloomington's case, commercial land use was not broken down into retail categories, such as grocery stores, retail goods, auto dealerships, etc., so the revenue could not be allocated to the organizations that collect the revenue. Furthermore, some would argue that sales taxes are paid by people who purchase retail items. Fiscal impact experts differ on who should be credited with sales tax revenue: the entities that collect the taxes or the people who pay them. This should be a topic of discussion for the decision-makers.

Special assessments are often part of the assessor's records but, if they are not, they should be geo-located by parcel ID.

Charges for services, fines and forfeits, licenses and permits, and franchise fees can cover a whole range of transactions. However, they could be tracked by the address of the person or entity paying for them. This would be a responsibility of the Finance Department, with support from the operating departments.

Intergovernmental revenue should be allocated based on the same formula that determined the amount incoming to the city. Often the formulas have population as a major factor and the Enterprise System should be able to track the location of population as well as other formula factors.

III Expenditures

Police and fire calls are already tracked by location and, with a little bit more structuring, the data could feed directly into a GIS format without a large amount of manipulating by staff. In the case of Anoka, MN, the locator was address. For Bloomington, IL, it was GPS point. Both used street-block segments for street calls. While the police may not want to reveal their patrolling schedules, a way of annually summarizing patrolling time by general location would enhance the allocation of police readiness costs instead of just using population, employment and building market values.

Parks and recreation departments account for significant amounts of a municipality's expenses: Anoka, MN – 11% and Bloomington, IL – 14%. In both cases, the costs were greater than the proportion devoted to public works. Yet, there generally has been a lack of detail on where staff time and resources are spent. Again, if staffing and maintenance records were tracked in the same way as public works might be doing, that would be one way of geolocating the costs. Another aspect of parks and recreation that is more difficult to measure would be the people who are using the parks, i.e., where do they live? There probably would be a proportion that comes from outside the municipality. However, there may be some functions, like swimming pools, where users are charged and it would be very helpful to know where they live and who is paying the costs. Local parks are intended to be used by local residents. How to allocate the revenues and costs from those coming into the city to use them would need to be decided. If the staff in the department were able to determine these costs on a spatial basis, it would be a significant input to the Enterprise System.

Public works operations could be better tracked by keeping their "transactions", or work orders, and time spent geocoded by address, street or intersection location so that the annual amount can be summarized by location rather than by local road frontage. To the extent capital outlay is directly related to public works, the expenses should be tracked by location. These expenses may vary significantly from one year to the next and also by location. Therefore, having a system that was updated annually would provide better insight as to what should be allocated to land uses, rather than averaging it by road frontage.

Many public works departments maintain a pavement management system that indicates the conditions of streets so that repairs can be anticipated. This information should also be related to parcels so that when improvements are made, the costs could also be allocated to them. However, if a parcel is located on a street badly in need of repair, there should be a consideration of equity, which would be in addition to fiscal impact. If capital expenses are mainly for maintaining facilities in the older developed area, then decision-makers would have a better idea of life-cycle costs and the possibility of establishing a TIF district which would replace the crumbling infrastructure and encourage new development.

Some fiscal impact methods use trip generation to measure the impact on roads. It would be helpful if the public works or transportation planning staff would include these measures by street segment as well so that trips could be correlated with road maintenance costs. However, trip generation measures generally do not distinguish between local traffic and traffic on county, state or US highways. The focus should only be on local roads and streets.

Expenses that can get obscured by time would be interest and princi- pal payments on debt. A city may be paying for a particular sewer and water extension that happened 10–15 years earlier. If it is possible, the project should be identified and the benefitted properties charged with these expenses. This can be difficult because records may no longer exist that specify the location and costs. In other cases, a bond issue may have been to pay for a variety of things. If the bonds were not for a specific geographic location, then the expenses can be charged off to the city parcels as a whole. In the future, parcels should have an indicator as to what bond issues were used if they were for a specific development. This way, the records for bond issues could be preserved rather than lost over time.

The spatial method described here allocates general government funds based on population, market value and employment. If there is a way for the administration to categorize specific developments that take up their time, it would be an improvement. In Bloomington, a major portion of the general-government expense was vehicle expenses and was allocated using a population, market value and distance factor. If more specific data were available, it would have been helpful.

IV Demographics

If the specific revenue and expenditure categories were geocoded as described above, there still would be a need to relate them to demographic factors.

The Economic Development Department should have an inventory of employment by address. In some cases, a business may occupy several par- cels so the employment should be distributed among them for the best sta- tistical results. Maintaining and updating the inventory should provide the city with measures that can be used to project the impact of future commer- cial/industrial projects. As mentioned above, the employment data should be supplemented with data on estimated trips generated by commercial/ industrial uses and employment to provide the basis for projecting local infrastructure investments needed for a proposed development.

There are some items that can only be approximately allocated using population, supplemented by employment and market value. Tracking new construction every year would provide a basis for updating population. Other measures, such as sewer and water billing, would also provide infor- mation as to the allocation of Enterprise Funds. In Anoka, electrical billing and usage was another way to track new or changing development.

Coupled with estimating population would also be the school-age popu- lation. If the school districts were able to share enrollment data with the city, it would help, but districts may not want to share this data for privacy reasons. Being able to track school enrollment by year would help the city project enrollment for new development, not just in the short term but also in the long term. If the city and school district are separate entities, this would be a subject for coordination that would help the district participate in the planning process and Enterprise Fiscal Analysis System.

V The Future

While some of these examples may be years off from being implemented, there are companies that deal specifically with some of the matters described earlier. For example, streamlining the permitting and construction inspection process already exists in some municipalities. As each of these types of functions is created they would be the small, incremental steps toward establishing an enterprise fiscal impact system, and developing a city's "information infrastructure". It may take many years before a municipality is able to implement a complete system, if at all. In the meantime, the spatial method described in this book can continue to be developed and improved upon.

References

Leistritz, F. L. (1994) "Economic and Fiscal Impact Assessment", *International Association for Impact Assessment*, https://ageconsearch.umn.edu/bitstream/1 21073/2/AAE%20No.94004.pdf.

Tomaselli, L, 2004 "The Enterprise Model of GIS, and the Implications for People and Organizations", Presented at the Troy State University GIS Conference, Troy, Alabama.

12 Summary of the Spatial Planning and Fiscal Impact Analysis Method

This book has been written to introduce the Spatial Planning and Fiscal Impact Analysis Method. It is intended to provide guidance to cities as to developing the data that is needed and ways to project fiscal impact. If a city lacks staff expertise or time to apply the method, it can be used to specify what a consultant should provide. Some key features are summarized below.

- The Spatial Fiscal Impact Analysis Method is based on the premise that nearly all city revenues and expenditures are spatially based and can be modeled using spatially distributed factors that are indicators.
- Existing methods rarely consider detailed land use categories or the spatial layout of cities.
- The parcel shapefile provides the organizing framework and generally provides the lowest common denominator for spatially defining land use, determining factors and modeling fiscal flows.
- Tax-exempt uses that benefit the city as a whole are properly considered, as well as residential, commercial/industrial and vacant.
- All components of a city's finances are taken into consideration, as appropriate. Nothing is double counted or omitted.
- It is costlier to apply but the results can be used on an ongoing basis.
- A robust planning database is developed in order to evaluate the characteristics of land use, which should be considered an investment in planning for the future as "information infrastructure".
- The method requires strong skills in Geographic Information Systems (GIS).
- Being able to show fiscal patterns as maps is a very effective way to present results to citizens or decision-makers.

The state of the art in previous fiscal impact methods has been described, including some that date back to the 1970s, along with an evaluation of their strengths and weaknesses identified by practitioners in the field. Some of the methods have been compared to the results from the Spatial Method to demonstrate the wide variation in results. Assuming that the results from the Spatial Method are more accurate, it appears that many of the older methods are not reliable and may tend to overstate expenses for dense development like apartments but underestimate them for single-family. They also appear to overstate the costs of commercial and industrial development.

The Spatial Method requires an in-depth analysis of a city's Comprehensive Annual Financial Report (CAFR) plus additional supporting information to clarify the factors that are needed to allocate revenues and expenditures to parcels.

Combining the financial data with the factor data results in multipliers to be used to calculate the revenues and expenditures applicable to each parcel, thus resulting in the calculation of the fiscal impact for each. The purpose is not to single out any one parcel but rather to be able to summarize the results by land use for similar parcels to be used to help project fiscal impact.

While assessed value is used to determine property taxes, market value, particularly building market value, provides the best way to measure the intensity of land development and the impact on revenues and expenditures.

While this is not a Per Capita approach, population is also an important factor.

The parcel shapefile is used to compile all of the factors that are indicators of revenues and expenditures, including detailed land use, population, school-aged population (SAP), employment, police and fire calls, road frontage, etc. In particular, estimating adult and school-aged populations would be time-consuming unless the census blocks upon which the analysis is based are more accurate than what was found in Bloomington. Nevertheless, the benefits of having census geography coincide with parcels will again be an investment.

Preparing the factor data by parcel requires a substantial amount of time. Much of the effort is just a one-time exercise that does not need to be repeated, such as reconciling census geography with parcels and census housing unit counts with the assessor's housing counts. Developing address-matching alternatives, measuring road frontage, and estimating census year adult and school-aged populations are other examples of a one-time effort; they only need to be updated as new development occurs or every decennial census year.

A major benefit of compiling the parcel shapefiles is that the data can be analyzed and cross-tabulated in many ways to allow the planner or practitioner better insight as to how the city functions.

The impact of employment is something that needs more research. Expressing commercial and industrial development costs on the basis of employment does not seem to be very reliable. The impact of employment is much like population, although to a lesser degree.

The method also allowed the analysis of fiscal impact summarized by the year built to be able to derive measures for recent development rather than city-wide averages. The results for more recent development allow for a better way to project the impact of new development. In summary, developing the parcel database is an investment in "information infrastructure".

The Spatial Method, as described in this book, deals with both operating and capital fiscal impacts. However, the practitioner could project operating fiscal impact separately and then also project capital impact based on a marginal analysis. Surpluses and deficits in Enterprise Funds should be considered if they are substantial.

The results can be used to evaluate redevelopment potentials, including providing the basis for establishing Tax Increment Financing (TIF) districts.

Examples of the impact of leapfrog or sprawl development were also a part of the Bloomington, IL study. This required the research back into the history of sewer and water infrastructure. In effect, this was a determination of marginal impacts "after the fact". Hopefully, in the future, cities will require major development proposals to include marginal impact assessments and city staff will be able to evaluate their plausibility.

Although not included in the original study, an examination of school fiscal impact has been demonstrated, including the process for estimating adult and school-age populations based on census data.

It should be noted that fiscal impact should not be the only concern when evaluating a development proposal. Certain commercial or industrial developments may require affordable housing for workers. Martin states that "fiscal impact should …be used to locate low income housing based on the 'net' impact or lowest cost to the City" (2008). Lastly, Bise cautions users to guard against basing "land-use decisions entirely upon fiscal considerations at the expense of achieving a healthy and balanced quality of life. This is referred to as fiscal zoning or the fiscalization of land uses. Communities must take care to consider all of their priorities, in addition to fiscal impacts" (2010, p. 4).

It is hoped that this book on Spatial Fiscal Impact Analysis will encourage others to begin to pursue this method and that perhaps eventually it can provide the basis for "Enterprise Fiscal Impact Analysis", joining together all operations of city government to not only estimate fiscal impact, but also to eliminate duplication, encourage the sharing of information, and contribute to greater efficiency. Being able to visually see the patterns, whether it be land use, population density, police and fire calls, and finally fiscal impact, can contribute greatly to an understanding of how a city functions. It is hoped that the method will be a milepost along the way in the evolution of spatial planning and fiscal impact analysis techniques.

References

Bise, L. C. (2010) *Fiscal Impact Analysis: Methodologies for Planners*, Chicago, IL: American Planning Association Planning Advisory Service.

Burchell, R. W., Nicholas, J. C., Martin, B., Flora, P. and Bise, L. C. (2008) *Fiscal Impact Roundup: Trends in Fiscal Impact Analysis*, Orlando, FL: Presentation at the National Impact Fee Roundtable.

Appendix A
Creating an Address-Matching File for Parcels

The parcel address is a key data item needed for the GIS approach to work. Transaction data on police calls, fire calls, electrical billing and water billing were available in various formats and all had addresses associated with them. For the transaction data to be useful, it needed to be matched to the parcels. The parcel addresses had to be standardized and the transaction data needed to be standardized as well. In Bloomington, the city also had an address point file, located with GPS. This was very helpful in matching data to parcels having more than one address or having the same address, plus unit numbers. In the examples provided in this Appendix, separate files were created containing the parcel identification number (*PIN*) and the address information contained in the assessor's parcel file or parcel point file. Address-matching alternatives were added to the files to account for different ways of expressing addresses in the transaction files. The condition of the addresses in the assessor's file and the presence of an address-point file greatly affects the amount of time needed to create address alternatives.

I Standardizing the Parcel Base Addresses

Standardizing means that each address needed to be broken down into its components: "house" number, street name, street type and street direction. GIS software has the capability of standardizing addresses and breaking them down. The house number means the numeric part of the address. Of course, in the case of businesses, this would be the structure number, not a house number. Street type would be whether the street is an avenue, a street, a circle, boulevard, etc. For example, standardization means that all of the "Av", "Ave", or "Avenue" words found in an address are standardized as "Ave". Street direction may or may not be needed. If all of the streets in a city can be classified as "west" then there is no need to worry about getting all the streets to have "west" as a prefix or a suffix. Sometimes transaction records will include a street direction and, in other cases, it is excluded.

What the GIS software standardization capability does not do is check the spelling. A street name may be "Arden View", but for some transaction records it may be "Ardenview". Therefore, some work should be done to develop a standard list of street names and street types for the city. The key here is *consistency*. If the city (and county) are able to adopt naming standards, the standards will be helpful in designing data entry systems for any transaction data in the future.

The GIS address-matching capability has its limitations. For example, if a transaction record refers to an address on a parcel that also has another address, only one address will be on the parcel record and the transaction may not match. GIS address-matching is also capable of matching to a street centerline file that has address ranges. When matching a transaction record to a centerline file, the record may fall within an address range but the results will be a point on one side of the street or other, depending on the house number being odd or even, and located approximately where it might be within the range of house numbers. This does not match the transaction record to the parcel. In this case, the transaction point would have to be manually coded with the nearest parcel's *PIN*.

Police and Fire make up the largest percentage of city expenditures. The best indicators of these costs are the calls for service. To allocate the time spent on calls to parcels, the calls must be matched to parcels. It may also be necessary to allocate other types of transactions, such as sewer and water billing, to parcels to estimate revenues and expenditures. Typically, transaction data has the address as the locator. Therefore, address-matching to the parcel-base file is needed, rather than matching to address ranges.

There are GIS tools to standardize addresses, both in the address locator file (the parcel base) and the file to be matched. However, since the parcel addresses will be used for many purposes, it is recommended that the addresses and alternatives be permanently standardized and stored in a parcel-base file. Usually, the assessor's parcel file will be somewhat standardized already but there may be spelling variations and other anomalies.

II Examples of Address Standardization

The situation for each county, and therefore each city, may be different, as shown in the examples provided below.

A Example of Parcel-Based Addresses

Table A.1 shows examples of typical street names and addresses coming directly from the assessor's parcel file. Generally, the addresses in the parcel file have been standardized well but, when it comes to addresses from other sources, there may be many variations.

In the first group, there is no *STRSUFDIR*, which is the street suffix direction. In the second group, there are directional values of "N" and "W" but, in this city, there are no "S" and "E" streets, so the direction

Table A.1 Examples of Addresses in a City's Parcel File

PARCELID	BLDGNUM	STRPRETYPE	STREETNAME	STRSUF-TYPE	STRSUF-DIR	STRNAMEALL	SITEADD
223023210129	1479		ARDEN VIEW	DR		Arden View Dr	1479 Arden View Dr
223023320070	1478		DAWN	CIR		Dawn Cir	1478 Dawn Cir
273023330009	1476		ARDEN OAKS	DR		Arden Oaks Dr	1476 Arden Oaks Dr
223023230030	1479		ARDEN VISTA	CT		Arden Vista Ct	1479 Arden Vista Ct
223023320025	1479		COLLEEN	AVE		Colleen Ave	1479 Colleen Ave
343023320011	1478		LAMETTI	LN		Lametti Ln	1478 Lametti Ln
223023340007	1371		FLORAL	DR	W	Floral Dr W	1371 Floral Dr W
223023120002	4490		HAMLINE	AVE	N	Hamline Ave N	4490 Hamline Ave N
333023330031	3192		CLEVELAND	AVE	N	Cleveland Ave N	3192 Cleveland Ave N
343023310047	3271		SNELLING	AVE	N	Snelling Ave N	3271 Snelling Ave N
343023440003	3235		LEXINGTON	AVE	N	Lexington Ave N	3235 Lexington Ave N
343023310025	3270		SNELLING	AVE	N	Snelling Ave N	3270 1/2 Snelling Ave N
343023130004	3390		DUNLAP	ST	N	Dunlap St N	3390 Dunlap St N
283023130015	3927		FAIRVIEW	AVE	N	Fairview Ave N	3927 Fairview Ave N
273023340047	3623		PASCAL	AVE	N	Pascal Ave N	3623 Pascal Ave N
283023310021	3766		BRIGHTON	WAY	N	Brighton Way N	3766 Brighton Way N
163023340003	4659	HIGHWAY	10			Highway 10	4659 Highway 10
163023340009	1845	HIGHWAY	96		W	Highway 96 W	1845 Highway 96 W
273023340041	1423	COUNTY ROAD	E		W	County Road E W	1423 County Road E W
333023340089	1865	COUNTY ROAD	D		W	County Road D W	1865 County Road D W
283023320028	1962	COUNTY ROAD	E2		W	County Road E2 W	1962 County Road E2 W
273023120006	1296	COUNTY ROAD	F		W	County Road F W	1296 County Road F W

may be superfluous. When other transactional records are matched to the file, the direction may often be often omitted. In other cases, the street type may be missing as well as the direction. Therefore, several different types of matching fields should be created. Furthermore, one may want to search street names to locate a parcel, so a field containing simply the street name and type should be created, with no directional suffix. Table A.2 shows the new fields to be added for purposes of address-matching other transactional data.

MATCHADD1 is the same as *SITEADD*, but the letters have been converted to all caps. *MATCHADD2* is the *SITEADD* without the direction. *MATCHADD3* is the *SITEADD* without the street type and direction. Lastly, *MATCHSNST* is the street name and street type. This field helps to locate all the parcels located on the street. With these variations, it should be possible to match most transaction data to the parcel-base file, although "3270 1/2 Snelling Ave" may still have some problems if the transaction records omit the "1/2".

B Example of Point Addresses

The city of Bloomington had an excellent address base for matching transactions, thanks to a consortium of members from the city and county, named McGIS, led by the county GIS director. Bloomington had an address point file, which also provided the *PIN* number, so it included points in cases where a parcel may have had more than one address associated with it. The parcel file itself did not contain addresses, but both files had the parcel *PIN* numbers. Figure A.1 shows an area in Bloomington as an example. Note that the point file has multiple points in some parcels. In the northwest corner, there were different addresses for each point. In the southeast corner, the house number and street were the same for all points, but the address also contained the unit number. The points within the parcel all had the same parcel ID or *PIN* number.

Table A.3 shows the relevant fields in the address point file, grouped by situation. Note that the first group of addresses had unique house numbers, but they all had the same *PIN*. These correspond to the parcel in the northwest corner of Figure A.1. Figure A.2 shows the second group in the southeast corner; the points all have the same *PIN* number, plus the unit number as part of the address. The last two groups show parcels with only one address and unique *PIN* numbers.

This parcel point file represents the best type of file to be used to match transaction records. When a transaction record is matched to it, it gets assigned the *PIN* number. In the case of cities that do not have an address point file, a transaction record will match to a parcel address and *PIN* if the addresses are the same. But, in the case of transaction records with other addresses on the parcel, there will not be a match to those. This will require

Table A.2 Example of Address-Matching Fields to be Added to the City's Address-Matching Parcel File

PARCELID	MATCHADD1	MATCHADD2	MATCHADD3	MATCHSNST
22302321012 9	1479 ARDEN VIEW DR		1479 ARDEN VIEW	ARDEN VIEW DR
22302332007 0	1478 DAWN CIR		1478 DAWN	DAWN CIR
27302333000 9	1476 ARDEN OAKS DR		1476 ARDEN OAKS	ARDEN OAKS DR
22302323003 0	1479 ARDEN VISTA CT		1479 ARDEN VISTA	ARDEN VISTA CT
22302332002 5	1479 COLLEEN AVE		1479 COLLEEN	COLLEEN AVE
34302332001 1	1478 LAMETTI LN		1478 LAMETTI	LAMETTI LN
22302334000 7	1371 FLORAL DR W	1371 FLORAL DR	1371 FLORAL	FLORAL DR
22302312000 2	4490 HAMLINE AVE N	4490 HAMLINE AVE	4490 HAMLINE	HAMLINE AVE
33302333003 1	3192 CLEVELAND AVE N	3192 CLEVELAND AVE	3192 CLEVELAND	CLEVELAND AVE
34302331004 7	3271 SNELLING AVE N	3271 SNELLING AVE	3271 SNELLING	SNELLING AVE
34302344000 3	3235 LEXINGTON AVE N	3235 LEXINGTON AVE	3235 LEXINGTON	LEXINGTON AVE
34302331002 5	3270 1/2 SNELLING AVE N	3270 1/2 SNELLING AVE	3270 1/2 SNELLING	SNELLING AVE
34302313000 4	3390 DUNLAP ST N	3390 DUNLAP ST	3390 DUNLAP	DUNLAP ST
28302313001 5	3927 FAIRVIEW AVE N	3927 FAIRVIEW AVE	3927 FAIRVIEW	FAIRVIEW AVE
27302334004 7	3623 PASCAL AVE N	3623 PASCAL AVE	3623 PASCAL	PASCAL AVE
28302331002 1	3766 BRIGHTON WAY N	3766 BRIGHTON WAY	3766 BRIGHTON	BRIGHTON WAY
16302334000 3	4659 HIGHWAY 10	4659 HIGHWAY 10		HIGHWAY 10
16302334000 9	1845 HIGHWAY 96 W	1845 HIGHWAY 96		HIGHWAY 96
27302334004 1	1423 COUNTY ROAD E W	1423 COUNTY ROAD E		COUNTY ROAD E
33302334008 9	1865 COUNTY ROAD D W	1865 COUNTY ROAD D		COUNTY ROAD D
28302332002 8	1962 COUNTY ROAD E2 W	1962 COUNTY ROAD E2		COUNTY ROAD E2
27302312000 6	1296 COUNTY ROAD F W	1296 COUNTY ROAD F		COUNTY ROAD F

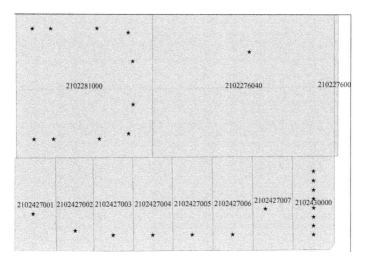

Figure A.1 Example of Parcel Polygons and Address Points, Bloomington, IL.

Table A.3 Example of Fields in the Address Point File, Bloomington, IL

PIN	ADDRESS
2102281000	105 N WILLIAMSBURG DR
2102281000	109 N WILLIAMSBURG DR
2102281000	115 N WILLIAMSBURG DR
2102281000	119 N WILLIAMSBURG DR
2102281000	123 N WILLIAMSBURG DR
2102281000	127 N WILLIAMSBURG DR
2102281000	131 N WILLIAMSBURG DR
2102281000	135 N WILLIAMSBURG DR
2102281000	139 N WILLIAMSBURG DR
2102281000	143 N WILLIAMSBURG DR
2102430000	2516 E WASHINGTON ST # UNIT A
2102430000	2516 E WASHINGTON ST # UNIT B
2102430000	2516 E WASHINGTON ST # UNIT C
2102430000	2516 E WASHINGTON ST # UNIT D
2102430000	2516 E WASHINGTON ST # UNIT E
2102430000	2516 E WASHINGTON ST # UNIT F
2102430000	2516 E WASHINGTON ST # UNIT G
2102430000	2516 E WASHINGTON ST # UNIT H
2102427002	2504 E WASHINGTON ST
2102427003	2506 E WASHINGTON ST
2102427004	2508 E WASHINGTON ST
2102427005	2510 E WASHINGTON ST
2102427006	2512 E WASHINGTON ST
2102427007	2514 E WASHINGTON ST
2102427001	101 N WILLIAMSBURG DR
2102276040	304 N HERSHEY RD

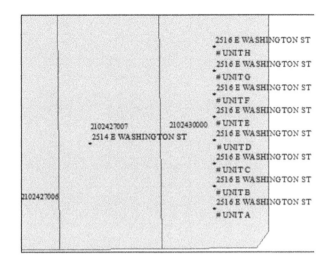

Figure A.2 Example of Parcel PIN Numbers and Address Point Addresses, Bloomington, IL.

additional work to try to locate the closest parcel, using the street centerline file with address ranges with ArcGIS.

However, even though the parcel point file has the most accurate addresses, transaction data may have abbreviated addresses and will not necessarily match. Anticipating the various ways addresses may be formatted in a transaction file, several alternatives should be created, similar to the example in Table A.2. To do this, the full address first needs to be broken down into its components by standardizing it. The fastest way to standardize the address is to use the *Geocoding Tools, Standardize Addresses* in ArcGIS. The results are shown in Table A.4. The field *ADDR_HN* is the house number, *ADDR_PD* is the direction as a prefix to the street name, *ADDR_SN* is the street name and *ADDR_ST* is the street type.

Creating matching alternatives was the next step. These are shown in Table A.5. The first field, *MATCHADD1*, was the original address in the point file. It was very complete but the transaction data may not be as complete. *MATCHADD2* dropped the unit number. *MATCHADD3* dropped the street type. *MATCHADD4* dropped the directional prefix. *MATCHADD5* dropped the directional prefix but kept the street type.

When matching transaction records, the first pass was to match to the original address, *MATCHADD1*. For those that did not match, an attempt was made to match to *MATCHADD2*. For those that still did not match, *MATCHADD3* was tried. Next, *MATCHADD4* was used. Lastly, *MATCHADD5* was used. The objective was to get as many transaction records to match on these first five passes. Those that did not match had to

Table A.4 Address Point File After Standardizing with ArcGIS Bloomington, IL

PIN	ADDRESS	ADDR_HN	ADDR_PD	ADDR_SN	ADDR_ST
2102281000	105 N WILLIAMSBURG DR	105	N	WILLIAMSBURG	DR
2102281000	109 N WILLIAMSBURG DR	109	N	WILLIAMSBURG	DR
2102281000	115 N WILLIAMSBURG DR	115	N	WILLIAMSBURG	DR
2102281000	119 N WILLIAMSBURG DR	119	N	WILLIAMSBURG	DR
2102281000	123 N WILLIAMSBURG DR	123	N	WILLIAMSBURG	DR
2102281000	127 N WILLIAMSBURG DR	127	N	WILLIAMSBURG	DR
2102281000	131 N WILLIAMSBURG DR	131	N	WILLIAMSBURG	DR
2102281000	135 N WILLIAMSBURG DR	135	N	WILLIAMSBURG	DR
2102281000	139 N WILLIAMSBURG DR	139	N	WILLIAMSBURG	DR
2102281000	143 N WILLIAMSBURG DR	143	N	WILLIAMSBURG	DR
2102430000	2516 E WASHINGTON ST # UNIT A	2516	E	WASHINGTON	ST
2102430000	2516 E WASHINGTON ST # UNIT B	2516	E	WASHINGTON	ST
2102430000	2516 E WASHINGTON ST # UNIT C	2516	E	WASHINGTON	ST
2102430000	2516 E WASHINGTON ST # UNIT D	2516	E	WASHINGTON	ST
2102430000	2516 E WASHINGTON ST # UNIT E	2516	E	WASHINGTON	ST
2102430000	2516 E WASHINGTON ST # UNIT F	2516	E	WASHINGTON	ST
2102430000	2516 E WASHINGTON ST # UNIT G	2516	E	WASHINGTON	ST
2102430000	2516 E WASHINGTON ST # UNIT H	2516	E	WASHINGTON	ST
2102427002	2504 E WASHINGTON ST	2504	E	WASHINGTON	ST
2102427005	2510 E WASHINGTON ST	2510	E	WASHINGTON	ST
2102427007	2514 E WASHINGTON ST	2514	E	WASHINGTON	ST
2102427006	2512 E WASHINGTON ST	2512	E	WASHINGTON	ST
2102427003	2506 E WASHINGTON ST	2506	E	WASHINGTON	ST
2102427004	2508 E WASHINGTON ST	2508	E	WASHINGTON	ST
2102427001	101 N WILLIAMSBURG DR	101	N	WILLIAMSBURG	DR
2102276040	304 N HERSHEY RD	304	N	HERSHEY	RD

Table A.5 Alternative Address-Matching Fields Bloomington, IL

PIN	MATCHADD1	MATCHADD2	MATCHADD3	MATCHADD4	MATCHADD5
2102281000	105 N WILLIAMSBURG DR		105 N WILLIAMSBURG	105 WILLIAMSBURG	105 WILLIAMSBURG DR
2102281000	109 N WILLIAMSBURG DR		109 N WILLIAMSBURG	109 WILLIAMSBURG	109 WILLIAMSBURG DR
2102281000	115 N WILLIAMSBURG DR		115 N WILLIAMSBURG	115 WILLIAMSBURG	115 WILLIAMSBURG DR
2102281000	119 N WILLIAMSBURG DR		119 N WILLIAMSBURG	119 WILLIAMSBURG	119 WILLIAMSBURG DR
2102281000	123 N WILLIAMSBURG DR		123 N WILLIAMSBURG	123 WILLIAMSBURG	123 WILLIAMSBURG DR
2102281000	127 N WILLIAMSBURG DR		127 N WILLIAMSBURG	127 WILLIAMSBURG	127 WILLIAMSBURG DR
2102281000	131 N WILLIAMSBURG DR		131 N WILLIAMSBURG	131 WILLIAMSBURG	131 WILLIAMSBURG DR
2102281000	135 N WILLIAMSBURG DR		135 N WILLIAMSBURG	135 WILLIAMSBURG	135 WILLIAMSBURG DR
2102281000	139 N WILLIAMSBURG DR		139 N WILLIAMSBURG	139 WILLIAMSBURG	139 WILLIAMSBURG DR
2102281000	143 N WILLIAMSBURG DR		143 N WILLIAMSBURG	143 WILLIAMSBURG	143 WILLIAMSBURG DR
2102430000	2516 E WASHINGTON ST # UNIT A	2516 E WASHINGTON ST	2516 E WASHINGTON	2516 WASHINGTON	2516 WASHINGTON ST
2102430000	2516 E WASHINGTON ST # UNIT B	2516 E WASHINGTON ST	2516 E WASHINGTON	2516 WASHINGTON	2516 WASHINGTON ST
2102430000	2516 E WASHINGTON ST # UNIT C	2516 E WASHINGTON ST	2516 E WASHINGTON	2516 WASHINGTON	2516 WASHINGTON ST

(*Continued*)

Table A.5 (Continued)

PIN	MATCHADD1	MATCHADD2	MATCHADD3	MATCHADD4	MATCHADD5
2102430000	2516 E WASHINGTON ST # UNIT D	2516 E WASHINGTON ST	2516 E WASHINGTON	2516 WASHINGTON	2516 WASHINGTON ST
2102430000	2516 E WASHINGTON ST # UNIT E	2516 E WASHINGTON ST	2516 E WASHINGTON	2516 WASHINGTON	2516 WASHINGTON ST
2102430000	2516 E WASHINGTON ST # UNIT F	2516 E WASHINGTON ST	2516 E WASHINGTON	2516 WASHINGTON	2516 WASHINGTON ST
2102430000	2516 E WASHINGTON ST # UNIT G	2516 E WASHINGTON ST	2516 E WASHINGTON	2516 WASHINGTON	2516 WASHINGTON ST
2102430000	2516 E WASHINGTON ST # UNIT H	2516 E WASHINGTON ST	2516 E WASHINGTON	2516 WASHINGTON	2516 WASHINGTON ST
2102427002	2504 E WASHINGTON ST		2504 E WASHINGTON	2504 WASHINGTON	2504 WASHINGTON ST
2102427005	2510 E WASHINGTON ST		2510 E WASHINGTON	2510 WASHINGTON	2510 WASHINGTON ST
2102427007	2514 E WASHINGTON ST		2514 E WASHINGTON	2514 WASHINGTON	2514 WASHINGTON ST
2102427006	2512 E WASHINGTON ST		2512 E WASHINGTON	2512 WASHINGTON	2512 WASHINGTON ST
2102427003	2506 E WASHINGTON ST		2506 E WASHINGTON	2506 WASHINGTON	2506 WASHINGTON ST
2102427004	2508 E WASHINGTON ST		2508 E WASHINGTON	2508 WASHINGTON	2508 WASHINGTON ST
2102427001	101 N WILLIAMSBURG DR		101 N WILLIAMSBURG	101 WILLIAMSBURG	101 WILLIAMSBURG ST
2102276040	304 N HERSHEY RD		304 N HERSHEY	304 HERSHEY	304 HERSHEY RD

be manually checked. The reasons for non-matches were typically spelling errors or records that were for a location not even in the city.

III Summary

In summary, the condition of the addresses in the assessor's file and the presence of an address point file greatly affect the amount of time needed to create addresses to which other transaction data can be matched. Since several transaction files (police, fire, sewer, water, utilities) may need to be matched to the parcel file, it is best to create alternative matching cases in an address-matching parcel file so that other transaction files can easily and quickly be matched to a *PIN* number.

Appendix B
Allocating Public Safety Data to Parcels

Police and fire calls are typically the largest operating expenditure item in a city's budget.

The city of Bloomington had an excellent system for recording their police and fire calls: using GPS, standardizing their addresses and keeping them in a Dbase format. All of the variations were taken care of in advance by the police department, working with McLean County. The fact that both police and fire/EMS records are in one file also streamlined the work. Each address in the city had an address point along with the parcel ID. In cities where the parcel file contains an address, there will be problems when there is more than one address on a parcel and manual matching will probably be necessary, as described in Appendix A.

I Locate the Calls by Address

When a call is to an address, it is matched to the appropriate parcel point. Figure B.1 shows an example of public safety call points to the same area. The stars represent the parcel points and the graduated symbols in gray represent police calls, with the number of calls located beside each.

Each public safety point could actually represent more than one call, as shown by the size of the symbol and the number by each. In fact, the public safety call file actually showed the number of personnel responding to each call. Many calls had two or more officers or responders and each was referenced as a point but, visually, the points "stacked up" on one another, which is why the graduated circles are shown here.

In addition to this information, the amount of time spent on each call was also recorded in the database. Therefore, the total amount of time for the call was documented, whether it be one, two, three or more officers responding to it. Table B.1 shows an example of the call records for the parcel with 2 calls with 2 officers, in other words, 4 "calls" for the parcel near the southeast corner of the map.

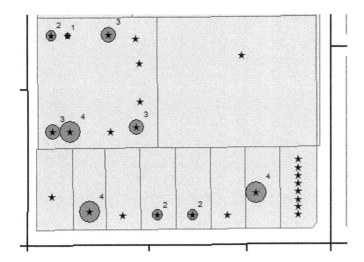

Figure B.1 Example of Parcel Points and Public Safety Address Calls.

II Allocate Intersection Call Time

In addition to the parcel address points, the police department had added points that represent the block and intersection records. Figure B.2 shows the intersection of S Williamsburg Dr and E Washington St. The point right at the intersection of the centerlines is the intersection point. In this case, there are two alternatives as to which name comes first. The point labeled 2500 E Washington actually represents the entire 2500 block of E Washington St and the point for 100 S Williamsburg Dr represents the entire 100 block of Williamsburg Dr.

With the calls geo-located to intersections, the amount of time can be summarized and then allocated to adjacent parcels. First, the amount of time is summarized for the example calls. This is shown in Table B.2. Note that E WASHINGTON ST/S WILLIAMSBURG DR and N WILLIAMSBURG DR/E WASHINGTON ST are the same intersection. The total amount of time for both police and fire is 283 minutes.

Figure B.3 shows a 300-foot buffer around the intersection which has *unioned*, using ArcGIS, with the parcels. Table B.3 shows the affected parcels and acreage within the buffer. The acreage has been totaled and the percentage of the total area for each parcel has been calculated. The 283 minutes are multiplied by the percentage to derive the allocation.

III Allocate Block Call Time

Often a police or fire call will just reference a block, such as "the 100 block of S. Williamsburg Dr", as shown in Table B.4.

Table B.1 Example of Public Safety Address Call Data for a Selected Parcel

SEQNO	CREATE	MINUTES	ADDRESS	TYPE	Responder	PIN
14556	2/12/2013	21	2514 E WASHINGTON ST	Check Well-Being	Police	2102427007
14557	2/12/2013	21	2514 E WASHINGTON ST	Check Well-Being	Police	2102427007
109615	11/4/2013	54	2514 E WASHINGTON ST	Check Well-Being	Police	2102427007
109616	11/4/2013	54	2514 E WASHINGTON ST	Check Well-Being	Police	2102427007

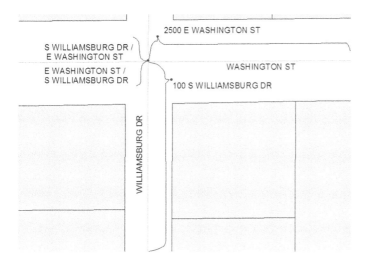

Figure B.2 Example of Intersection and Block Points.

For the 100 block of Williamsburg Dr, the total call time is 36 minutes. For the 2500 block of Washington St, it is 15 minutes.

Figure B.4 shows the way to allocate the call time for the 2500 block of Washington St to the adjacent parcels. A rather narrow buffer of 50 feet was used to locate only the parcels adjacent to the street and not so large as to include parcels in adjacent blocks. Table B.5 shows how the 15 minutes of call time were allocated to the adjacent parcels. While 15 minutes may seem minuscule, it is important to include all calls so that the city-wide results can be summarized and checked for accuracy, ensuring that nothing is omitted or double counted. Certainly, in other parts of the city, for other blocks, the amounts of time might be much greater.

IV Summarize All Call Time Allocated to Parcels

The last step in the process was to summarize all of the call minute data by parcel. Figure B.5 shows parcels within the example area and Table B.6 shows the totals by *PIN*. These were the numbers that were used to allocate the police expenditures to parcels. For Bloomington, police and fire/EMS calls were expressed as call equivalents rather than dealing with minutes. The average call time for police was about 47 minutes and 46 minutes for fire. Therefore, the call minutes for each parcel were divided by these averages to get call equivalents. For example, if the total minutes equaled 47 for police, the call equivalent was 1. If the call time was 60 minutes, the call equivalent was 1.2765. If the call time was 30 minutes, the equivalent was .63829. Table B.7 shows the call time as call equivalents.

Table B.2 Example of Public Safety Intersection Calls

SEQNO	DATE	MINUTES		INTERSECTION	SOURCE	TYPE
		POLICE	FIRE			
21634	3/6/2013	38		E WASHINGTON ST/N WILLIAMSBURG DR	Telephone	MVA
21635	3/6/2013	38		E WASHINGTON ST/N WILLIAMSBURG DR	Telephone	MVA
25932	3/21/2013	4		E WASHINGTON ST/N WILLIAMSBURG DR	Officer Initiated	TS
25933	3/21/2013	4		E WASHINGTON ST/N WILLIAMSBURG DR	Officer Initiated	TS
61725	6/27/2013	66		E WASHINGTON ST/N WILLIAMSBURG DR	911	MVA
97396	10/1/2013		34	E WASHINGTON ST/N WILLIAMSBURG DR	Telephone	GAS LEAK
121075	12/9/2013		38	E WASHINGTON ST/N WILLIAMSBURG DR	911	CHEST PAIN
121076	12/9/2013		38	E WASHINGTON ST/N WILLIAMSBURG DR	911	CHEST PAIN
121077	12/9/2013	16		E WASHINGTON ST/N WILLIAMSBURG DR	911	Assist
67507	7/12/2013	4		N WILLIAMSBURG DR/E WASHINGTON ST	Officer Initiated	TS
102695	10/16/2013	3		N WILLIAMSBURG DR/E WASHINGTON ST	Officer Initiated	TS
Total		173	110			

Table B.3 Call Time Allocated to Parcels within the Intersection Buffer

PIN	Acres	Percent of Acreage	Allocated Minutes	
			Police	Fire/EMS
2102428003	0.26974	0.97%	1.68	1.07
2102427002	0.49746	1.79%	3.1	1.97
2102428015	10.91195	39.34%	68.07	43.28
2102428001	0.32748	1.18%	2.04	1.3
2102428002	0.26974	0.97%	1.68	1.07
2102426008	0.28173	1.02%	1.76	1.12
2102431000	6.98763	25.20%	43.59	27.71
2102432000	0.91831	3.31%	5.73	3.64
2102426007	0.36186	1.30%	2.26	1.44
2102426009	0.27873	1.01%	1.74	1.11
2102427003	0.52365	1.89%	3.27	2.08
2102427001	0.54273	1.96%	3.39	2.15
2102404015	0.71475	2.58%	4.46	2.83
2102280004	0.69889	2.52%	4.36	2.77
2102404013	1.25675	4.53%	7.84	4.98
2102281000	2.89268	10.43%	18.04	11.47
Total	27.73408	100.00%	173	110

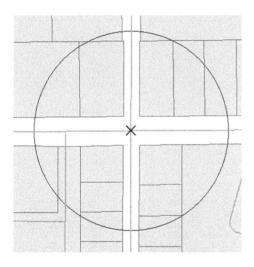

Figure B.3 Parcel Areas Within a 300-Foot Buffer of E WASHINGTON ST/S WILLIAMSBURG DR.

Table B.4 Examples of Public Safety Call Records Allocated to Blocks

SEQNO	DATE	MINUTES	ADDRESS	SOURCE	TYPE
60699	6/24/2013	8	100 S WILLIAMSBURG DR	Officer Initiated	XP
127724	12/31/2013	28	100 S WILLIAMSBURG DR	Telephone	911 Hang-up
Subtotal		36			
103245	10/17/2013	15	2500 E WASHINGTON ST	Telephone	911 Hang-up
Subtotal		15			

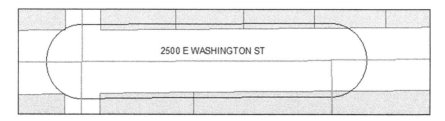

Figure B.4 Parcels Within a 50-Foot Buffer of the 2500 Block of Washington St.

Table B.5 Call Time Allocated to Parcels Within The Block Buffer

PIN	Acres	Percent of Acreage	Allocated Minutes	
			Police	Fire/EMS
2102427002	0.49746	5.27%	0.79	0
2102431000	6.98763	74.05%	11.11	0
2102426007	0.36186	3.83%	0.58	0
2102427003	0.52365	5.55%	0.83	0
2102427001	0.54273	5.75%	0.86	0
2102427004	0.52365	5.55%	0.83	0
Totals	9.43698	100.00%	15	0

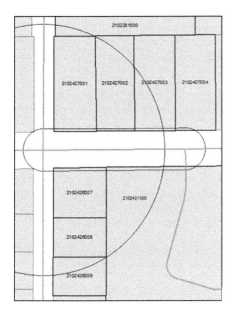

Figure B.5 Example of Allocating Intersection and Block Call Time to Parcels.

Table B.6 Summary of Police and Fire Call Minutes for the Example Parcels

	Calls to Addresses		Intersection Calls		Block Calls		Total Call Minutes	
PIN	Police	Fire	Police	Fire	Police	Fire	Police	Fire
2102427002	239	0	3.1	1.97	0.79	0	242.89	1.97
2102426008	0	0	1.76	1.12	0	0	1.76	1.12
2102431000	720	287	43.59	27.71	11.11	0	774.69	314.71
2102426007	0	0	2.26	1.44	0.58	0	2.83	1.44
2102426009	0	0	1.74	1.11	0	0	1.74	1.11
2102427003	0	0	3.27	2.08	0.83	0	4.1	2.08
2102427001	0	0	3.39	2.15	0.86	0	4.25	2.15
2102427004	45	0	0	0	0.83	0	45.83	0
2102281000	657	139	18.04	11.47	0	0	0	0
Totals	1661	426	77.14	49.05	15	0	1078.1	324.58

V Summary

Police and fire calls are typically the largest operating expenditure item in a city's budget. Therefore, it is essential that they be allocated to parcels as much as possible. In the case of Bloomington, IL, the task was simplified because the GIS department had worked to integrate the parcel address points and the police call points.

Table B.7 Police and Fire Call time Expressed as Call Equivalents

	Total Call Minutes		Total Call Equivalents	
PIN	Police	Fire	Police	Fire
2102427002	242.89	1.97	5.168	0.043
2102426008	1.76	1.12	0.037	0.024
2102431000	774.69	314.71	16.483	6.842
2102426007	2.83	1.44	0.06	0.031
2102426009	1.74	1.11	0.037	0.024
2102427003	4.1	2.08	0.087	0.045
2102427001	4.25	2.15	0.09	0.047
2102427004	45.83	0	0.975	0
2102281000	0	0	0	0
Totals	1,078.10	324.58	22.938	7.056

One should check with the police and fire departments to see what they may have done to process their records. One may find that they have done some of the work already.

Appendix C
Determining Local Road Frontage for Parcels

Road or street maintenance costs are typically the second or third largest expenditures for a city. These costs are part of the public works expenditures and need to be allocated to local roads and streets and then to the parcels that front on them based on the amount of frontage.

Often the assessor's file may have frontage measurements, but only for the street upon which the address is based. Parcels on corners actually have two frontages. As a result, the side-street frontage may be ignored if the assessor's numbers are used. Even if the assessor has accurate frontage measurements, the jurisdiction of the frontage may not be in the file. For fiscal analysis, the jurisdiction that maintains the road or street is needed to allocate the city maintenance costs. Locally maintained road frontage is needed, as opposed to county or state highways. Furthermore, if there are certain streets that the city maintains for which it receives state aid, frontage for the state-aid streets must also be known so that the revenue can be allocated. This type of street will be referred to as "Municipal Street Aid", or MSA streets.

There are several ways of measuring road or street frontage. The method described below seems to be the least time-consuming to accomplish fiscal impact analysis and was developed for a more recent project than the one for Bloomington, IL. The method shown here requires GIS skills to create and edit a right-of-way file and estimate the amount of local road frontage for each parcel. This method will also make it possible to allocate police and fire calls to blocks and intersections, which was described in Appendix B.

Before starting on creating a right-of-way file, check with your public works or streets departments and find out if they already have such a file. They may have already done this work for you. This chapter describes one way to create the right-of-way file, as well as to create a point file for intersections and a line file for blocks to be used to allocate public safety calls.

I Create a Right-of-Way (ROW) File

The assessor's parcel map typically consists of just the land parcels as polygons with empty spaces in between, which represent road rights-of-way.

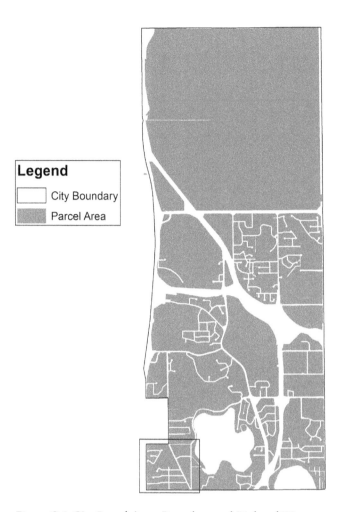

Figure C.1 City Parcel Area, Boundary and Right-of-Way.

If there is not already a GIS file available which has rights-of-way as polygons, one must be created. Figure C.1 shows the blank area between parcels that represents right-of-way, and the city boundary. Figure C.2 is an inset of a smaller area showing the detail.

The right-of-way file was created by using the GIS *Union* function to merge the city boundary file with the parcel file so that the blank spaces between the parcels can be converted to road polygons. Note that the blank right-of-way area was now a large polygon in the new file, along with the parcels, shown collectively as gray. An attribute was added to the GIS file named polytype. The row polygon was labeled "right of way" and the parcels labeled "parcel".

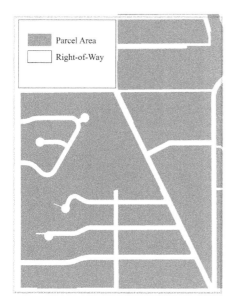

Figure C.2 Inset Area Showing Parcels and of Right-of-Way.

II Obtain a Centerline File

The next step was to obtain the road centerline GIS file which had attributes such as street name, jurisdiction and state-aid status. By selecting out only the shape that has "right of way" as the polytype, a separate shapefile was created. Figure C.3 in the color insert section shows the right-of-way polygon file and the road centerline file. The red centerlines were county roads. The blue centerlines were local roads that receive municipal street aid (MSA) funding toward their maintenance. The green roads were strictly local roads and are totally maintained and financed by the city.

III Edit the Right-of-Way Polygons

The next task was to edit the right of way polygon to separate the local, MSA and county rights- of-way from each other. This required some editing skills because the right-of-way polygon is very large and difficult to edit. In this example, the editing was done with ArcView 3.x, although ArcGIS could also have been used.

Figure C.4 in the color insert section shows an example of the edited right-of-way polygons that were created from the large, city-wide, right-of-way polygon. It is important that the editing be done as accurately as possible to ensure the most accurate frontage measurements. The highlighted lines in bold red show how the right-of-way polygon was split. The light green shaded rights-of-way were local, the light blue were MSA and the

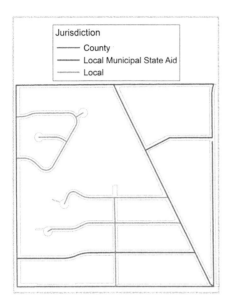

Figure C.3 Right-of-Way Polygon and Centerlines. (See Color Figure C.3 in the color insert section.)

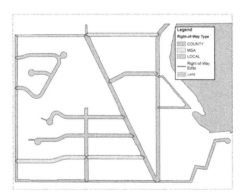

Figure C.4 Edited Right-of-Way Polygons. (See Color Figure C.4 in the color insert section.)

light red were county and state. At this point, attributes were added to the right-of-way polygons, indicating an ID, the type of right-of-way, and also road names for the county and state roads. While parcels that only front on county or state roads do not have locally maintained frontage, this information will be useful when allocating police and fire calls to streets, as was described previously. Table C.1 shows the attributes of the right-of-way polygons for the example area.

Table C.1 Example of Attribute Table for the Right-of-Way Polygons

ID	ROWTYPE	ROADNAME
2	COUNTY/STATE	CLEVELAND AVE
3	LOCAL	
4	MSA	
5	MSA	
6	LOCAL	
7	MSA	
8	LOCAL	
9	COUNTY/STATE	CLEVELAND AVE
10	LOCAL	
11	MSA	
12	COUNTY/STATE	LAKE JOHANNA
13	COUNTY/STATE	CLEVELAND AVE
14	COUNTY/STATE	COUNTY ROAD D
15	COUNTY/STATE	NEW BRIGHTON
16	COUNTY/STATE	LAKE JOHANNA
17	MSA	
18	COUNTY/STATE	NEW BRIGHTON

IV Buffer the Right-of-Way Polygons

The next step was to buffer around each right-of-way polygon using the GIS *buffer* tool. Up to this point, all of the processing had been in ArcView. For buffering, however, ArcGIS was used because the right-of-way attributes are preserved in the buffer file. Figure C.5 shows the result of a .5-foot buffer around the outside of each right-of-way polygon. The smaller the buffer, the more accurate the frontage measurement. The buffer file has the right-of-way type and road name as attributes. Figure C.5 is windowed in closely on a parcel that has both local frontage and MSA frontage.

V Union the Right-of-Way Buffer with Parcels

The next step was to use the GIS *union* function to join just the buffer file with the original parcel file. As a result of the union, parcel number 333023330046

Figure C.5 Example of a Parcel Located on a Corner and 0.5-Foot Buffers.

has been split into 3 parts: the body of the parcel and two narrow strips that are .5-foot-wide and have the designation of "Local" and "MSA".

VI Calculate the Road Frontage for Each Parcel

Next, the perimeter of each buffered parcel part was calculated. Since the buffer was so small, frontage can be estimated by subtracting .5 plus .5 from the perimeter, to allow for the buffer distance, and then dividing by two to get the approximate amount of frontage. In the case of parcels that are perfectly square, the estimate was very accurate. Small variations will be present in parcels that are on curves, corners or on cul-de-sacs, but the variance would be small. As stated earlier, the smaller the buffer distance, the more accurate the estimate. Table C.2 shows the results for the example parcel. It should be noted that the polygons for local and MSA actually overlap at the corner, giving the true perimeter and frontage estimate.

VII Add Frontage Measurements to a Parcel Base File

The last step was to put the road frontage measurements into a format that can be used to allocate road maintenance costs. Figure C.6 in the color insert section shows some examples of parcels with their road frontage polygons. The parcels have been selected because they front on more than one right-of-way type. Most parcels will have only one type. Table C.3 shows the measurements for the example parcels.

VIII Summarize Parcels by Individual Right-of-Way Type

Next, the records in the file were selected by each right-of-way type and summarized by PIN: one summary file for local, one file for MSA and one for county/state. The reason they are summarized by *PIN* is that in some rare cases a parcel may have more than one of the same type of ROW polygon with multiple frontages. These must eventually be summed. The results for this example are shown in Tables C.4, C.5 and C.6.

Table C.2 Estimated Local and MSA Frontage Compared to the Actual Measured Frontage for an Example Parcel

PARCELID	ROW Type	Buffer Distance in Feet	Perimeter in Feet	Estimated Frontage in Feet	Actual Measured Frontage	Difference
333023330046	MSA	0.5	170.996	84.998	85	−0.002
333023330046	Local	0.5	374.999	186.9995	187.03	−0.0305
333023330046	None	0	542.001	0		

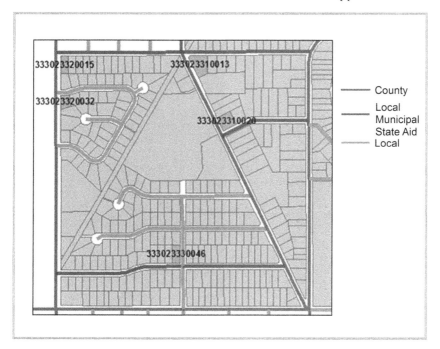

Figure C.6 Example of Selected Parcels Located on Corners with Different Street Jurisdictions. (See Color Figure C.6 in the color insert section.)

IX Add Road Frontage Measurements to the *Parcel_Factor* Shapefile

The last step was to add fields to the *Parcel_Factor* shapefile to store the frontage measurements. In this example, the fields were *MSA_FRTG, LOC_FRTG, CO_ST_FRTG, CO_ST_NAME* and *COST_ID* (Note: the last two fields were used for processing police and fire calls to streets). Then, each of the tables above was joined with the shapefile using the *PIN*. Table C.7 shows the results after the three join and the calculation operations for the five example parcels.

At this point, one will have the measurements needed to calculate the total amounts of local and MSA frontage to be used to calculate the road maintenance multiplier by dividing the amount spent on road maintenance by the total amount of local frontage. One will also have just the total amount of MSA frontage to calculate the revenue multiplier by dividing the amount of Municipal Street Aid by the MSA frontage.

X Intersections and Blocks

In the previous appendix on allocating police calls for intersections and blocks to adjacent parcels, the city of Bloomington already had a means of identifying them because of the GPS designations identifying them.

Table C.3 Examples of Selected Parcels and Their Right-of-Way Frontage Measurements

Parcel ID (PIN)	ROW Type	Road Name	Road ID	Buffer Distance in Feet	Perimeter in Feet	Calculated Frontage in Feet*
333023310013	COUNTY/STATE	NEW BRIGHTON	15	0.5	475.4	237
333023310013	MSA		17	0.5	391.3	195
333023310020	MSA		5	0.5	300.7	150
333023310020	COUNTY/STATE	NEW BRIGHTON	15	0.5	300.1	150
333023320015	COUNTY/STATE	CLEVELAND AVE	9	0.5	356.8	178
333023320015	MSA		4	0.5	152.6	76
333023320032	COUNTY/STATE	CLEVELAND AVE	2	0.5	286	142
333023320032	LOCAL		3	0.5	181.6	90
333023330046	MSA		7	0.5	171	85
333023330046	LOCAL		10	0.5	375	187

* Calculated Frontage = (Perimeter) minus (.5 +.5) divided by 2

Table C.4 Local Frontage by Parcel

Parcel ID (PIN)	ROW Type	Road Name	Road ID	Buffer Distance in Feet	Calculated Frontage in Feet
333023320032	LOCAL		3	0.5	90
333023330046	LOCAL		10	0.5	187

Table C.5 MSA Frontage by Parcel

Parcel ID (PIN)	ROW Type	Road Name	Road ID	Buffer Distance in Feet	Calculated Frontage in Feet
333023310013	MSA		17	0.5	195
333023310020	MSA		5	0.5	150
333023320015	MSA		4	0.5	76
333023330046	MSA		7	0.5	85

Table C.6 County/State Frontage by Parcel

Parcel ID (PIN)	ROW Type	Road Name	Road ID	Buffer Distance in Feet	Calculated Frontage in Feet
333023310013	COUNTY/ STATE	NEW BRIGHTON	15	0.5	237
333023310020	COUNTY/ STATE	NEW BRIGHTON	15	0.5	150
333023320015	COUNTY/ STATE	CLEVELAND AVE	9	0.5	178
333023320032	COUNTY/ STATE	CLEVELAND AVE	2	0.5	142

Table C.7 Example of Parcel File with Road Frontage Measurements

Parcel ID (PIN)	LOC_ FRTG	MSA_ FRTG	CO_ST_ FRTG	COST_NAME	CO_ST_ID
333023310013		195	237	NEW BRIGHTON	15
333023310020		150	150	NEW BRIGHTON	15
333023320015		76	178	CLEVELAND AVE	9
333023320032	90		142	CLEVELAND AVE	2
333023330046	187	85			

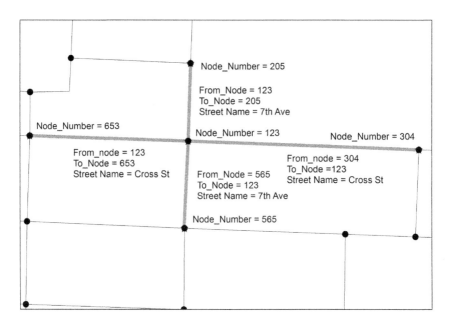

Figure C.7 Example of Centerline File, Intersecting Streets and Node Numbers.

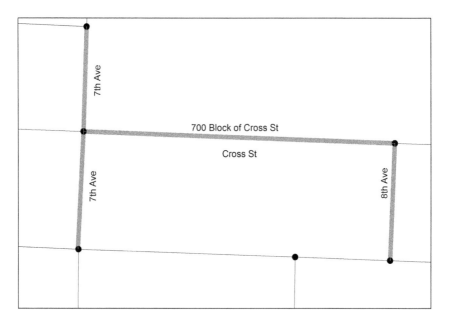

Figure C.8 Example of Using the Centerline File to Identify a Street Block and Number.

Without such a sophisticated police and fire geocoding system, shapefiles for intersections and blocks will need to be created.

A city will typically have a centerline file, containing the names of the streets and address ranges. Where streets meet one another, there are intersections. Each line or segment in the centerline shapefile, when processed with ArcInfo, will have a *from_node* and a *to_node*. Each node will have a unique identifier or node number. The file can be further processed to extract the node points with their unique node numbers. Where streets intersect, the *from_node* or *to_node* will be the same as the other intersecting streets, as shown in Figure C.7.

Note that the intersection of Cross St and 7th Ave has a node number of 123. The streets that intersect have either a *from_node* or a *to_node* that is 123. By processing the centerline file and the intersection file, node 123 can be given the name of "7th & Cross St". Police or fire calls to "7th & Cross St" can then be assigned to the node number, tabulated and then allocated to the surrounding parcels.

Based on the address ranges in the centerline file, blocks can also be identified and named. Figure C.8 shows the "700 Block of Cross St". Again, calls to the "700 Block of Cross St" can be assigned to that street segment, tabulated and then allocated to the parcels along that street.

XI Summary

This chapter has described how to create a right-of-way file to measure local road frontage so that the revenues and costs for maintaining local streets can be allocated to parcels.

The chapter also described how to create an intersection file and a city block file to locate police and fire calls that do not have addresses.

The method shown here requires GIS skills to create and edit a right-of-way file and estimate the amount of local road frontage for each parcel.

Remember to check with your public works or streets department first to see if they already have done some of this work for you.

It should also be noted that ArcGIS has tools for performing some of these tasks, but the author has not evaluated them.

Appendix D
Reconciling Census Blocks with Parcels

For purposes of estimating existing fiscal impacts using a Spatial Approach, knowing the estimated adult and school-aged population (SAP) by parcel, and thereby land use, is essential. Before being able to use census data for analysis, census geography, especially census blocks, must be reconciled with the parcels.

If one is lucky, the census block boundaries will coincide with parcel boundaries. But, in most cases, they will not. This appendix will describe how to identify and fix the errors. The census block file will probably need to be edited extensively so that the parcel points fall within the appropriate block. There may also be blocks with strange or ambiguous boundaries. These will need to be combined into larger blocks. A detailed description of how to download and process census shapefiles and data will be provided, as well as examples of errors one might find and how to correct them. ArcGIS models will be shown for some of the processing.

I Assemble and Edit Census Block Shapefiles

A Download State Census Block File

Obtain the latest census block shapefile. It is a *TIGER* file and can be found at:

https://www.census.gov/geo/maps-data/data/tiger-data.html. Figure D.1 shows the website page.

Select *Population and Housing Unit Counts*, then select the state and download it. The shapefile will include the population and housing unit counts as attributes.

This file will contain all of the blocks for the selected state, so one will need to select out the particular city. The file name will be something like *tabblock_2010_st_pophu.shp*, where *st* is the state number, e.g., 17 = IL (Illinois).

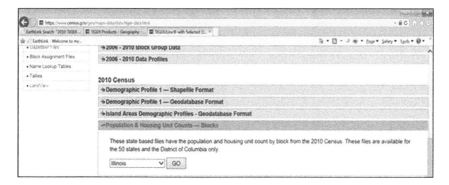

Figure D.1 Location of *TIGER* Polygon File of Census Blocks.

B Download County Subdivisions File

On the same page, shown above, another item is *Demographic Profile 1 - Shapefile Format*. Under this, one will see another shapefile that will be needed: *County Subdivisions*. Figure D.2 shows this website page. Also, download this file.

C Select City Census Blocks

The *County Subdivisions* file contains all county subdivisions for the entire country. To easily select just one's the city area, ArcGIS can simplify this task.

1.   Start a new map file (*MXD*) and name it *Census_Blocks*.

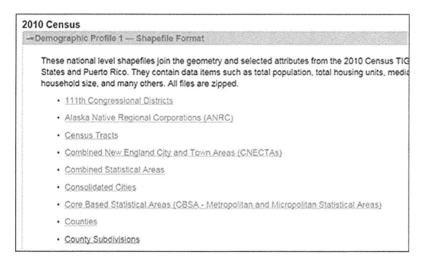

Figure D.2 Demographic Profile 1 Containing *County Subdivisions* Shapefile.

Figure D.3 Initial View of City Extent.

2.   Add the parcel file containing the parcel boundaries in the desired coordinate system (in this case, *Parcel_Factor*).

This will create a view that shows the extent of the city and will be in the desired coordinate system. This is very important.
   Your view should look like Figure D.3.

3.   Add the *County Subdivisions* shapefile to the view. Since it is a file covering the whole nation, only the part within the extent of the city will show up on top of the parcel file. An outline of the city will be seen, as shown in Figure D.4.

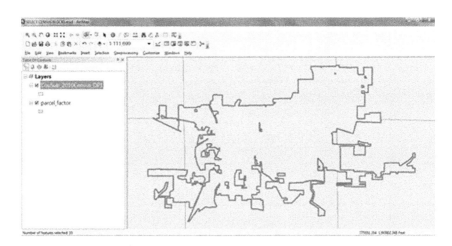

Figure D.4 Selected Polygon of City Boundary from *County Subdivisions* Shapefile, City of Bloomington, IL.

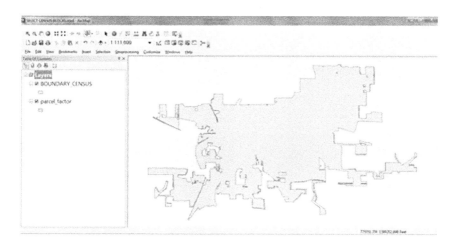

Figure D.5 BOUNDARY_CENSUS Shapefile.

4. Select the city boundary shape.
5. Save the selected polygon and save it as a *BOUNDARY_CENSUS* shapefile, as shown in Figure D.5. For simplicity, remove the *CouSub_2010Census_DP1* shapefile from the view.
6. Add the state census block map to the view: *tabblock2010_st_pophu*. While the file is for the entire state, only the blocks within the extent of the city boundary will be visible. One now can use the *BOUNDARY_ CENSUS* file to select only the blocks for the city from the state file. Figure D.6 below shows the statewide block file overlaid by the *BOUNDARY_CENSUS* shapefile.

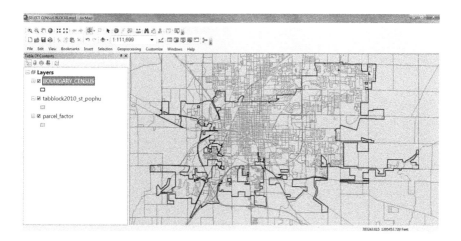

Figure D.6 Boundary and Illinois Census Block Polygons, City of Bloomington, IL.

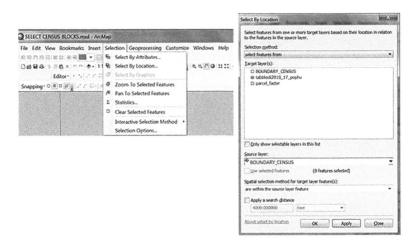

Figure D.7 Select by Location Tool: Selecting Bloomington's Census Blocks from Illinois Census Blocks Using the *BOUNDARY_CENSUS* Shapefile.

7. Using the *BOUNDARY_CENSUS* file, select the city's census blocks by using *Select by Location*, found under the item *Selection* on the top menu bar. Make sure you select *are within the source layer feature.* Figure D.7 shows the dialog boxes to accomplish this. The selected blocks will be highlighted as shown in Figure D.8.

8. Save the selected blocks as *ORIGINAL_BLOCKS*. For simplicity, remove *tabblock2010_17_pophu* from the view. Your view should look like Figure D.9.

At this point, one will have a preliminary census block file for Bloomington (or one's city) with the attributes of *POP10* and *HOUSING10*. The shapefile

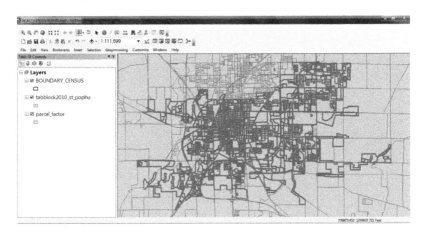

Figure D.8 Boundary and Illinois Census Block Polygons, City of Bloomington, IL.

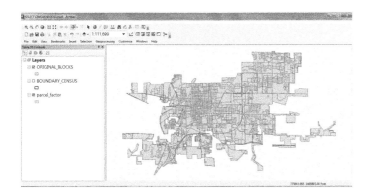

Figure D.9 *BOUNDARY_CENSUS* and *ORIGINAL_BLOCKS* Shapefiles, City of Bloomington, IL.

is still preliminary because there will probably be a lot of spatial errors when comparing census blocks to parcels.

9. Verify the housing and population counts for the city.

    1. Add a field named *SHP* to the *ORIGINAL_BLOCKS* file.
    2. Calculate *SHP* = 1.
    3. Summarize the fields *POP10* and *HOUSING10* on the *SHP* field.

    Figure D.10 shows a model that accomplishes these tasks.

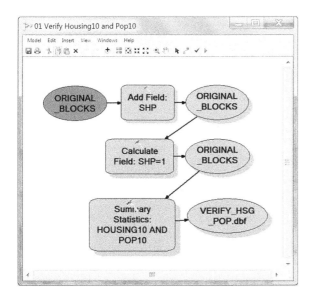

Figure D.10 Model to Summarize Census Statistics.

FID	Shape	STATEFP10	COUNTYFP10	TRACTCE10	BLOCKCE	BLOCKID10	PARTFLG	HOUSING10	POP10	SHP
0	Polygon	17	113	001106	1004	171130011061004	N	0	0	1
1	Polygon	17	113	001302	1006	171130013021006	N	14	132	1
2	Polygon	17	113	001301	2031	171130013012031	N	32	75	1
3	Polygon	17	113	005400	1036	171130054001036	N	0	0	1
4	Polygon	17	113	000302	3082	171130003023082	N	0	0	1

(0 out of 1744 Selected)

ORIGINAL_BLOCKS

Figure D.11 Example of *ORIGINAL_BLOCKS* Attribute File.

Verify that the sums are equal to known census counts for the city. Figure D.11 shows some sample records from the *ORIGINAL_BLOCKS* file.

II Edit Census Block Boundaries and Revise Block Numbers

In order for census data to be used with the parcel data, the block boundaries need to be edited so that they conform to parcel boundaries. The main objective is to make sure that a parcel point file, when overlaid, falls into the correct census block.

A. Create a file named *EDITED BLOCKS* by copying the *ORIGINAL_ BLOCK* file.
B. Add the field *REVBLK10* to store block numbers for blocks that need to be merged due to errors in the census shapefile. Figure D.12 shows a model to accomplish these tasks.
C. Edit the *EDITED BLOCKS* file as needed by changing the shapes and/ or specifying which blocks need to be merged. This will probably be the most time-consuming task, but it will be well worth the effort.

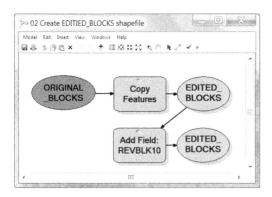

Figure D.12 Model to Create an *EDITED_BLOCKS* File with a *REVBLK10* Field.

There are ways to use ArcGIS to flag census block errors by intersecting parcel boundaries and block boundaries. Then, one would summarize the resulting file on the *PIN* number and select the parcels that are split by the blocks and would thus have a frequency of more than 1. The selected polygons would be saved in a file named *BLOCK_ERRORS*, as described below.

1. Create a simplified version of the parcel file (POPCALC)

The parcel file (*PARCEL_FACTOR*) that was used to identify the city's location in the national county subdivision file probably contains a lot of fields that are not needed for editing or estimating population. To create a simplified file, copy the parcel to another file named *POPCALC* and then delete the fields that are not needed. For Bloomington, the land use fields (*LUSE0, LUSE1, LUSE1B, LUSE2* and *LUSE3*) were retained, along with *ACRES*, parcel identification number (*PIN*), building square feet (*BLDSQFT*), lot square feet (*LOT_SQFT*), year built (*YBBUILT*), assessor's unit counts (*ASSR_UNITS*) and number of bedrooms (*NO_BDRMS*). Figure D.13 shows a model to accomplish this task.

2. Intersect the ORIGINAL BLOCKS file and POPCALC to create BLOCK_PARCEL and BLOCK_ERRORS shapefiles

Intersecting the *ORIGINAL BLOCKS* and *POPCALC* shapefiles will help to identify block errors. The file named *BLOCK_PARCEL* can be summarized on the *PIN*, creating a database file named *PARCEL_SPLITS*. This summary file can then be joined back with the *BLOCK_PARCEL* file on the

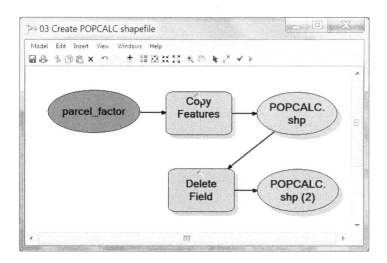

Figure D.13 Model to Create the *POPCALC* File.

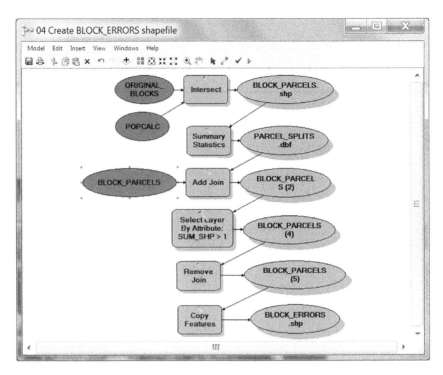

Figure D.14 Model to Create *BLOCK_PARCELS* and *BLOCK_ERRORS* Shapefiles.

PIN and then the polygons can be selected that have a count of more than 1. The selected polygons will identify areas where parcels have been split by the block boundaries. Figure D.14 shows a model to accomplish these tasks.

Figure D.15 shows the block boundary errors in dark gray (*BLOCK_ ERRORS*). This method will produce a bunch of "false errors", where only a tiny bit of a parcel may be intersected but they will be visually obvious and can be quickly discarded.

3. Create a parcel point file: POPCALC_POINT

The way that census blocks can be accurately assigned to parcels is that the parcel points must fall within the correct census block. To consider this when editing block boundaries, a parcel point file named *POPCALC_ POINT* must be created. It is not necessary to have all the block boundaries exactly coincide with the parcel boundaries. It is only necessary that the parcel points fall within the correct block. However, if one has the staff time available, all of the errors could be corrected, even the minor ones. Figure D.16 shows a model to create the *POPCALC_POINT* shapefile.

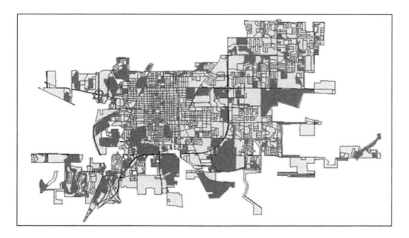

Figure D.15 Map Showing *BLOCK_ERRORS.*

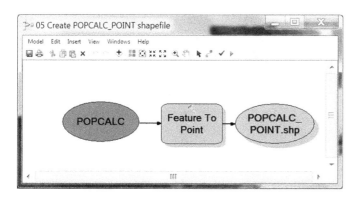

Figure D.16 Model to Create the *POPCALC_POINT* Shapefile.

4. Correct block boundary errors

Figure D.17 shows an example of a block boundary error. The *BLOCK_ ERRORS* are shown in a light gray, the *ORIGINAL_BLOCKS* boundary is shown in a medium gray and the corrected boundary in black. With the block boundary corrected, the parcel points will fall within the appropriate block when assigning block numbers to parcels.

5. Identify ambiguous block boundaries and provide a revised block number in the *REVBLK10* field

Where block boundaries are ambiguous, combine blocks by assigning a new, revised block number to each group of blocks. Figure D.18, below, provides an example of ambiguous blocks.

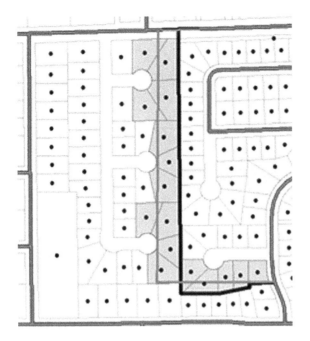

Figure D.17 Example of Census Block Boundary Error before and after Correction.

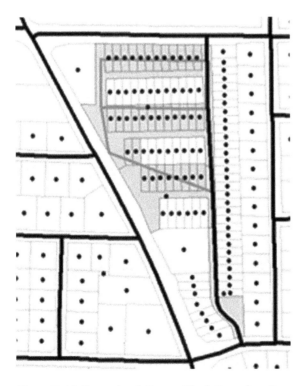

Figure D.18 Example of Census Block Boundary Error and New Combined Block Boundary.

Table

EDITED_BLOCKS

OID	STATEFP10	COUNTYFP10	TRACTCE10	BLOCKCE	BLOCKID10	PARTFLG	HOUSING10	POP10	REVBLK10	SHP
0	17	113	005800	3020	171130058003020	N	18	27	171130058003020	1
1	17	113	005800	3018	171130058003018	N	24	49	171130058003020	1
2	17	113	005800	3019	171130058003019	N	26	55	171130058003020	1

1 (0 out of 3 Selected)

EDITED BLOCKS

Figure D.19 Example of Records for Three Census Blocks with Ambiguous Borders that Will Be Dissolved into a Single Block.

The original block boundary is shown in gray. Rather than guess at the correct boundaries, the three blocks were given the same block number under the field *REVBLK10,* as shown in Figure D.19. Later the three blocks were combined by dissolving on the *REVBLK10* field and the boundary will be as shown in black.

The *EDITED_BLOCKS* file should have the original block numbers in one field (*BLOCKID10*) and a revised block number (*REVBLK10*) in another field. In this instance, the three blocks involved have been given a block number in the *REVBLK10* field equal to one of the original block numbers. Doing this will make sure that one will not duplicate any other block numbers and will be the most convenient way of editing. When summarized in either field, the results should be the known population and housing unit counts for the city. Once all the editing was done, the *EDITED_BLOCKS* file was dissolved on the *REVBLK10* field and the housing and population numbers were also summarized.

As stated previously, this will be the most tedious part of this exercise but, once the block boundaries have been edited, there will be a much better block file for future GIS applications, beyond just this one.

This would be a good task for a GIS technician or planning intern.

III Summary

In order for one to use the detailed block statistics from the census in combination with the parcels, the census block file will probably need to be edited extensively so that the parcels fall within the appropriate block or the census blocks will need to be combined where they are ambiguous. While this will be a somewhat tedious task, it will be an investment that will not only be useful for measuring fiscal impact, but also for other uses of census data in the future. It would be a good project for a GIS technician or intern.

Appendix E
Using Census Data to Estimate Adult and School-Age Population by Parcel

Census data contains housing and population counts by block. But, when using this data, the analyst does not know what land uses are in the block and the different housing types. For purposes of estimating existing fiscal impacts using a Spatial Approach, knowing the estimated adult and school-aged populations by parcel, and thereby land use, is essential. While the Spatial Method is not a "Per Capita" approach, population is an important component, as are police and fire/EMS calls, road frontage and building market value. This appendix will provide instructions on estimating demographic data at the parcel level. The examples are for the city of Bloomington, IL, using the 2010 census data. Since the project was for fiscal impact in 2013, examples of how to update it to 2013 are also provided. The process should be equally applicable to the 2020 (or 2030) census and any year that follows.

The redistricting file contains key demographic items at the block level that are needed to allocate population and school-aged population (*SAP*) to parcels: population and voter-age population (*VAP*) over 18 years. There are also other block-level files that are available for housing units and population in group quarters. Unfortunately, there is no one single file containing all of these attributes, so one must be created by accessing and then creating a file with all of these attributes that then can be compared to the land parcels in the blocks.

This section describes a way to go about creating a single data file with these attributes, and then, how to allocate housing units, population and school-aged children to parcels. There are two parts to this process. The first is to download and combine the demographic data needed by census block. The second part will deal with refining the assessor's housing unit counts and estimating adult and school-aged population by parcel. Models created using ArcGIS Model Builder are provided to suggest ways in which the tasks can be accomplished.

I Locate and Join Other Data to the *EDITED_BLOCKS* File

Appendix D showed how to download and create a block boundary shapefile named *EDITED_BLOCKS*. It also showed how to correct the block boundary file by editing the shapes or combining blocks that are ambiguous in relation to the parcel file. The first step in locating the census block data needed to allocate adult and student populations to parcels is to download the data and join it with the *EDITED_BLOCKS* shapefile. This section will describe how to do it for the 2010 census. For future censuses, the process should be similar.

A Download Basic Demographic Data

The first thing to be done is to download the Redistricting and Group Quarters files. The redistricting file will provide data on the under-age-18 population and the group quarters will identify blocks where people do not live in traditional housing units, which is important to accurately estimate both populations in, and not in, housing units. Both files can be found in the following location as illustrated in Figure E.1: https://www2.census.gov/census_2010/.

The basic data that are needed can be found in the *01-Redistricting_File* and *02-Advance_Group_Quarters*. The initial work will be done in Excel, creating the tab-delimited files that can be brought into and used in ArcGIS.

Other data on population under the age of 20, by year, is also available in *04-Summary_File_1*, if one wants to break down the *SAP* by age year and by block. However, it will not be discussed here, to keep things simple.

1 Obtain VAP data

The redistricting file contains total population counts for the block (*POP10*), plus counts of the *VAP*, which is the population aged 18 and over.

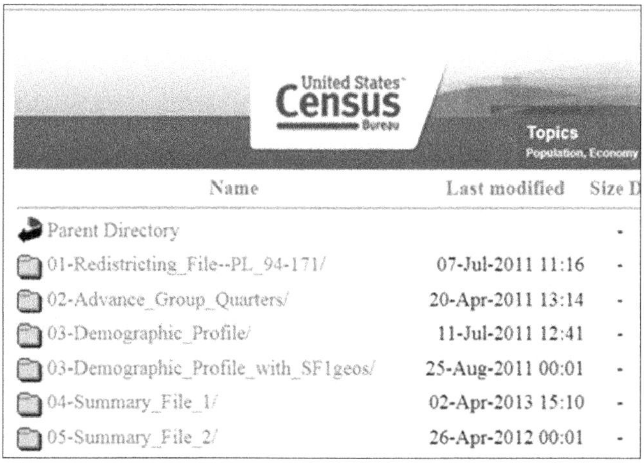

Name	Last modified	Size D
Parent Directory		-
01-Redistricting_File--PL_94-171/	07-Jul-2011 11:16	-
02-Advance_Group_Quarters/	20-Apr-2011 13:14	-
03-Demographic_Profile/	11-Jul-2011 12:41	-
03-Demographic_Profile_with_SF1geos/	25-Aug-2011 00:01	-
04-Summary_File_1/	02-Apr-2013 15:10	-
05-Summary_File_2/	26-Apr-2012 00:01	-

Figure E.1 Census File Selection Screen.

Subtracting the *VAP* from the total population will result in the age 0–17 population by block. Adjustments will be made to estimate the age 5–18 population, as described later. The *EDITED_BLOCKS* file already has the population counts, along with housing unit counts by block. The objective here is to get the *VAP*. Go to https://www2.census.gov/census_2010/, select *01-Redistricting_File—PL_94-171/* and then select the state to download the data. For Illinois, the file was named *17_REDIST_DATA.zip* and unzips to *17_REDIST_DATA.CSV*.

a   Create an ArcGIS Map (*MXD*)
      Assembling the redistricting and group quarters will initially use Excel to extract the data and ArcGIS will be used to assemble it into the desired data file. To be imported into ArcGIS, the redistricting file will need to be saved as a tab-delimited text file: *17_REDIST_DATA. TXT*.
b   Open ArcGIS and save the map as *POP_HSG_ALLOCATION.MXD*.
c   Add *17_REDIST_DATA.TXT* to the ArcGIS project and save it as a dbf file (*17_REDIST_DATA.DBF*).
d   Add the *EDITED_BLOCKS* file that was created in Appendix D.
e   Add *BLOCKID10* to the redistricting file.

For some reason, the block identifier does not import into the file properly, so, using ArcGIS, one will have to create a text field named *BLOCKID10* with a length of 15. Then, use the expression (((((*[STATE]* *1000) + *[COUNTY]*) *1000000) + *[TRACT]*)*10000) + *[BLOCK]* to calculate the value. The following model shows this step (Figure E.2).

f   Add the *VAP* to *EDITED_BLOCKS* file.
g   Add the *VAP* field to the *EDITED_BLOCKS* file.

2 *Join the redistricting file to the EDITED_BLOCKS*

Join the redistricting file (*17_REDIST_DATA.DBF*) to the *EDITED_ BLOCKS* file by *BLOCKID10*. Select the matching records. Calculate *VAP* to be equal to *17_REDIST_DATA.VAP*. Then, remove the join. The model to do this is shown in Figure E.3.

3 *Obtain data on population in group quarters*

Data on group quarters population is needed to be able to subtract it from the total population in the block to derive the remaining population to be allocated to parcels based on housing units.

      Group Quarters data can also be found at: https://www2.census. gov/census_2010/. The files are under the heading *02-Advance_Group_ Quarters/*.

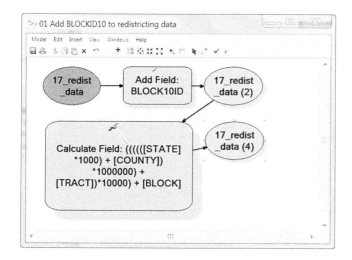

Figure E.2 Model to Add *BLOCKID10* to Redistricting Data.

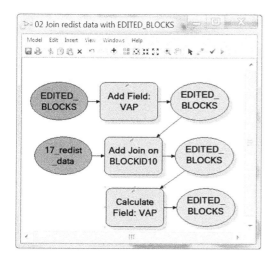

Figure E.3 Model to Join Redistricting Data to *EDITED_BLOCKS*.

a   Select your state, download and unzip it.

For Illinois, the zip file name was *il2010.sgq.zip*. After unzipping you will see two files *ilgeo2010.sgq* and *il000012010.sgq*. The "geo" file will have the geographic information and the other will contain the actual data.

b   Process the geographic header file.

Figure 2-4.
Geographic Header Record

Field	Data dictionary reference	Field size	Starting position	Data type	Summary level 040	050	140	750
RECORD CODES								
File Identification	FILEID	6	1	A/N	X	X	X	X
State/U.S. Abbreviation (USPS)	STUSAB	2	7	A	X	X	X	X
Summary Level	SUMLEV	3	9	A/N	X	X	X	X
Geographic Component	GEOCOMP	2	12	A/N	X	X	X	X
Characteristic Iteration	CHARITER	3	14	A/N	X	X	X	X
Characteristic Iteration File Sequence Number	CIFSN	2	17	A/N	X	X	X	X
Logical Record Number	LOGRECNO	7	19	N	X	X	X	X
GEOGRAPHIC AREA CODES								
Region	REGION	1	26	A/N	X	X	X	X
Division	DIVISION	1	27	A/N	X	X	X	X
State (FIPS)	STATE	2	28	A/N	X	X	X	X
County	COUNTY	3	30	A/N		X	X	X
FIPS County Class Code	COUNTYCC	2	33	A/N		X	X	X
County Size Code	COUNTYSC	2	35	A/N				
County Subdivision (FIPS)	COUSUB	5	37	A/N				X
FIPS County Subdivision Class Code	COUSUBCC	2	42	A/N				X
County Subdivision Size Code	COUSUBSC	2	44	A/N				
Place (FIPS)	PLACE	5	46	A/N				X
FIPS Place Class Code	PLACECC	2	51	A/N				X
Place Size Code	PLACESC	2	53	A/N				
Census Tract	TRACT	6	55	A/N			X	X
Block Group	BLKGRP	1	61	A/N				X
Block	BLOCK	4	62	A/N				X

Figure E.4 Layout Specifications for the Geographic Header File.

Unfortunately, one will have to deal with a flat *ASCII* file to process the geographic header. The geo-file has the format shown in Figure E.4. One needs to rename *ilgeo2010.sgq* to *ilgeo2010sgq.txt* and then open the text file in Excel. It has a fixed width, so one will need to specify the fields based on their position. Figure E.5 shows the dialog box in Excel for defining the fields by length.

After the file is created, the field names can be added to the columns, also as shown in Table E.1.

The field *LOGRECNO* will be the way to link the geographic file to the data file. Once created, delete the fields that are not needed: *MISC1, REG, DIV, MISC2* and *MISC3*. Afterward, the file should look like the following. Save it as a tab-delimited file to open in ArcGIS: *ILGEO2010GQ.TXT*.

c   Create the *BLOCKID10* field using ArcGIS.

After opening *ILGEO2010GQ.TXT* in ArcGIS and then exporting it into a dbf file (*ILGEO2010GQ.DBF*), one needs to add and calculate the *BLOCKID10* field because, for some reason, the block identifier does not import into the geographic file properly. Add a field named *BLOCKID10* as text, with a length of 15. Then use the expression (((((([ST] *1000) + [CO]) *1000000) + [TRACT])*10000) + [BLOCK]. Also, add a short field named *DBF* and calculate it to a value of 1. This will be used later when summarizing the data.

d   Process the data file.

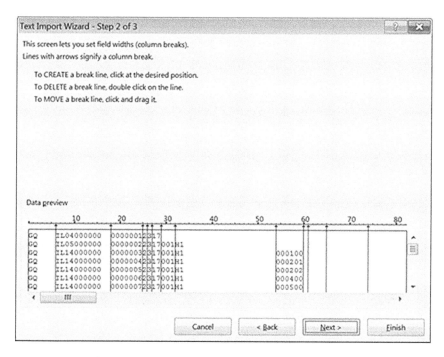

Figure E.5 Excel Text Import Wizard to Define Fields by Length.

The data file, named *il000012010.sgq*, will need to be renamed *il000012010sgq.txt*. Fortunately, it is not a flat *ASCII* file and it can be opened directly in Excel as a comma delimited file.

After opening the file, insert a top row for the field names. The File Linking Fields, shown in Figure E.8, should be used for the field names: *FILEID, STUSAB, CHARITER, CIFSN* and *LOGRECNO*.

Table E.1 Fields for the Geographic Header File

Columns	Description	Field Name
1–6	File ID	FILEID
7–18	State and Other Miscellaneous Data	MISC1
19–25	Logical Record Number	LOGRECNO
26	Region	REG
27	Division	DIV
28–29	State	ST
30–32	County	CO
33–54	Miscellaneous Data	MISC2
55–60	Tract	TRACT
61	Block Group	BG
62–65	Block	BLOCK
65–477	Miscellaneous Data	MISC3

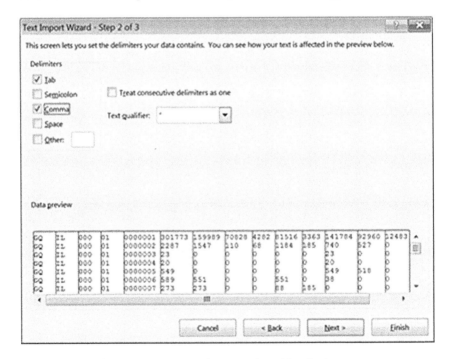

A	B	C	D	E	F	G
1 FILEID	LOGRECNO ST	CO	TRACT	BG	BLOCK	
22 GQ	21	17	1	10200	4	4009
23 GQ	22	17	1	10200	4	4010
24 GQ	23	17	1	10200	4	4011
25 GQ	24	17	1	10200	4	4012
26 GQ	25	17	1	10200	4	4013
27 GQ	26	17	1	10200	4	4014
28 GQ	27	17	1	10200	4	4015

Figure E.6 Example Records in the Geographic Header file.

The remainder of the fields contain the group quarters data, as listed under "Group Quarters Population by Group Quarters Type". To make them more meaningful, use the names listed below in Table E.2 when adding field names. The fields *STUSAB, CHARITER* and *CIFSN* are not needed and can be deleted. The important field is *LOGRECNO*. Figure E.9 shows a sample of what the table should look like. Save the file as a tab-delimited text file that can be opened in ArcGIS, named *IL2010GQ.TXT*.

Figure E.7 Excel Text Import Wizard to Specify Field Delimiters.

Table number	Table contents	Data dictionary reference name	Seg-ment	Max size

File 01—File Linking Fields (comma delimited). These fields link File 01 with the geographic header.

Field name	Data dictionary reference name	Max size	Data type
File Identification	FILEID	6	A/N
State/U.S. Abbreviation (USPS)	STUSAB	2	A
Characteristic Iteration	CHARITER	3	A/N
Characteristic Iteration File Sequence Number	CIFSN	2	A/N
Logical Record Number	LOGRECNO	7	N

P42.	GROUP QUARTERS POPULATION BY GROUP QUARTERS TYPE [10]			
	Universe: Population in group quarters			
	Total:	p0420001	01	9
	Institutionalized population (101–106, 201–203, 301, 401–405):	p0420002	01	9
	Correctional facilities for adults (101–106)	p0420003	01	9
	Juvenile facilities (201–203)	p0420004	01	9
	Nursing facilities/Skilled-nursing facilities (301)	p0420005	01	9
	Other institutional facilities (401–405)	p0420006	01	9
	Noninstitutionalized population (501, 601–602, 701–702, 704, 706, 801–802, 900–901, 903–904):	p0420007	01	9
	College/University student housing (501)	p0420008	01	9
	Military quarters (601–602)	p0420009	01	9
	Other noninstitutional facilities (701–702, 704, 706, 801–802, 900–901, 903–904)	p0420010	01	9

Figure E.8 Census Fields for the Group Quarters Data File.

e   Open the file in ArcGIS and join the header file to the data file.

Open the group quarters data file, *IL2010GQ.txt* and then save it as *IL2010GQ.dbf.*

Next, the two dbf files, *ILGEO2010* and *IL2010GQ*, can be joined on *LOGRECNO* and saved with an appropriate name, such as

Table E.2 Fields for the Group Quarters Data

Census Field	Descriptive Field	Description
P420001	POPGQ	Number in Group Quarters (Total)
P420002	INST	Number in Institutions (Subtotal)
P420003	CORRF	Number in Correctional Facilities
P420004	JUVF	Number in Juvenile Facilities
P420005	NURS	Number in Nursing Homes
P420006	OTHINST	Number in Other Institutions
P420007	NONINS	Number in Non-Institutional Housing (Subtotal)
P420008	COLL_U	Number in Colleges and Universities
P420009	MIL	Number in Military
P420010	OTHERNON	Number in Other Non-Institutional Housing

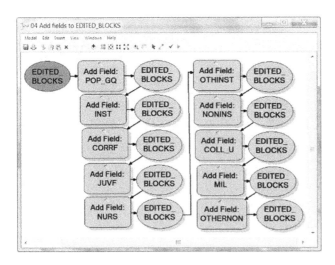

Figure E.9 Example Records from the Group Quarters Data File.

ILLINOIS_GROUP_QUARTERS. Redundant fields can also be deleted, such as *OID_1, LOGRECNO_1* and *FILEID_1.*

f   Add group quarters fields to the *EDITED_BLOCKS* shapefile.

Add group quarters text fields to *EDITED_BLOCKS: POPGQ, INST, CORRF, JUVF, NURS, OTHINST, NONINS, COLL_U, MIL* and *OTHERNON.* Figure E.10 shows the model to do this.

At this point, the *ILLINOIS_GROUP_QUARTERS* file will still contain the data for all blocks in the state. To select out only the data for the city, join the state file to the *EDITED_BLOCKS* file on *BLOCKID10.*

Figure E.10 Model to Add Group Quarters Fields to *EDITED_BLOCKS.*

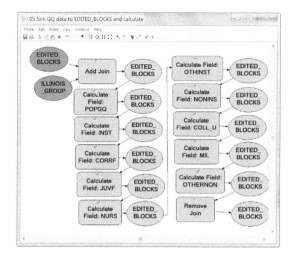

Figure E.11 Model to Join and Calculate the Group Quarters Fields.

Calculate the group quarters fields in *EDITED_BLOCKS*. Remove the join. Figure E.11 shows the model to do this.

B Dissolve the *EDITED_BLOCKS* file to create a *NEW_BLOCKS* file

Since one probably has had to make edits to the *EDITED_BLOCKS* file, by combining blocks, the next step is to create a *NEW_BLOCKS* shapefile by dissolving the blocks that need to be combined. Figure E.12 shows the model to do this.

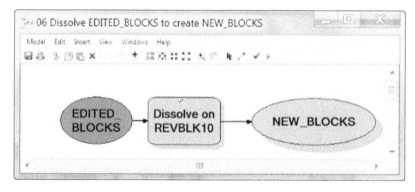

Figure E.12 Model to Dissolve *EDITED_BLOCKS* to Create the *NEW_BLOCKS* Shapefile.

Figure E.13 Dialog Box to Specify Fields to be Summarized.

Figure E.13 shows part of the dialog box where one specifies the fields to be summarized in the *NEW_BLOCKS* shapefile. This will result in fields named *SUM_POP10, SUM_VAP*, etc. Some names will be truncated, like *SUM_HOUSIN*, due to length limitations.

An example of records in the *NEW_BLOCKS* attribute file is provided in Figure E.14.

II Allocate Housing Units and Adult and School-Aged Populations to Parcels

A *Add Fields to the Parcel file*

The process for allocating housing units and adult and school populations will require variables to hold the calculations. Table E.3 lists all the fields that are needed. One can add all the fields at once, or in stages. They are all presented here to serve as a reference and a data dictionary as one goes through the process of calculating the results.

FID	Shape	REVBLK10	SUM_HOUSIN	SUM_POP10	SUM_VAP	SUM_POP_GQ	SUM_INST	SUM_CORRF	SUM_JUVF	SUM_NURS	SUM_OTHINS	SUM_NONIN	SUM_COLL_U	SUM_MIL	SUM_OTHERN
0	Polygon	171130003013014	0	0	0	0	0	0	0	0	0	0	0	0	0
1	Polygon	171130003013019	0	0	0	0	0	0	0	0	0	0	0	0	0
2	Polygon	171130003023045	429	810	517	0	0	0	0	0	0	0	0	0	0
3	Polygon	171130003023046	0	0	0	0	0	0	0	0	0	0	0	0	0
4	Polygon	171130003023047	0	0	0	0	0	0	0	0	0	0	0	0	0
5	Polygon	171130003023048	0	0	0	0	0	0	0	0	0	0	0	0	0
6	Polygon	171130003023049	24	40	31	0	0	0	0	0	0	0	0	0	0
7	Polygon	171130003023053	0	0	0	0	0	0	0	0	0	0	0	0	0
8	Polygon	171130003023054	0	0	0	0	0	0	0	0	0	0	0	0	0
9	Polygon	171130003023065	0	0	0	0	0	0	0	0	0	0	0	0	0
10	Polygon	171130003023072	0	0	0	0	0	0	0	0	0	0	0	0	0

Figure E.14 Example Records in the *NEW_BLOCKS* Attribute File.

Table E.3 Fields to be Added to the Parcel File

Census Data Fields:

REVBLK10	revised block number (text)
TPOP10	Census population count in the block (short integer)
THSG10	Census housing unit count in the block (short integer)
TVAP	Census voting-age population count in the block (short integer)
TPOPGQ	Census total population in group quarters in the block (short integer)
TINST	Census total institutionalized population in the block (short integer)
TCORRF	Census total population in correctional facilities in the block (short integer)
TJUVF	Census total population in juvenile facilities in the block (short integer)
TNURS	Census total population in nursing homes in the block (short integer)
TOTHINST	Census total population in other institutional facilities in the block (short integer)
TNONINS	Census total non-institutionalized population in the block (short integer)
TCOLL_U	Census total population in colleges and universities in the block (short integer)
TMIL	Census total population in the military in the block (short integer)
TOTHERNON	Census total population in other non-institutions in the block (short integer)

Housing Fields:

RESHSG10	Field to select all residential parcels with a YRBUILT < 2010 (short integer = 1)
ASSR_HSG	Backup field to hold assessor's housing counts – ASSR_UNITS (short integer)
NEWASSRHSG	Assessor's unit count by parcel, as corrected (short integer)
NEWCENHSG	Revised census housing block counts, due to errors (short integer)
SUM_HSGBLK	Sum of NEWASSRHSG by block (short integer)
DIF_HSG	Difference between census housing totals (THSG10) and SUM_HSGBLK (short integer)
ADJ_HSG	Adjustment factor for small differences by block (float)
ADJ_HSG2	Final adjustment based on census total housing unit count (float)
COMMENT	A field to note errors or inconsistencies (text)
FINALHSG10	Final housing estimate by parcel (float)
ERR_CENHSG	Difference between THSG10 and FINALHSG10 (float)
CORRCENERR	Census housing error multiplier: FINALHSG10 / THSG10

Group Quarters Allocation Field:

ALLOC_GQ	Allocated group quarters population for parcel (short integer)

Population Allocation Fields:

CLASS10	Classification of residential units in 2010 (text)
CLASS13	Classification of residential units in 2013 (text)
POPHU	Starting population per housing unit (float)

(Continued)

Table E.3 (Continued)

OLDCENPOP	Original census population: equals TPOP10
NEWCENPOP	Adjusted census population based on housing error: OLDCENPOP * CORCENERR
CALC_POP	Calculated population for parcel (float)
TCALC_POP	Total calculated population for block (float)
DIFCALCPOP	TNET_POP minus TCALC_POP (float)
ADJPOP10	Preliminary adjustment percentage (float)
PRE_POP10	Preliminary population in parcel (float)
ADJPOP10B	Final adjustment percentage (float)
PARC_POP10	Total allocated population for parcel (float)
ERRCENPOP	Difference between original census population and adjusted for evaluating: NEWCENPOP - OLDCENPOP

School-Aged Population Fields:

OLDCENVAP	Original census voting-age population: VAP10
NEWCENVAP	Adjusted voting-age population based on housing error: OLDCENVAP * CORCENERR
POP_0_17	Adjusted population aged 0–17 (float)
POP_0_4	Estimated population under the age of 5 (float)
POP_18	Estimated population aged 18 (float)
POP_5_18	Estimated population 5–18 (float)
PROP_SAP	Proportion school-aged population in the block (float)
SAP	Probable school-aged population in the parcel (float)

Update Fields:

ADDHSG_13	Housing units built between 2009 and 2013 (short integer)
FINALHSG13	Total housing units in 2013 (float)
ADDPOP_13	Additional population since 2009 (float)
PREPOP13	Total population in 2013 (float)
ADJPOP13	Adjustment factor for city (float)
PARCPOP13	Final estimated 2013 population for the parcel (float)
ADDSAP_13	Probable additional school-aged population since 2009 (float)
TOTALSAP13	Total probable school-aged population in 2013 (float)
POPHU10	population per housing unit

B Determine Housing Unit Counts by Parcel

Reconciling the parcel level counts of housing units with the census counts will take some time and effort. But it is very essential to the ability to accurately estimate the adult and school-aged populations by parcel.

1 Assign NEW_BLOCKS Data to Parcels

As part of the instructions in Appendix D, files named *POPCALC* and *POPCALC_POINT* were created. These are simplified polygon and point files containing only the attributes that are needed to allocate housing units and population. These shapefiles should be added to the view in ArcGIS.

a   Add fields to *POPCALC*

In preparation for spatially joining the block data to parcels, the fields listed in Table E.3 under the heading "Census Data Fields" must be added to join and hold the data.

The model to do this will be similar to Figure E.10.

b   Spatially join *POPCALC_POINTS* with *NEW_BLOCKS* and join the data with *POPCALC.*

c   Calculate the fields in *POPCALC.*

Parcels will be assigned block numbers by spatially joining the parcel points with the *NEW_BLOCKS* shapefile, created as described in Appendix D. The resulting joined point file will then be joined with the *POPCALC* polygon file. Figure E.15 shows the model to accomplish this.

The *POPCALC* polygon shapefile will still be joined to the *POPCALC_POINT_CENSUS_DATA* file.

A model similar to the one previously shown in Figure E.11 will calculate the values for the fields added to the *POPCALC* file based on the values in the *POPCALC_POINT_CENSUS_DATA* file.

The *POPCALC* parcel file will now have all of the data needed to allocate population and school-age children to parcels. Remember to remove the join with *POPCALC_POINT_CENSUS_DATA.*

C Reconcile Assessor's Housing Unit Counts with Census Counts

This is when work needs to be done reconciling detailed land use categories, assessor's housing unit counts and census housing unit counts. A first assumption is that the assessor's counts are correct, but that may not necessarily be the case. Also, the census numbers, in rare instances, may not be accurate, usually due to undercounting or ambiguous census block boundaries. To preserve the work that has been done so far and to create a parcel

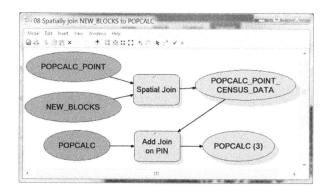

Figure E.15 Model to Spatially Join Parcel Points with *NEW_BLOCKS* and Then Join the Data to the Parcels.

file to allocate housing, copy *POPCALC* to a new file named *POPCALC_HSG*, using the *COPY FEATURES* tool in ArcGIS.

1 Add housing fields to POPCALC_HSG

Add the fields listed under "Housing Fields" in Table E.3.

2 Verify the accuracy of the assessor's housing unit counts

The assessor's file has the number of housing units for each parcel, but they may not always be accurate.

a   Summarize the assessor's housing unit counts by block.

For Bloomington, the assessor had a field named *YR_BUILT*, mostly just for single-family. The residential parcels with housing units built before 2010 (the census year) were selected for processing. The field *RESHSG10* was calculated to be equal to 1 to provide an easy way to select only the parcels to be involved in the initial calculations.

The *NEWASSRHSG* field was initially calculated to be the same as *ASSR_UNITS* and *NEWCENHSG* were calculated to be equal to *THSG10* (the census count for the block). As errors are found, these two fields will also hold the corrections. Figure E.16 shows a model to accomplish these tasks.

b   Compare the assessor's units by block to census block data.

To compare the assessor's counts to the census counts, one needs to summarize the assessor's counts (*NEWASSRHSG*) by block (*REVBLK10*), as shown in Figure E.17.

c   Join the assessor's housing counts by block and calculate the difference with the census.

The summary file (*SUM_ASSR_HSG*) is then be joined with the parcel file (*POPCALC_HSG*) on *REVBLK10*, using a model similar shown in Figure E.18.

d   Calculate preliminary housing.

Before doing any editing of assessor unit counts or census counts, preliminary housing is calculated as shown in Figure E.19 shown below. The first part of the model deals with census blocks that have a difference compared to the assessor's counts by block. The second part of the model shows that, if there are no differences, the housing counts for the parcel can be calculated to be the same as the assessor's.

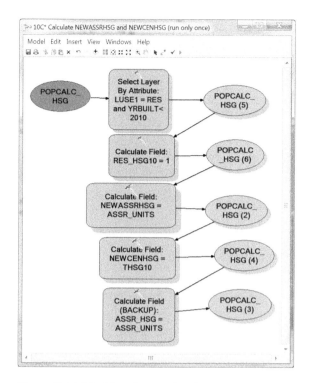

Figure E.16 Model to Summarize Assessor's Unit Counts.

Where there are differences, the field *DIF_HSG* will show the absolute number of unit differences. The field *ADJ_HSG* will show the relative differences. If the census count is greater than the assessor's count, the value in *ADJ_HSG* will be greater than one and, if the assessor's count is greater than the census count, the value will be less than one. When

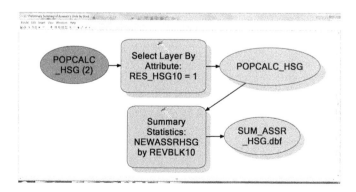

Figure E.17 Preliminary Summary of Assessor's Units by Census Block.

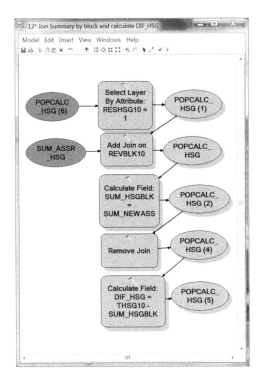

Figure E.18 Model to Join Assessor's Unit Count by Block and Calculate the Difference with the Census.

trying to reconcile the differences, it is best to focus on the very large and very small values. If the absolute difference (DIF_HSG) is only +1 or +2, or –1 or –2, the discrepancy can be ignored. Using the relative measures, if ADJ_HSG >=0.95 or ADJ_HSG <=1.05, the discrepancy can also be ignored.

Figure E.20 shows a model that could be used to select the errors to focus on when working on making corrections. It starts by selecting all records with a DIF_HSG = 0 and then switching the selection. It continues on to remove other records from the selection that do not represent major differences. What will be left are the parcels in blocks that have major differences. These will need to be investigated to figure out if the differences are due to census errors or due to assessor's errors. The fields $NEWASSRHSG$ can initially be calculated to be equal to the assessor's counts ($ASSR\_UNITS$) and $NEWCENHSG$ calculated to be equal to the original census housing counts ($THSG10$). As errors are found, $NEWASSRHSG$ will hold the corrections to the assessor counts and $NEWCENHSG$ will hold the corrections to the census counts.

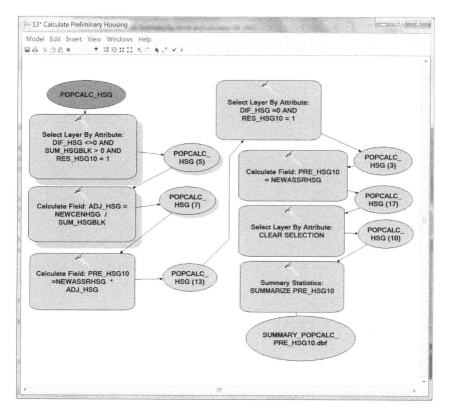

Figure E.19 Model to Calculate Preliminary Housing.

e   Examples of assessor's errors.

Figure E.21, below, shows the parcels for an example block outlined in a heavy black line. An aerial photograph is shown in the background. For the large parcels with several structures, the assessor only listed 13 housing units. It should be noted that all four of what appear to be single large parcels are actually only one parcel in the shapefile.

According to the census, the block contains 131 units, while the total of the assessor's units in the block is only 56, including 33 single-family units. Further research revealed that the one parcel that looked like four actually contained 88, rather than only 13 public housing units owned by the US Department of Housing and Urban Development (HUD). Perhaps since this was tax-exempt property, the assessor was not concerned with the number of units. For fiscal impact purposes, however, it is important to know the impact of public housing on city finances. To correct this error for this public housing parcel, the field *NEWASSRHSG* was calculated to be 88 rather than 13, according to the assessor. As a result, the assessor's count equaled the census count, as shown in Table E.4.

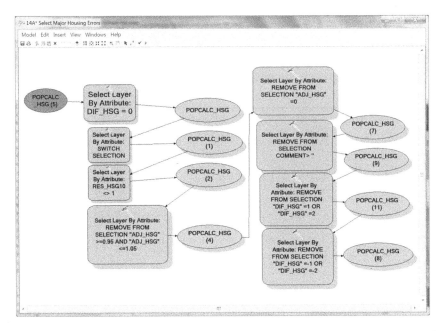

Figure E.20 Model to Select Major Differences Between Assessor's Unit Counts and Census Block Counts.

Figure E.21 Example of Assessor's Housing Unit Count Error Compared to the Census.

Table E.4 Example of Assessor Housing Unit Count Errors Compared to the Census

Block ID	Land Use	Number of	Assessor's Units	New Assessor's Units
REVBLK10	LUSE1B	Parcels	ASSR_UNITS	NEWASSRHSG
171130014033056	Apartments	2	10	10
171130014033056	Apartments Public Housing	1	13	88
171130014033056	Single-Family	33	33	33
171130014033056	Recreation And Open-Space Recreational Public Park	1	0	0
171130014033056	Vacant Government City	1	0	0
171130014033056	Vacant Residential	2	0	0
Totals		40	56	131
Census Housing Units			131	131
Missing Units			−75	0

f   Example of census error.

Figure E.22 shows a census error. According to the census, there are only 7 housing units in the block (outlined in a heavy black line). Yet, the air photo from 2009 shows 61 units, which agrees with the assessor's count. In this case, the field *NEWCENHSG* was corrected to be 61 rather than seven.

g   Example of other errors for apartments.

The method shown above helps to correct for the assessor's and census errors, but there may still be other blocks with regard to apartments with large errors. One big problem in Bloomington was the lack of *YR_BUILT* data for apartments. If one assumed that they all were built before the last census, but they were actually built after, then the *SUM_HSGBLK* would be greater than the census counts and the *DIF_HSG* amounts would be greatly less than zero.

One way to determine the year built, when the data is missing from the Assessor, is to use the aerial photography for the year of or one year before the census year, plus photography for the study year. By looking at parcels with apartments in particular and then comparing the photographs, one can determine if they existed before the census year or not. See the maps below. The first one is from 2009 and the one below it is from 2012 (The photo for

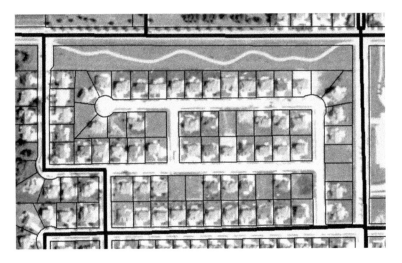

Figure E.22 Example of Census Error, Verified by Aerial Photography.

2013 was not available). One can see that two large buildings were added by 2012, as shown by comparing the structure in the lower right corner.

This reconciliation process is as much an art as a science. There may be cases where the differences cannot be totally reconciled. As one gets down to very small values under *DIF_HSG*, such as 1 or 2 units in a block, or the *ADJ_HSG* values range between 0.95 and 1.05, one may assume that the differences are minimal and can simply be corrected by multiplying

Figure E.23 Apartments in a Block, 2009.

ADJ_HSG by *NEWASSRHSG* to calculate the preliminary housing numbers (*PRE_HSG10*).

h   Calculate final housing.

At this point, preliminary housing unit counts per parcel have been calculated but, if they are summed for the city as a whole, they may be less than or more than the census count for the city. To maintain the housing counts as equal to the census counts, as a control, a final adjustment factor (*ADJ_HSG2*) is calculated to be the census housing total divided by the sum of the preliminary housing total. One may ask, "Why do this?". Working with such large amounts of data, it is important to work within some control totals to make sure nothing is over- or under-counted, even though there are probably some errors. In Bloomington's case, the housing unit census control total was 34,325, but the total of the preliminary housing was 34,714. Dividing the census amount by the preliminary total resulted in an adjustment factor of 0.988791, or nearly 99%.

The value of *FINALHSG10* was calculated to be the preliminary housing (*PRE_HSG10*) multiplied by *ADJ_HSG2* (0.988791). At the very end, summarize the values for *FINALHSG10* to make sure that they equal the known counts for the city. Some parcels that started out with an assessor count of 1 will end up with a final value of 0.988791.

Figure E.25 shows a model to be used to perform these tasks.

i   Calculate census housing errors.

Since some blocks have census housing errors, it is presumed that there are population count errors as well. Two fields will contain data on the housing

Figure E.24 Apartments in a Block, 2012.

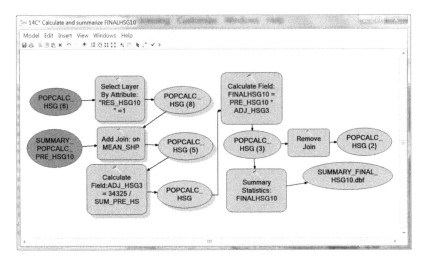

Figure E.25 Model to Calculate Final Housing by Parcel.

errors: *ERR_CENHSG* and *CORRCENERR*. The first will just contain the absolute number of units where *NEWCENHSG* is different from *THSG10* for the block. *CORCENERR* will contain the relative difference between the two by dividing *NEWCWNHSG* by *THSG10*. *CORCENERR* will be used later to adjust the census population and *VAP* per block. Figure E.26 shows a model that will accomplish these tasks.

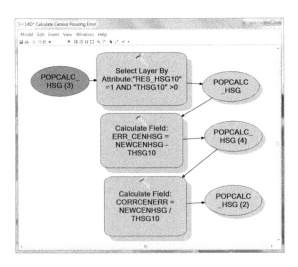

Figure E.26 Model to Calculate Housing Errors.

D Allocate Population to Parcels

Once housing units are reconciled with the census counts, the allocation of population is relatively straightforward. To preserve the work done so far in *POPCALC_HSG*, make a copy of it and name it *POPCALC_POP* to hold the population calculations, using the *COPY FEATURES* tool in ArcGIS.

1 Determine which parcels represent group quarters population

It is very important to identify the parcels that contain group quarters population so that the amounts can be deducted from the total population. The remainder is the amount that will be allocated to parcels with housing units. Add the following field to the *POPCALC_POP* file, if it has not already been added:

ALLOC_GQ – Allocated group quarters population for parcel

Select all the parcels in *POPCALC_POP* that have blocks that have group quarters (*TPOPGQ* > 0).

Start by determining which parcels house group quarters population. Here, it helps if one has detailed land use categories, such as university or college dormitories, nursing homes, government buildings for correctional facilities or juvenile facilities. Check with the police or fire/EMS departments to perhaps help identify them.

When the parcels are located, allocate the group quarters numbers to the *ALLOC_GQ* field. Make sure that the housing unit counts for those parcels are also equal to zero.

2 Allocate the remaining non-group-quarters population to parcels

At this point, one will have determined how much of the population in each block is housed by the housing units in the block.

a   Classify residential housing types.

It is a well-established fact that different housing types have different numbers of populations living in them. In this step, each parcel's housing type will be identified.

1   Add the "Class and population per unit" fields if they have not already been added: *CLASS10, CLASS13, POPHU*.
2   Classify residential parcels.

Classify the residential parcels based on the type of residential and numbers with bedrooms, if available. This step will have to be done interactively.

Start by selecting all parcels with bedroom counts (in Bloomington, it was mostly for single-family).

Based on the detailed land use category, determine the class of each residential parcel and record it in the field *CLASS13*. For example:

SF1 – one-bedroom single-family
SF2 – two-bedroom single-family
.
.
.
SF7 – seven-bedroom single-family

For single-family parcels with no bedroom count, classify them as *SFBLEND*.

Do the same for apartments, duplexes, townhouses, mobile homes or other residential types.

After classifying all residential parcels, select only those built before 2010. Calculate the value of *CLASS10* to be equal to *CLASS13*.

b   Define housing multipliers.

After one has classified all of the residential parcels, search for a recent table of reliable population multipliers and have a field that corresponds to the classes in *CLASS13*. Table E.2 shows the one that was used for Bloomington, named *PPHU2006.dbf*.

Table E.5 was based on a table from 1980, appearing in the *New Practitioner's Guide to Fiscal Impact Analysis* and then updated with some numbers from a publication from Rutgers University, titled "Who Lives in New Jersey Housing?", published in 2006, which also includes numbers from a project in Connecticut (CONN):

http://bloustein.rutgers.edu/wp-content/uploads/2015/03/NJDM.pdf

Household size has been decreasing since 1980 and the 2006 numbers reflect this decline. Since most of the 1980 numbers were much higher than those for 2006, some of them were adjusted downward by the author, noted as GISRDC_ADJ. Others that were not in that study were added based on interpretations of the 1980 data and Rutgers data. For Bloomington, the bedroom counts were mostly available only for single-family. Therefore, for the other uses, blended numbers had to be used. The important thing was to use numbers that were relative to one another. When doing the final allocation by block, the allocated population will be increased or decreased based on the total population within the block, as will be described in detail below. The table has been named *PPHU2006* based on the source of the data, but one can give it another name.

The first line in the table is a description of the field. Of course, that would not be included in the dbf file. The second line is the field name used when creating the dbf file.

Table E.5 Example of Population Multipliers that Could Be Used to Allocate Population to Parcels Based on Housing Type

Number of Bedrooms	Class	Number of Occupants	Source
NO_BDRMS	CLASS	NOCC	SOURCE
One Bedroom	SF1	1.774	APT
Two Bedroom	SF2	2.14	RUTGERS – CONN
Three Bedroom	SF3	3.1	RUTGERS – CONN
Four Bedroom	SF4	3.64	RUTGERS – CONN
Five Bedroom	SF5	4.37	RUTGERS – CONN
Six Bedroom	SF6	5.1	GISRDC_ADJ
Seven Bedroom	SF7	5.83	GISRDC_ADJ
Blended	SFBLEND	3.31	GISRDC_ADJ
One Bedroom	APT1	1.28	RUTGERS – CONN
Two Bedroom	APT2	1.69	RUTGERS – CONN
Three Bedroom	APT3	2.1	GISRDC_ADJ
Blended	APTBLEND	1.69	GISRDC_ADJ
One Bedroom	TH1	1.342	NPG – 1980
Two Bedroom	TH2	1.97	RUTGERS – CONN
Three Bedroom	TH3	2.74	RUTGERS – CONN
Blended	THBLEND	2.286	NPG – 1980
One Bedroom	MH1	1.774	SF
Two Bedroom	MH2	2.14	SF & RUTGERS
Three Bedroom	MH3	3.1	SF & RUTGERS
Blended	MHBLEND	2.726	NPG – 1980
One Bedroom	DUP1	1.76	RUTGERS – CONN
Two Bedroom	DUP2	2.38	RUTGERS – CONN
Three Bedroom	DUP3	3.61	RUTGERS – CONN
Blended	DUPBLEND	2.233	NPG – 1980
Blended	MIXBLEND	1.774	APT & RUTGERS
Blended	MFBLEND	2.233	DUP BLEND
One Bedroom	CONDO1	1.28	APT & RUTGERS
Two Bedroom	CONDO2	1.69	APT & RUTGERS
Three Bedroom	CONDO3	2.5	APT & RUTGERS
Blended	CONDOBLEND	1.774	GISRDC_ADJ

Join *POPCALC_POP* and *PPHU2006* on *CLASS13* and then calculate the field *POPHU* to be equal to the value of *NOCC*. For parcels with *YR_BUILT* less than 2010, *CLASS10* should be equal to *CLASS13*. In other words, *CLASS10* should be blank for parcels with *YR_BUILT* greater than or equal to 2010.

Here is an area of ambiguity. A parcel may be built upon during 2010 but not yet completed and occupied and counted in the census. Others may be occupied and counted.

Figure E.27 shows a model that could be used to accomplish this task.

c   Roughly calculate 2010 parcel population.

1   Add the fields to *POPCALC_POP* listed under "Population Allocation" on Table E.3, if they have not already been added.

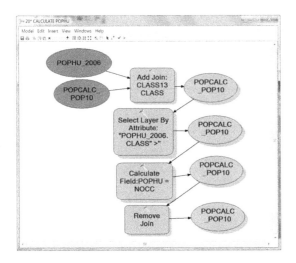

Figure E.27 Model to Calculate the Number of Occupants *(NOCC)*.

2 Select the parcels with housing units in 2010.
3 Calculate *CLASS10* to be equal to *CLASS13*.
4 Calculate *OLDCENPOP* to be equal to *TPOP10*.
5 Correct 2010 population based on the errors found in the housing counts: *NEWCENPOP = OLDCENPOP * CORCENERR*.
6 Calculate *TNET_POP* to be equal to *NEWCENPOP* minus population in group quarters *(POPGQ)*.
7 Select the parcels with a value for *ALLOC_GQ* > 0, then calculate *PARC_POP10 = ALLOC_GQ*.
8 Select the parcels with *CLASS10* > '' and a value of *ALLOC_GQ = 0*.
9 Calculate the field *POPCALC_POP* to be equal to the values of *FINALHSG10* times the population multiplier *(POPHU)*.
10 Calculate *PARC_POP10* to be equal to *CALC_POP*.
11 Select the 2010 residential parcels: *RES_HSG10 = 1* or *ALLOC_ GQ > 0*.
12 Summarize the values of *CALC_POP* by *REVBLK10*.

Figure E.28 shows a model to accomplish these tasks.

d Calculate the preliminary population.

1 Join the summary table with *POPCALC_POP10* on the *REVBLK10*.
2 Calculate the field *TCALC_POP* to be equal to *SUM_CALC_P*.
3 Select parcels with *TCALC_POP* greater than zero.
4 Calculate *ADJ_POP10* to be equal to *TNETPOP* divided by *TCALC_POP*.

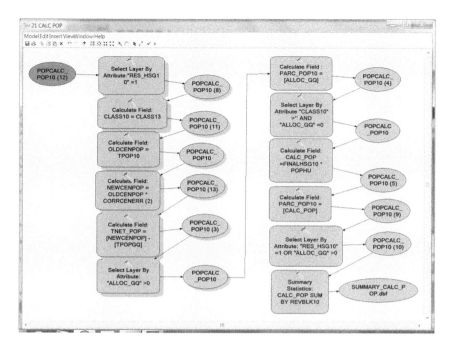

Figure E.28 Model to Calculate *PARC_POP10*.

5. Calculate the field *PRE_POP10* to be equal to *POP_CALC* times *ADJ_POP10*, plus *ALLOC_GQ*.
6. Remove the join.
7. Summarize the city's preliminary population.

Figure E.29 shows a model to accomplish these tasks

e   Calculate the final population.

At this point, examine the values of *ADJ_POP10*. Some may represent very large adjustments (greater than 2, or less than .95). These may be valid because the calculations are based on the *POPHU* assumptions. Those with an adjustment less than .95 are probably due to the *POPHU* values being too high. If large errors are otherwise found, they should be corrected and then *POP_CALC* recalculated as shown in steps c. and d., above.

The last steps in the process make final adjustments to *PRE_POP10*.

1 Clear the selection so that group quarters population is included.
2 Summarize to get the city total of *PRE_POP10* to derive and compare it to the census total for the city.

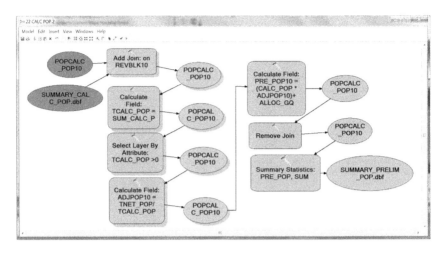

Figure E.29 Model to Calculate the Preliminary Population.

3 Calculate a final adjustment factor (*ADJPOP10B*) by dividing the census total of the population for the city (the control total) by the sum of *PRE_POP10*. The adjustment should be relatively small.
4 Calculate the final population (*PARC_POP10*) by multiplying *PRE_POP10* times *ADJPOP10B*.
5 Remove the join and summarize *PARC_POP10* for the entire city to verify that the values in *PARC_POP10* equal the total known population for the city.

Figure E.30 shows a model to accomplish the above tasks.

E Allocate SAP to Parcels

The instructions so far have dealt with obtaining the *VAP* by block, assuming that it can be used to estimate the *SAP*. However, if the voting-age population is subtracted from the total population, one will have the population aged 0–17, not really the *SAP*.

If one wanted to be more precise in the allocation of the *SAP* to parcels, there is other data in the census that would provide the block breakdown by individual age year and sex. This is contained in Summary File 1, Table P14.

For purposes of this example, the adjusted 0–17 population will be used to estimate the approximate *SAP*, by subtracting the under-5 population and adding in the age-18 population.

1 Calculate the SAP based on the VAP

a   Copy *POPCALC_POP10* to *POPCALC_SAP*.

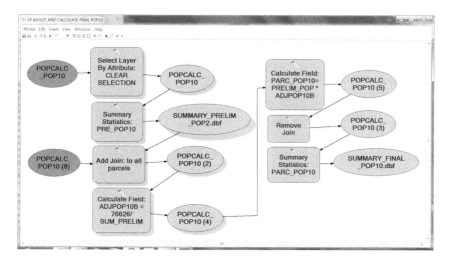

Figure E.30 Model to Calculate the Final 2010 Population.

b   Add the fields listed in Table E.3, under the heading "School-Aged Population", if they have not already been added.
c   Adjust the *VAP* based on the housing errors. It has been assumed that the housing errors are indicators of population and *VAP* errors as well.
   1   Calculate *OLDCENVAP* to be equal to the *VAP* numbers from the census *(TVAP)*.
   2   Calculate the *NEWCENVAP* to be equal to the *OLDCENVAP* multiplied by the *CORCENERR*.
d   Calculate the *SAP*.

Using 2010 census data for the Bloomington School District as a guide, it was found that the relationship of the population aged 18 was about 8% of the population aged 0–17. Therefore, the first thing to be done is to calculate *POP_18* to be approximately 8% of the POP_0_17.
   The percentage of the 0–17 population under age 5 was about 30%. Therefore, the calculations would be as follows:

POP_0_17 = TPOP10 – TVAP
*POP_0_4 = POP_0_17 * .3*
*POP_18 = POP_0_17 * .08*
POP_5_18 = POP_0_17 – POP_0_4 + POP_18

Figure E.31 shows a model to accomplish the tasks c. and d. above.

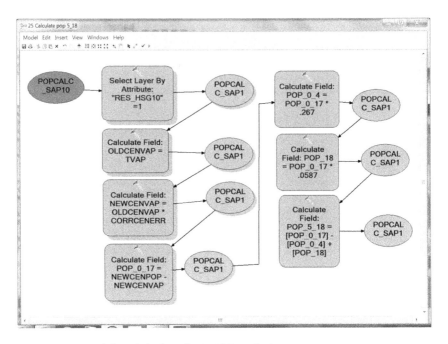

Figure E.31 Model to Calculate the 5–18 Population.

2 Estimate the SAP (SAP10)

Like the housing and population estimates per parcel that may have values based on decimal places rather than whole numbers, the *SAP* can be thought of as the "probable" *SAP*. To be sure, the numbers will have decimal places.

  a Select parcels with a value for *TNET_POP* greater than zero.

  b Calculate the proportion of *SAP* per block to the total block population: *PROP_SAP* = *POP_5_18* divided by *TNET_POP*

  c Calculate the probable *SAP* by parcel: *SAP10* = *PROP_SAP* * *PARC_POP10*.

  d Add the population in juvenile facilities.

     1) Select the parcel (s) with a value >0 in *ALLOC_GQ* and a value > 0 in *T_JUVF*.

     2) Calculate *SAP10* to be equal to *ALLOC_GQ*.

  e Clear the selection and summarize *SAP* by the city as a whole and also by land use.

Figure E.32 shows a model to accomplish the tasks described above.

F Update the Population to the Current Year

  1 Copy *POPCALC_SAP* to *POPCALC_UPDATE*.

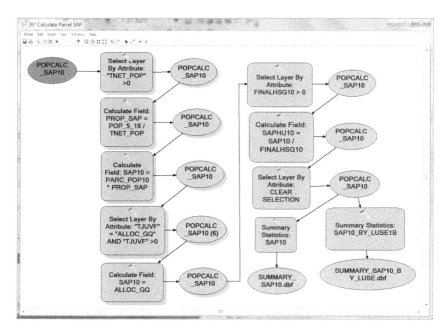

Figure E.32 Model to Calculate Probable School-Aged Population.

2 Add the fields listed in Table E.3, under the heading "Update", if they have not already been added.

3 Determine the average population per housing unit by land use for the city as a whole. This will be used to calculate the new population.

   a Select the parcels with a value for 2010 housing units: *FINALHSG10* > 0.

   b Calculate the population per housing unit for all 2010 parcels with housing units.

   c Summarize to get the city-wide mean population per housing unit by land use category.

Figure E.33 shows a model to accomplish these tasks.

4 Determine the new housing units based on the assessor's units that have been identified as having been built since the census.

   a Select parcels with housing units with a value for *YRBUILT* greater than or equal to 2010. This will mostly be single-family.

   b Calculate *ADDHSG_13 = ASSR_UNITS*

   c Select parcels with *NEWASSRHSG* less than the *ASSR_HSG*. The difference will mostly be new apartment units.

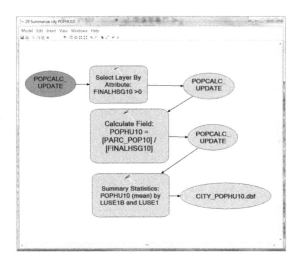

Figure E.33 Model to Calculate the Estimated 2010 Population per Housing Unit.

d   Calculate *ADDHSG_13 = ASSR_UNITS*.
e   Select parcels with a value greater than zero for *ADDHSG_13*.
f   Join with the city summary file of the mean values of population per housing unit by land use (*CITY_POPHU.dbf*).
g   Select *LUSE1* = residential.
h   Calculate *ADDPOP_13 = ADDHSG13 * MEAN_POPHU*.
i   Calculate *PREPOP13* to be equal to *ADDPOP_13* plus *PARC_POP10*.
j   Remove the join.
k   Summarize the total of *PREPOP13* for the city.

Figure E.34 shows a model to perform the above tasks a. through k.

5   Calculate the final 2013 housing units. Figure E.35 shows a model to accomplish this.
6   Calculate the final 2013 population.

There may be an outside source, such as the state demographer, that has the official population counts for the city. In this case, the number for Bloomington was 77,680. This served as a control total to adjust the preliminary population. Figure E.36 shows a model to accomplish this.

7   Calculate the 2013 school-age population.

a   Create a city-wide table of students per housing type.

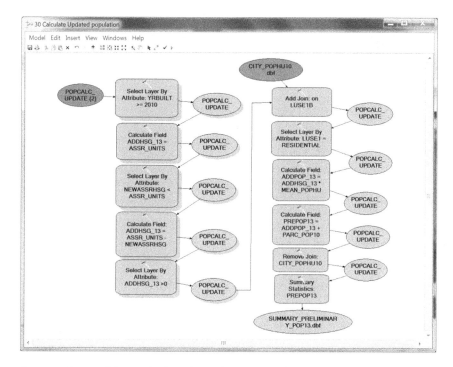

Figure E.34 Model to Calculate the Preliminary Updated 2013 Population.

Since some of the new parcels may be in census blocks that did not have 2010 housing or population, average proportions of school-age population (*PCT_SAP13*) are first calculated to provide a multiplier to estimate the new *SAP* (*ADDSAP_13*) coming from the new housing units.

b   Calculate SAP13.

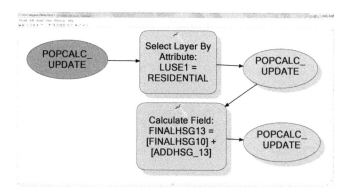

Figure E.35 Model to Calculate the Final 2013 Housing Units.

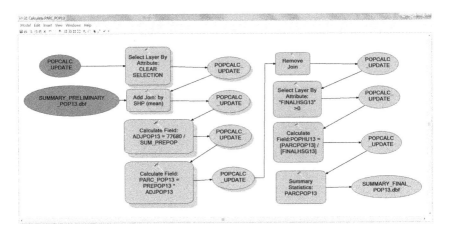

Figure E.36 Model to Calculate the Final 2013 Population.

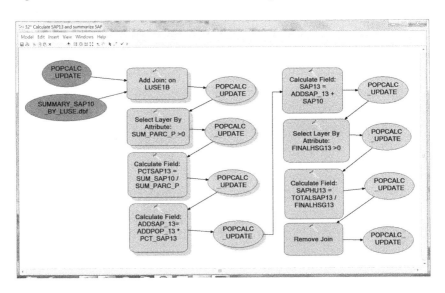

Figure E.37 Model to Calculate the 2013 School-Age Population.

The estimated additional *SAP* is then added to the 2010 estimated *SAP*: $SAP13 = SAP10 + ADDSAP\_13$.

Figure E.37 shows a model to accomplish these tasks.

III Summary

This appendix is intended to give some instructions as to how to allocate adult and student-age populations based on the corrected number of housing units per parcel. One may have other ways to do this, but this is an attempt to describe the actual models used to accomplish this for the city of Bloomington, based on census year 2010 and updated to 2013. The same process could be applied to the 2020 census and update years. Of course, it will require substantial GIS skills.

References

US Census Bureau (2011) "US Census Statistics", *United States Census Bureau*, https://www2.census.gov/census_2010/.
"Who Lives in New Jersey Housing?"(2006). Retrieved from http://pppolicy.rutg ers.edu/cupr/otherreports/Multipliers_QuickGuide.pdf.

Appendix F
Modeling Fiscal Impact Using ArcGIS

The process for calculating fiscal impact can be accomplished in two ways. One is to build models using the ArcGIS Model Builder, which is part of the GIS software from ESRI, the other is to use custom spreadsheets that the user develops for the municipality. The spreadsheet approach is more applicable to smaller jurisdictions and was used for the city of Anoka. However, spreadsheets do have size limitations and make it difficult to update as changes or selections are made. The more complicated fiscal situations, and the larger the city, can be more effectively modeled using Model Builder.

I ArcGIS Model Builder

The process for calculating Bloomington's Net Taxable Fiscal Impact using ESRI's Model Builder capabilities in ArcGIS is described in this chapter. As noted previously, each city's financial situation is unique. Therefore, there is no one model that will work for every city. The modeling needs to be developed individually. The examples in this chapter can provide a general guide as to how to develop a city's model. There may be other ways that it may be done in ArcGIS but this is the way it was done for Bloomington. The effort was made exclusively using very basic Model Builder skills. There are many fields and variables but, once they are grouped according to their function, customized models are a very effective way of processing the information to produce meaningful and verifiable results. They also provide an excellent means of documenting the processes.

1. Add the fiscal impact fields to the fiscal factor database

The first step is to copy the *Parcel_Factor* shapefile to another named *Fiscal_ Impact* and then add the field names to contain the results of the calculations. Rather than just adding fields to the *Parcel_Factor* shapefile, it was decided to keep the *Parcel_Factor* shapefile separate from the *Fiscal_Impact* shapefile. That way, as adjustments were made to the attributes of individual parcels, such as land use or police calls, the fiscal impact would need to be recalculated. To avoid the need to reset all of the calculation fields to

Table F.1 Parcel_Factors Fields

FIELD NAME	Description
OBJECTID	Object ID assigned by ArcGIS
PIN	Parcel Identification Number
AREA	Area in square feet
ACRES	Area in acres
BLOCKID	Census Block ID (modified)
TAZ	Traffic Assignment Zone (modified)
SHP	Summary item, all records equal to 1
LUSE0	Tax status: "TAXABLE" or "TAX EXEMPT"
LUSE1	Generalized Land Use Category: Commercial, Industrial, Institutional, Recreation and Open Space, Residential, Transportation and Vacant
LUSE1B	More detailed categories, especially with regard to residential
LUSE2	Very detailed categories when applicable
LUSE3	Concatenation of LUSE1, LUSE1B and LUSE2
POP10	Estimated 2010 population
HSG10	Estimated 2010 housing units
POP13	Estimated 2013 population
HSG13	Estimated 2013 housing units
EMPLOYMENT	Estimated 2013 employment based on disaggregating TAZ data
F_CALLS	Fire call equivalent (Fire call minutes divided by average of 47.28 minutes)
P_CALLS	Police call equivalent (Police call minutes divided by average of 46.24 minutes)
FRTG_ART	Arterial road frontage
FRTG_COLLE	Collector road frontage
FRTG_LOCAL	Local road frontage
FRTG_CNTY	County road frontage
FRTG_PRIV	Private road frontage (not complete data)
FRTG_S_HWY	State highway frontage
FRTG_USHWY	US highway frontage
FRTG_ALLEY	Alley frontage
TOT_FRTG	Total locally maintained road frontage
SWALK_FRTG	Sidewalk frontage (incomplete data)
BLTUSECODE	BLTUSE code from assessor
LAND_MV	Land market value from Assessor
BLDING_MV	Building market value from Assessor
ASSESSEDMV	Total land and building market value from Assessor
NETMV	Net market value after subtracting credits from assessed value
COMMERCMV	Commercial market value (NETMV for commercial/ industrial land use)
TOT_LMV	Estimated land market value, including tax-exempt properties
TOT_BMV	Estimated building market value, including tax-exempt properties
TOT_TMV	Total estimated land and building market values, including tax-exempt properties
TIFMV	TIF total market value
BLDSQFT	Building square footage from Assessor

(*Continued*)

Table F.1 (Continued)

FIELD NAME	Description
LOT_SQFT	Lot square footage from Assessor
ASSR_UNITS	Number of units according to the Assessor (errors were found)
ERR_ASSR	Flag of 1 used to locate the errors
LOW_INC_IX	Low Income Index: residential parcels with a low building market value
DILAP_ST	Index based on pavement condition. Applies only to very dilapidated streets.
PUB_HSG_NA	City public housing complex name
PUB_HSG_UN	City public housing number of units
METROZONE	Parcels in the Metrozone have a value of 1
DISCONTIG	Parcels considered to be dis-contiguous
BP_YEAR	Year of building permit if since 2007
PARC2010	Parcels that existed in 2010 (accuracy is questionable)
PARC2005	Parcels that existed in 2005 (accuracy is questionable)
DBF	Summary field to get totals, like SHP. All values equal 1
BUF_MILES	Distance from the center of the city, in quarter mile increments
FIRE_MIN	Total minutes spent on fire calls
POL_MIN	Total minutes spent on police calls
NEW_FCALL	Number of fire calls, based on second match, February, 2015
NEW_PCALL	Number of police calls, based on second match, Feb., 2015
PCT_POP	Percentage of total population
PCT_MV	Percentage of total building market value
PCT_TOT	Total of PCT_POP and PCT_MV
PCT_MI	PCT_TOT multiplied times BUF_MILES
DISTF	Distance factor: each parcel's percentage of the total PCT_MI for the city.
NBHD2	Neighborhood number
NBHD_NAME	Neighborhood name
CI_NBHD	Commercial/industrial neighborhood for C/I Parcels
CI_NBHD2	Concatenation of NBHD_NAME and CI_NBHD
NBHD_LUSE	Concatenation of NBHD_NAME and LUSE1

zero each time, it was decided to simply copy the *Parcel_Factor* shapefile to a new *Fiscal_Impact* shapefile each time and add all of the calculation fields, which would be automatically be equal to zero. For reference, the list of fields in the *Parcel_Factor* shapefile are provided below in Table F.1, below.

A Add Revenue and Expenditure Fields

The multipliers from Table 6.06 from Chapter 6 were combined into a single database file named "*Multipliers*" that was used to do the calculations of fiscal impact. The key components of the file are shown below in Table F.2. The names listed under *MULT_JOIN* are the values that were iteratively calculated to a *MULT_JOIN* field in the *Fiscal_Impact* shapefile. With each

Table F.2 The *Multipliers* File Values

Operating Revenue		
Allocation Factor	*MULT_JOIN*	*FF_MULT*
Population	*ORPOP*	449.60157
Employment	*OREMP*	114.68941
Nert Assessed Value	*ORNETAV*	0.01376179
Police Calls	*ORPCALLS*	29.08362
Fire Calls	*ORFCALLS*	295.22529
Residential Building Market Value	*ORRESBMV*	0.00600745
Commercial/Industrial Market Value	*ORCMV*	0.02403136
City Maintained Road Frontage	*ORRF*	0.28424
Operating Expense		
Allocation Factor	*MULT_JOIN*	*FF_MULT*
Population	*OEPOP*	253.79115
Employment	*OEEMP*	96.15847
Police Calls	*OEPCALLS*	104.75800
Fire Calls	*OEFCALLS*	735.28601
Police and Fire Street Calls	*OESTCALLEQ*	110.04200
Arterial Streets	*OEFAR*	5.70341
Collector Streets	*OEFCO*	4.73052
Local Streets	*OEFLOC*	1.18033
Alleys	*OEFAL*	0.48442
Commercial/Industrial/Apartment Building Market Value	*OECIAMV*	0.00414
Total Building Market Value	*OETBMV*	0.00544
Population Mile	*OEPOPMI*	5.37502
Distance Factor	*OEDISTF*	8,614,980
Capital and Special Revenue		
Allocation Factor	*MULT_JOIN*	*FF_MULT*
Population	*CRPOP*	35.96565
Nert Assessed Value	*CRNETAV*	0.00111371
Total Building Market Value	*CRTBMV*	0.00042861
2013 Building Permits	*CRFY13DEV*	118.94000
Low- and Moderate-Income Index	*CRLMINDX*	0.00492
TIF Market Value	*CRTIFMV*	0.01702610
Metrozone	*CRTN*	236,819
Capital and Special Expenditures		
Allocation Factor	*MULT_JOIN*	*FF_MULT*
Population	*CEPOP*	73.05776
Employment	*CEEMP*	21.46461
Police Calls	*CEPCALLS*	1.60974
Fire Calls	*CEFCALLS*	39.03160
Police and Fire Street Calls	*CESTCALLEQ*	4.28370
Arterial Streets	*CEFAR*	4.90055
Collector Streets	*CEFCO*	5.72057
Local Streets	*CEFLOC*	1.47731
Alleys	*CEFAL*	0.52723
Total Building Market Value	*CETBMV*	0.00180218
Commercial/Industrial/Apartment Building Market Value	*CECIAMV*	0.00012098
Population Mile	*CEPOPMI*	0.72939
Dilapidated Streets	*CEDILAP_ST*	2.87486
Low- and Moderate-Income Index	*CELMINDX*	0.01495
TIF Market Value	*CETIFMV*	0.04194510
Metrozone	*CETN*	1,204,011

iteration, the appropriate multiplier was used to do the calculations. The multipliers are listed below under *FF_MULT* (fiscal factor multiplier).

The illustrations below show an example of a Model Builder dialog box to add the operating revenue fields. It starts with adding the field named *MULT_JOIN*, which will be used to join the *Multipliers* file with the *Fiscal_Impact* shapefile, as shown in Figure F.1.

Figure F.2 shows the addition of the *"ORAV"* field.

The model also included similar operations to add the remaining operating revenue fields listed under *MULT_JOIN: OREMP, ORFCALLS, ORPCALLS, ORPOP, ORRESBMV and ORRF*.

Other similar models were created to add the fields for operating expenses, capital and special revenue and expenditures.

B Add Summary Fields

Fields were also added to contain the summary data for each parcel, shown in Table F.3.

C Add Adjustment Fields

More fields were added to contain the numbers that would be needed to make adjustments to fiscal impact, such as allocating the tax-exempt fiscal impact to the taxable parcels, as shown in Table F.4.

Figure F.1 Example of Adding Operating Revenue Fields.

Figure F.2 Example Dialog Box to Define the Fields.

D Add Final Fiscal Impact Fields

The fields needed to contain the final fiscal impact calculations were also added, shown in Table F.5.

2. Calculate the revenues and expenditures using the multipliers

The models to calculate revenues and expenditures are described below, starting with operating revenue.

Table F.3 Summary Fields Added to *Fiscal_Impact* Shapefile

Field Name	Description
OPER_REV	Total operating revenue (sum of all OR fields)
OPER_EXP	Total operating expense (sum of all OE fields)
CAP_REV	Total capital revenue (sum of all CR fields)
CAP_EXP	Total capital expense (sum of all CE fields)
TOT_REV	Total revenue (OPER_REV plus CAP_REV)
TOT_EXP	Total expense (OPER_EXP plus CAP_EXP)
OPER_FI	Operating fiscal impact (OPER_REV minus OPER_EXP)
CAP_FI	Capital fiscal impact (CAP_REV minus CAP_EXP)
TOTAL_FI	Total fiscal impact before adjustments (OPER_FI plus CAP_FI)
PCT_OREV	Percent operating revenue for each parcel
TRANS2CAP	Transfer surplus operating revenue to capital revenue using PCT_OREV
NET_0_FI	Net operating fiscal impact (OPER_FI minus TRANS2CAP)
NETCAPFI	Net capital fiscal impact (CAP_FI plus TRANS2CAP)
T_NET_FI	Preliminary fiscal impact (NET_O_FI plus NETCAPFI)

Table F.4 Adjustment Fields Added to *Fiscal_Impact* Shapefile

Field Name	Description
T_TBL_OE	City total taxable operating expense
T_TBL_CE	City total taxable capital expense
PCT_TBL_OE	Percent taxable operating expense by parcel
PCT_TBL_CE	Percent taxable capital expense by parcel
ALLOCEXOFI	Exempt operating fiscal impact for the central city allocated to all taxable parcels
ALLOCEXCFI	Exempt capital fiscal impact for the central city allocated to all taxable parcels
ALLOCEXOFI2	Exempt operating fiscal impact for the each outlying neighborhood allocated to the taxable parcels in the neighborhood
ALLOCEXCFI2	Exempt capital fiscal impact for the each outlying neighborhood allocated to the taxable parcels in the neighborhood
TBL_0_FI	Taxable operating fiscal impact by parcel
TBL_C_FI	Taxable capital fiscal impact by parcel
TBL_FI	Total taxable fiscal impact by parcel

Table F.5 Final Fiscal Impact Fields Added to *Fiscal_Impact* Shapefile

Field Name	Description
TBLOREV	Total operating revenue of taxable properties
PCT_TBOREV	Percent of total operating revenue for taxable properties
TRANSOUT	Share of city surplus deducted based on *PCT_TBOREV*
NET_TB_OFI	Net taxable operating fiscal impact (same as *TBL_O_FI*)
NET_TB_CFI	Net taxable capital fiscal impact (*TBL_C_FI* minus *TRANSOUT*)
NET_TBL_FI	Net taxable fiscal impact (total city summary equals zero)

The *Multipliers* file had a field called *MULT_JOIN* with text values that correspond to the type of multiplier (see Table F.2). For example, the record with the value of *MULT_JOIN* = "*ORRESBMV*" signifies Operating Revenue based on Residential Building Market Value. This record in the *Multipliers* file has the value 0.00600745 under the *Sum_FF_Mult* field.

The *Fiscal_Impact* shapefile also had a field named *MULT_JOIN*. As was stated previously, this field was iteratively calculated to the same names in the *Multipliers* file so that the *Multipliers* file could be joined with it to do the calculations. With each iteration, the values in the fiscal impact fields were calculated based on the fiscal factor, such as "*RESBMV*", times the multiplier value in the *Multipliers* file.

Figure F.3, below, conceptually shows the join and calculation for seven representative parcels in the file. For the first record, the parcel has a residential building market value (*RESBMV*) of 45,741. The arrows indicate that the *Multipliers* file and the *Fiscal_Impact* shapefile have been joined

Multiplier File					Fiscal_Impact File		
					Calculate Mult_join to be valvue from multiplier file for joining		Calculate the value ORRESBMV to be RESBMV times 0.00601
MULT_JOIN	SUM_DIST_A	MEAN_FACT_	SUM_FF_MUL		MULT_JOIN	RESBMV	ORRESBMV
OREMP	7145150.50	62300.00	114.68941		ORRESBMV	45741	274.78654
ORFCALLS	3630680.45	12298.00	295.22528		ORRESBMV	50865	305.56869
ORAV	23625440.00	1716746188	0.01376		ORRESBMV	50372	302.60702
ORPCALLS	2168124.44	74548.00	29.08360		ORRESBMV	0	0
ORPOP	34925019.49	77679.00	449.60697		ORRESBMV	50442	303.02754
ORRESBMV	6352768.00	1057482518	0.00601		ORRESBMV	0	0
ORRF	914495.12	3217386.00	0.28424		ORRESBMV	70031	420.70738

Figure F.3 Example of the *Multiplier* File Joined with the *Fiscal_Impact* File.

on the *MULT_JOIN* field of *ORRESBMV*. The field *Sum_FF_Mult* in the Multiplier file has a value of .00601 (rounded from 0.00600745). Multiplying the 45,741 by .00601 yields the operating revenue based on residential building market value equal to $274.78654 for that parcel.

Figure F.4 shows the first iteration of the model to calculate operating revenue based on residential building market value. Components of the model to calculate the other operating revenue fields would be similar.

The first operation, *Calculate Field*, was to calculate the field *MULT_JOIN* in the *Fiscal_Impact* shapefile to be *ORRESBMV*, as shown in Figure F.5.

The next operation, *Add Join*, joined the *Multipliers* file with the *Fiscal_Impact* shapefile on the common fields named *MULT_JOIN*, which happen to be *ORRESBMV*, as shown in Figure F.6.

The next operation, *Calculate Field*, calculated the value for the *ORRESBMV* field in the *Fiscal_Impact* shapefile for all parcels to be equal to the product of *RES_BMV* times the multiplier *Sum_FF_Mult* from the *Multipliers* file, as shown in Figure F.7.

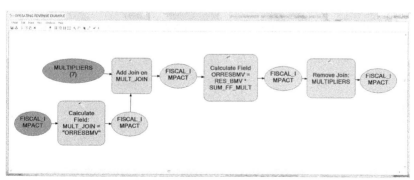

Figure F.4 Example Model to Calculate *ORRESBMV*.

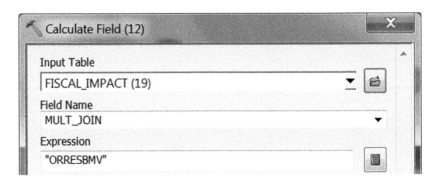

Figure F.5 Calculate *Mult_Join* Field to be *ORRESBMV*.

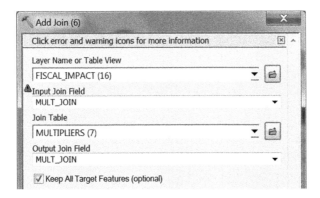

Figure F.6 Join the *MULTIPLIER* File with *Fiscal_Impact* on Common *MULT_JOIN* Field: *ORRESBMV*.

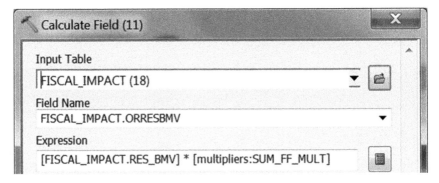

Figure F.7 Calculate ORRESBMV to be *RES_BMV* Times the Multiplier, *SUM_FF_MULT*.

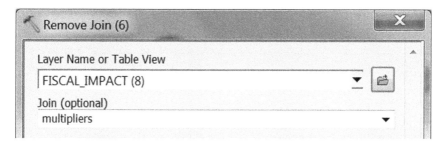

Figure F.8 Remove Join.

The next operation, *Remove Join*, removed the join of the *Multiplier* file with *Fiscal_Impact*, as shown in Figure F.8

Similar models were used to calculate operating expenses, capital revenue and capital expenditures.

3. Calculate the preliminary fiscal impact

With all of the operating and capital revenues and expenditures calculated, it was then possible to calculate some preliminary fiscal impact measures. Figure F.9 shows the model and the calculated fields for each parcel.

4. Transfer the operating surplus to capital revenue

The revenue items for operations far exceeded the operating expenses and the surplus was used to finance capital and special projects. The objective was to develop an accurate measure of operating fiscal impact, so the excess revenue needed to be transferred out. The transfer was accomplished by calculating each parcel's percentage share of the total operating revenue for the city and thus allocating the share of the surplus. This amount was subtracted from each parcel's operating fiscal impact (the same as subtracting it from the operating revenue and then recalculating the operating fiscal impact). The same amount was, in turn, added to each parcel's capital revenue and thus the capital fiscal impact. Figure F.10 shows the calculations.

It should be noted that all of the summary results were output as DBF tables, which had a field length maximum of 10. As a result, the field names in the summary files were often truncated. For example, the sum of operating revenue (*OPER_REV*) appears in the output file as *SUM_OPER_R*. This should be kept in mind when viewing any of the models with summary statistics. Figure F.10 notes this situation.

5. Allocate the tax-exempt fiscal impact

To derive the taxable fiscal impact, the tax-exempt fiscal impact had to be allocated to the taxable parcels. The premise behind giving some parcels a

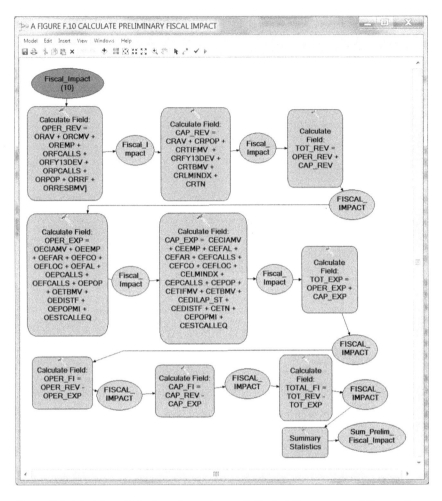

Figure F.9 Model to Calculate Operating and Capital Revenues and Expenditures and Preliminary Fiscal Impact.

tax-exempt status is that they generally benefit the other parcels, whether it be government properties, churches, cemeteries, parks, golf courses, etc. Therefore, the taxable parcels support the tax-exempt uses.

A. Allocate Central City Tax-Exempt

In Bloomington's case, the central city neighborhood really benefitted all areas in the city, while the outlying neighborhoods had tax-exempt uses that benefitted each neighborhood. Therefore, the first task was to allocate the central city's tax-exempt fiscal impact to all of the parcels in the city. The parcels in the central city neighborhood had a value of *NBHD2* equal to 1.

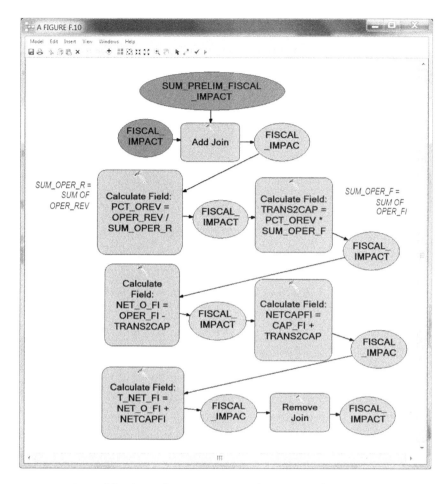

Figure F.10 Model to Transfer Operating Surplus to Capital Revenue.

Figure F.11 shows the model to summarize the central city's operating and capital tax-exempt fiscal impact (a deficit).

Figure F.12 shows the model to allocate the tax-exempt fiscal impact for the central city to all parcels in the city. It begins by summarizing the operating and capital taxable expenditures. The expenditure sums were then joined with *Fiscal_Impact* and each parcel gets the total operating expenses in field *T_TBL_OE* and the total capital expenditures in the field *T_TBL_CE*. Next, each parcel's share of the city's total operating expenses is calculated as *PCT_TBL_OE* and its share of capital expenditures is calculated as *PCT_TBL_CE*. Using these percentages, each parcel's share of the total tax-exempt operating and capital fiscal impact from the central city was allocated. The allocated amount fields were named *ALLOCEXOFI* for operating expenses and *ALLOCEXCFI* for capital expenditures.

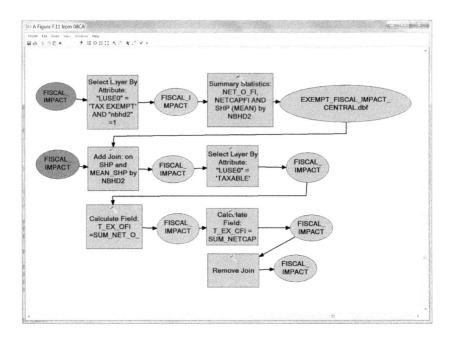

Figure F.11 Model to Summarize the Fiscal Impact of Tax-Exempt Parcels in the Central City.

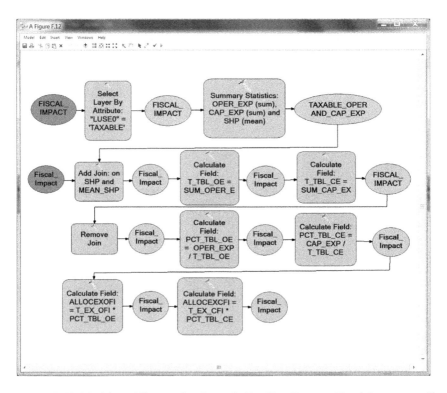

Figure F.12 Model to Allocate the Central City Tax-Exempt Fiscal Impact to all Taxable Parcels.

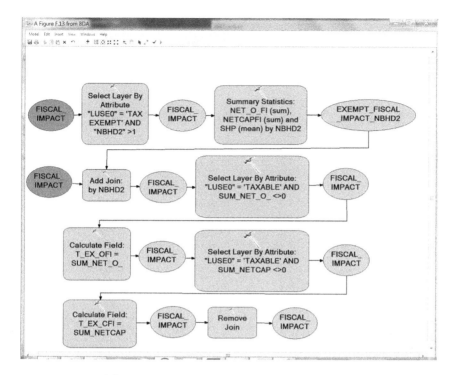

Figure F.13 Model to Summarize Tax-Exempt Fiscal Impact by Neighborhood.

B Allocate Neighborhood Tax-Exempt

A similar process was used to allocate each outlying neighborhood's tax-exempt fiscal impact to parcels, the difference being that it was done by each neighborhood rather than city-wide. The neighborhoods were those with NBHD2 > 1. Figure F.13 shows the selection and calculation of the operating and capital tax-exempt fiscal impacts for each neighborhood.

Figure F.14 shows the allocation to the neighborhoods. The field names for the neighborhood allocations were *ALLOCEXOFI2* and *ALLOCEXCFI2*.

C Add each parcel's share of the central city tax-
   exempt and the neighborhood tax-exempt

The allocations of exempt operating and capital fiscal impact (deficits) were added to (or subtracted from) the preliminary operating and capital fiscal impact for each parcel to get the TBL_O_FI and TBL_C_FI. Then the two were added together to get the taxable fiscal impact (TBL_FI), as shown in Figure F.15.

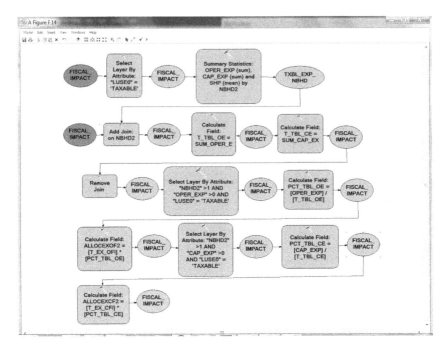

Figure F.14 Model to Allocate Each Neighborhood's Tax-Exempt Fiscal Impact to the Neighborhood's Taxable Parcels.

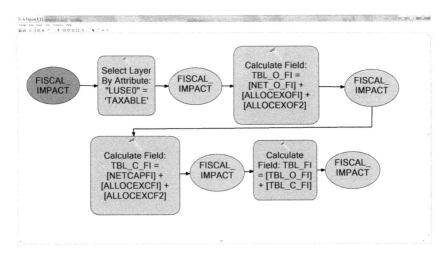

Figure F.15 Model to Calculate the Taxable Operating, Capital and Total Fiscal Impact.

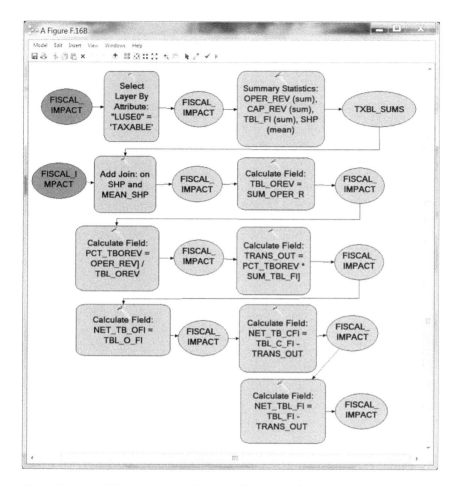

Figure F.16 Model to *Zero_Out* the Overall City Surplus.

6. Zero-out the overall city surplus

The city had a surplus of $2.15 million in 2013. To get the final measure of fiscal impact, the surplus was subtracted from each parcel's fiscal impact in proportion to its share of total revenue. The result was the net taxable fiscal impact (NET_TBL_FI). Figure F.16 shows the model to make this final adjustment.

II Summary

As stated previously, every city is unique as to its fiscal components and spatial characteristics, so the above models are only examples. The Spatial Fiscal Impact Analysis Method is a method, not a model. It may seem that there are too many fields and variables but, once they are grouped according to their function, building customized models can be a very effective way of processing the information to produce meaningful and verifiable results. They also provide an excellent means of documenting the processes.

Index

Page numbers in *italics* mark figures, while page numbers in **bold** denote tables.